Education
and the
social condition

Harold Silver

Education
and the
social condition

METHUEN *London & New York*

First published in 1980 by
Methuen & Co. Ltd
11 New Fetter Lane, London EC4P 4EE
Published in the USA by
Methuen & Co.
in association with Methuen, Inc.
733 Third Avenue, New York, NY 10017
© 1980 Harold Silver
Photoset by Northampton Phototypesetters Ltd and
printed in Great Britain at the
University Press, Cambridge

British Library Cataloguing in Publication Data

Silver, Harold
Education and the social condition.
1. Educational sociology
I. Title
370.19′3   LC191   80–40304
ISBN 0–416–74020–0
ISBN 0–416–74030–8 Pbk

Contents

Acknowledgements

Parts of this book contain adaptations of material previously published as indicated below. My thanks are due to the publishers concerned for permission to use this material.

New Society
'Teaching: the death of a meal-ticket', 16 September 1976 (ch. 10).
'The Political Quest for Educational Standards', written jointly with Pamela Silver, 24 February 1977 (ch. 4).
'Public Control and Choice in Education', 1 September 1977 (ch. 5).
'Education and Social Policy', 30 November 1978 (ch. 2).
'Education and Public Opinion', 7 December 1978 (ch. 2).
Westminster Studies in Education
'Higher Education and Lower Learning', vol. 1, 1978 (ch. 8).
The Times Higher Education Supplement
'Institutes of the 1970s – flotsam and jetsam?', 22 September 1978 (ch. 9).
The Guardian
'What's in a Name?', 13 February 1979 (ch. 9).

My thanks are also due to the following, to whom versions of some of this material were presented in one form or another, and who provided valuable opportunities for discussion:

King Alfred's College, Winchester, where the Winton Lecture was delivered under the title 'Education and the Social Condition', on 23 May 1979 (ch. 1).

Manchester University and the Centre for the Study of Disadvantage, under whose joint auspices a lecture was delivered on 22 March 1979 on 'Equality of Educational Opportunity: a reconsideration' – subsequently printed by the Centre (ch. 3).

The History of Education Society, to whom a paper was read at Birmingham Polytechnic on 5 May 1979 entitled 'Endless Agendas: interpreting the history of education in the United States and Britain' (ch. 4).

The Institute of Education, University of London, to whose MA students in curriculum studies a paper was read on 'Knowledge as Power' (ch. 8).

The Social Science Research Council, for whom a version of 'Accountability in Education: towards a history of some English features' was written in 1979 (ch. 6).

I am indebted to Chelsea College, to the University of London and to the Social Science Research Council for assistance with research for other purposes in the United States, where some of this material originated and where some of the ideas were discussed. Without John Naylor the book would never have been started, and without Pam it would never have been finished.

H.S.
Bulmershe College of Higher Education

1 The social condition: a framework for discussion

My main concern in this book is with education and society now, with education as it is and as it is not. My central assumption is that without a serious historical input it is difficult to know how to discuss education in the present. Not that the history provides the answers, or merely helps to identify the questions: it is necessary for any sense of judging the nature and dimensions of the questions. If a high proportion of this book is concerned with twentieth-century educational history, and to a lesser extent with its nineteenth-century foundations, it is in order to suggest ways of beginning to think about the present. If it contains material about the United States, it is the better to be able to think about Britain.

Increasingly in the 1960s and 1970s it has become difficult to recognize educational orthodoxy, to know what is progressive, to identify what is radical. In matters of school provision, what is taught, when and how, there has been endless controversy, experiment, disillusion, and abandonment of the field to whatever and whoever happens at the moment to have the largest visible amount of confidence. Going forward has come to be interpreted as going backward, or nowhere. Discussions of higher education become trapped in what higher education is, with decreasing certainty as to what it might be. Plans for action diversify until the central theme becomes the reasons for inaction. Locating the issues in a historical discussion is not an evasion of the issues: it is an attempt to find out if the issues exist.

If my concerns with contemporary education lead me into its recent history, this is not to say that there is *a* history that tells all, *one* inescapable sequence of historical explanations. Historically and in the present we achieve our best possible approximations: what stands as the predominant account of our present or our past does so by virtue of the sophistication of its message, or the authority of its author, or the power of its sponsors, or the accident of its inception – just occasionally by some consensus as to its truth. Such confusions may tell us that something is wrong with our society, or with our ways of making history or analysing our present – or both, or all. Education is one of many social battlegrounds and an understanding of the battles can be arrived at from their present or their past (or their intended future). History is written roughly in two ways. It may attempt to elucidate the present by starting with the present, and tracing the steps which seem to have led to the present events, or structure, or process, or to some known end-point. Or it may start with the past – trying to picture *their* world, *their* structures, *their* interpretations, and seeking some kind of contemporary message about or from them. History which does neither may cease to be history: at one end it becomes disembodied theory, at the other – a compendium, a depository of antiques.

Not, of course, that all accounts of our present or our past have equal value. We assess the data, the method, the interpretation, the judgement. We take our pick, our preference. We take sides. We cast our historical or contemporary vote in selecting the problem, its present and its past, the interpretation of the past and the present, and the solution. Cut off from concern with the past we are involved with contemporary problems presented as logic, or as models, or as passionate prejudice. Cut off from concern with the present we are involved in passionless encounters with the meaningless bric-à-brac of yesterday.

There is a danger. Too much of the history of education has been concerned with derivations, and much of the discussion in this book is concerned with historical derivations of some precise areas of British, or more specifically, English, education in the 1970s. Past attempts at unilinear explanations of the educational system in particular have accompanied excessive concern with major features of our contemporary world – notably the strong, centralized State. A second failure has been the refusal or the inability to grasp, or even consider, the complex discussions by social scientists of the concepts that are the very stock-in-trade of the historians of education – the family, social class, industrialization and democracy, for example. Since these questions of history and ideology have been explored, in relation to the history of education, most extensively in the United States, we shall in a later chapter return to the nature and implications of that exploration. In Britain historical explanation has often tended to be a self-perpetuating concern with *apparently* understood concepts and *apparently* agreed priorities. Historical explanation needs to exchange illuminations with the attempts of social scientists to disentangle the elements of our social condition. The historical *parallel* is of importance only if it suggests otherwise unavailable insights into that condition. From the contemporary analysis historians can learn the limitations of their emphases and frameworks when they approach the past. Present uncertainties, confusions, controversies, conflicting explanations, are reminders of the danger of neglecting in the past the complexities that surround apparently simple events, and that makes it difficult to match causes with effects. It is important to understanding our past and how we moved from there into the present, to be aware of the forgotten and the defeated, the alternative explanations, the conflicting ideologies – in other words, the world as its denizens knew and explained it variously, not the world as chronological sequences and current obsessions suggest.

The 'social condition', however vague it may be, seems a useful working concept for the discussion of education in this book. Not the 'human condition' because this is not an attempt at philosophical stock-taking. The theme cannot be described as the 'historical condition', because the intention is not to encompass a long time-scale of historical change, or the lack of it. The theme is social. Not the 'social context' – that ultra-fashionable phrase – because it is too inert, as if education is surrounded by, framed by, perhaps even affected by the big out-there, but is not in any serious kind of relationship with it, *in* but not *of* it. Not 'education and society', because that implies more of a theoretical commitment than is claimed here to explain how we relate to one another as a social complexity, and how education is located in all of that. Not even 'education and social change' – which, by repeating the title of Sir Fred Clarke's 1940 book, would have implied too much that we are at the kind of significant moment that Clarke perceived would follow the war, when things are expected to happen, and when education was destined to play a major part in the happening. At the end of the 1970s that may, of course, be the case, but it is not particularly obvious that it is. The 'social condition' therefore offers the opportunity to emphasize the present and a manageable time-scale of discussion, to ask what are some of the main features of the way we *are* together, and what we still want or can expect of education. A 'condition' is something that it is sensible to try to understand, and to wish to improve. It calls us to reflect on recent experience, and to expose anxieties.

The publication of Clarke's little book, *Education and Social Change* is a useful starting-point. It has an important ancestry. There have been a small number of important books written in this country in what can be broadly described as a sociological tradition, books that have in the nineteenth and twentieth centuries had an impact far beyond what might have been expected from their scale – and usually with no small surprise to their authors. The first was Robert Owen's *A New View of Society* – four essays written in the 1810s and offering the first humane educational analysis of and programme for the new industrial society. Radical and epoch-making in a totally different way was Herbert Spencer's *Education: Intellectual, Moral and Physical*, four essays published as a book in 1861, exploring education in relation to the Victorian social dynamic and containing his great essay on 'What Knowledge Is of Most Worth?' – the answer being science, broadly (socially) interpreted. The two outstanding twentieth-century texts in the tradition are R. H. Tawney's 1922 *Secondary Education for All*, and Clarke's *Education and Social Change*. All four (and there are other candidates for the list, including Matthew Arnold's *Culture and Anarchy*) are acutely aware of aspects of social change, of the social definition of education, of a relationship between education and any improvement in the social condition. In a period when some research and important sections of opinion internationally question whether education does and can contribute to such an improvement, it is imperative – especially in Britain – to be aware of the tradition, and to try to make sense of it.

Clarke's basis for thinking about education and the future was liberal and social-democratic as well as Christian, though the Christianity does not play an important, or at least a very central and explicit, part in his argument. Clarke had had considerable international experience, including many years in South Africa, and he had a strong sense of justice at the level both of policy and of social experience. He was committed to a radical view of educational reform: he had felt in 1922 that Tawney's *Secondary Education for All* programme did not go far enough. Tawney, he wrote, seemed to accept the present order of things in secondary education and confines himself to the demand that all who are mentally fit should be admitted to its opportunities. . . . The task of the Labour Party . . . is not merely to get the children of the working-man into the free secondary school. It is to point the way to a social order where, in and through the educative function of that social order itself, what was for the Greeks the special privilege of the few may become for us the common heritage of the many.[1]

Clarke's early understanding of the limitations of Tawney's programme, and his emphasis on 'the educative function' of the 'social order itself' point towards the strengths of the book he was to write nearly two decades later. By 1940 Clarke was also firmly committed to the need for a sociology of education that would contribute both to understanding and to change. He later acknowledged that *Education and Social Change* owed much to Karl Mannheim, the great refugee sociologist with whom Clarke was in close contact.[2] By 1940 wartime reconstructionist ideals were already being formulated and Clarke was given reason to believe, as he put it, that his book 'had some influence on the course of events',[3] helping as it did to guide and crystallize the body of opinion out of which came the Education Act of 1944. Clarke was in this respect the Beveridge of education.

The importance of Clarke's analysis lies in its sense of intersection – between history and the present, between tradition and the critical need to understand, respond to and influence change. In the book he talks a good deal about the liberal tradition and the need to adapt it to new demands, but the overwhelming sense is of a long-delayed need for new educational structures which would advance social justice. *Education and Social Change* offered four main, related messages. *First,* the old class-divided education would be intolerable after the war. 'We can hardly continue,' he wrote, 'to contemplate an England where the mass of the people coming on by one educational path are to be governed for the most part by a minority advancing by a quite separate and more favoured path.'[4] In the context of a brief but important discussion of cultural history Clarke recognized that 'the effects of a long past during which it was the rule that the many should be schooled for the service and convenience of the few are not thus easily to be thrown off'.[5] But the message is crisp and emphatic. *Second,* it is particularly so in relation to secondary education. It was necessary, he believed, to see 'with clear eyes that great field of *secondary* education in which our main task of reconstruction lies'.[6] And with a clarity that many people failed to develop until long after the 1944 Act had been implemented, he wrote in this connection: 'It is surely a little naive to imagine that in the present state of English society real parity of status can be established between the "modern" school for the unselected goats and the "grammar" school for the carefully selected sheep.'[7] *Third*, at various points in the book Clarke points to the lack of a solid sociology of educational and social differences: 'So far as we are aware there are no studies of English social structure and class distinction which have set themselves to estimate with some precision the real social effects of these diverse routes to the goal.'[8] He is anxious to thrust the discussion of apparently 'neutral' educational issues into their social and political dimensions. English writers, he complains, 'often in the most ingenious way . . . give vigorous expression to quite English politico-social ideals while believing themselves to be discussing pure educational theory . . . our English authors show little explicit awareness of the social presuppositions of their thought.'[9] *Fourth*, he suggests that the future pattern of education requires increased State intervention. He discounts anxieties about 'Whitehall bureaucracy' because forty years of vigorous State action had already by that time resulted in no two counties being alike 'in the individual interpretation they have each worked out of a common national policy for the mass'.[10]

It is worth underlining these main points in Clarke's book for two reasons: to indicate the directions in which we have travelled since 1940, and to raise some issues for which Clarke still provides relevant starting-points. The directions are fairly clear. We have since the Second World War become massively engaged with the notion that education may or should contribute to greater social justice and economic opportunities, and we have across four decades pursued educational policies that have started from that assumption. We have to a considerable extent remodelled our secondary education, at the same time as having to debate the 'politico-social ideals' which relate to such strategies. No one can any longer doubt, therefore, that education is a significant political issue. We also have a quarter-century of extensive educational sociology behind us, a sociology which has increasingly sought to reveal underlying relationships between education, the social structure, culture, social class, the family, the State – relationships central to Clarke's own analysis. The State, finally, has become increasingly involved in educational policy-making, planning and provision. Clarke did not invent such criteria and emphases, but – like the 1944 Act itself – he helped to raise them to the level of comprehensive national policy.

We have not, of course, gone forward since 1940 to accomplish all that the rhetoric has often suggested, nor have we proceeded uniformly and in agreement. We have not shared an agreed national policy for education, or even an agreed framework of discussion. We have not agreed as a nation on what has constituted success or failure. The discussion of educational expansion, access and social mobility has to some of us been central, to others a distraction from the real educational enterprise – that concerned with educational 'quality' and 'standards'. We have not agreed about the relevance or the operation of social class, the need for or the effectiveness of positive discrimination and compensatory policies. We have clashed over progressive methods, selection, the comprehensive school, the raising of the school leaving age, public examinations, direct grant schools, school milk, school management, discipline, and priorities in the allocation of resources. We have not agreed about the way to handle resistance to authority inside or outside the school, and we have not agreed about its causes. We have reacted differently to the findings of an impressive list of committee and commission reports since Clarke wrote his book – reports on teachers, on schools, on technology, higher and adult education, and in general the problems of education in a period of rapid social change.

Behind our political and ideological disagreements, however, lies a crucial, common confidence in the educational process. Since the early nineteenth century education has become our religion – and we have in education our fundamentalists, our evangelicals, our latitudinarians, but above all our similar faiths. In this Clarke reflects a confidence that expresses our feelings about education since the Second World War, and indeed in this century – our confidence in its ability both to change and to protect, what Clarke referred to elsewhere as Matthew Arnold's 'overwhelming sense of the school as a civilizing agent'.[11] We have for the most part disagreed about the shape of that civilization and the behaviour of the agent, about the extent of social coherence and division, about classroom tactics and national strategies – but not about the centrality of schools and of education. The short life in this country of the deschooling debate and the limited nature of experimental 'alternatives' to the school system in the 1960s and 1970s, indicate the strength of our belief, or of our inertia.

We do not all want to use education for the same ends, but we all want to use it. Here lies the central difficulty of talking about what 'we' want, and equally about the 'social condition'. We have as many conditions as we have categories of people thinking about them. Before we turn to the implications, however, it is important to re-emphasize what I called Clarke's 'sense of intersection' between history and the present. Clarke's whole discussion reinforces how critical it is to locate education in a contemporary *and* historical sense of our social condition, requiring more attention to an understanding of our recent experience than we have been prepared to devote, and a heightened awareness of the politico-social nature of our educational enterprise.

'Much good work has been done, and is being done,' wrote Clarke in 1950, 'on the history of English education in the nineteenth century. We shall understand ourselves and our situation better when that work has been carried nearer completion. It cannot yet be called "adequate".'[12] We need a more 'adequate' view of our history since the Second World War, particularly our attempts to reorganize, redeploy, rethink our educational resources, procedures and aims (or too often the 'common sense' and unexamined assumptions that we have assumed to be legitimate aims). Our assessment of our present condition rests on too many speculative accounts of our recent educational history, and to gain more clarity on the central features of that history is of mounting importance if we are not to claim too much for it, or to dismiss it contemptuously without having even properly examined it.

The lack of such a historical sense has produced the sterile educational non-dialogues of the 1970s. Much in the conservative and radical critiques of educational policy has been trapped in an unhistorical present, erecting politico-social models which do not intersect with any historical understandings. The more stringent conservative critique has tried to pull education from the contamination of the social, to restore the 'purity' of its 'standards', and to deny the social imprint on our educational condition. Clarke was profoundly convinced that schools were important, but in addition that 'the general life of society is also a "school"'.[13] The conservative critique does not work, in Clarke's view or mine, because it simply ignores the socio-historical processes that have remodelled our lives in the recent past. The *Black Papers*, for example, have since the end of the 1960s waged unhistorical war on our recent educational experience, wishing that the social pressures that have shaped changes in educational policy and practice would simply go away. They have not gone away. The conservative response has been to try to restore education to a definition that will conjure the pressures away. The conservative attack has therefore – in the way Clarke diagnosed – substituted for the understandings we need, an ingenuous politico-social ideal disguised as pure educational theory.

The attempts at a radical critique of educational reform as it has been pursued in the 1970s in particular have combined theoretical political models with a historical picture as thin and as crude as that of the most conservative one. They have portrayed the main educational policies and experiences of the 1960s and 1970s as having been naively social-democratic, and the actors as being trapped in large historical forces, producing liberal reforms aimed at stabilizing and improving on the capitalist *status quo*. The grains of truth in the argument are wrapped in unhistorical judgements which debase it. The argument is conducted to the point at which historical forces and contemporary motives are trivialized, so that the research of the 1950s and afterwards is divorced from the situation in which clarity and reform were being sought, so that A. H. Halsey ends up resembling Rhodes Boyson, and educational priority areas might just as well have been designed by Margaret Thatcher.

If the conservative and radical positions have led to a huge admixture of socio-historical fantasy, that is no argument for seeking an anodyne, compromise, cosily liberal middle ground. Locating education in the texture of the social condition is still the need; and as radical a position as it was when Clarke was defining it. Since the conservative view survives only by clinging to romantic and illusory pictures of the past, the only place where history and the present *can* intersect is on that socially committed part of the spectrum that is radical in one way or another.

Clearly we are now in a situation where there is little certainty either about the problems to which education should be addressing itself, or about how to place educational advance outside the narrow limits of the party political see-saw, or about the extent to which education can change anything anyway. In terms of the social condition our experience since the Second World War has not been reassuring, in spite of the constant extension of 'education' beyond its definition as 'schooling', and of thrusts into new educational directions in the community, in adult education, in higher education, 'the educative function of the social order itself'. The educational responses to underprivilege, disadvantage, inequality, poverty (the history of the vocabulary itself is important) have produced not only uncertain results but arguably no results. In the 1950s and 1960s we sought to equalize opportunities by means of institutional reorganization. From the late 1960s we sought means of applying positive discrimination in ways which would improve the life chances of the poor, the minorities, the immigrant, the black, the inner-city child (again the vocabulary bears scrutiny). Educational priority areas, urban aid, compensatory schemes of various kinds – these were designed at least in part to use educational channels and economic resources to tilt a social balance, and it is clearly the case that the achievement has been disappointing, and expectations may – we can judge with hindsight – seem to have been exaggerated and naive.

Poverty is still a major element in our condition. The educational paths to positions of leadership and followership are still as clearly exemplified by Mrs Thatcher's cabinet and the main positions of power today as they were in pre-1940 England. The structure of education in the State sector may have been remodelled, social and occupational mobility may be notionally more accessible, and the language of socio-economic divisions may have been softened from time to time, but the social injustices and problems indicated by Clarke are not very different. One argument would be that educational programmes such as Clarke's or those of the 1950s and 1960s are inevitably and by definition palliatives, adapting traditions based on exploitation and injustice and bound to fail. It is not surprising, therefore, the argument continues, if little or nothing has changed, because the very attempt at reform has perpetuated a system which can be reformed *only* by fundamental political, revolutionary changes. Since this argument brings us no nearer to an analysis of education and the social condition – indeed it denies the legitimacy of the attempt – it can be by-passed here, though we shall return to it. We are left, therefore, with two major ways of responding to the disappointing outcomes of our educational strategies. Either we can argue that education should not have concerned itself with these things in the first place, and should abandon the attempt, or we can argue that it was right to do so, and we now need to do more and better. The former is the conservative version of the revolutionary message – education is not an instrument of social change and should not be distorted by confusing its aims with those of other social agencies. The latter keeps open the possibility of pursuing present anxieties and seeking in the past the sources of understanding and change. If education has not solved the dilemmas of our condition it is because it has not engaged *sufficiently* with them. In attempting to combat disadvantage and discrimination it has not *sufficiently* related to other partners whose roles need similar attention – housing, the social services, and the possible range of social and political measures which can constitute a coherent campaigning whole. Education has not *sufficiently* and explicitly enough sought to disentangle rival enquiries, rival conclusions and rival versions, rival policies, and it has not *sufficiently* committed itself to improvements in the condition of society.

'Improvements' of what and for whom are obviously the critical questions. If as a nation we look to education for improvements in technology, in productive power, in the supply of necessary and usable competencies, in access to culture and the sources of human satisfaction, then these are proper dimensions of educational design and provision. But unless they are supplemented with an equal commitment to improving social justice, to taking part in processes that point towards greater equality and the elimination of profound social divisions and grievances, these are disembodied targets. Educational goals for all are not equally achieved for all, and the results are not evenly distributed. The concept of positive discrimination has been a relatively recent newcomer to our thinking, and after barely a decade of trying to manipulate it we ought not to let it too easily out of sight.

One of the main things we have learned since 1940 is how difficult it is to achieve change through education, if it is seen in isolation from other strategies for intervention. Clarke has been proved wrong in assuming that a convincing sociology plus a determined restructuring of the secondary school would alone make major inroads into the problems of a divided and unequal society. Our concern with opportunities and structural changes has not upheld such a belief, though the vision was justified and laudable, and in the decades since 1940 we have learned to incorporate those emphases in our analysis of education at all levels and in all its forms. That may prove to have been an important beginning. This is still something rationalist and eighteenth-century in Clarke's view that somehow truth will triumph. It was there in Owen's *A New View of Society*, and Spencer's proclamation of the virtues of science shared it. We still share it, but the message since 1940 is that a great deal more is necessary in education than sensible people producing sensible policies. What Clarke thought would be intolerable after the war is still tolerated.

Social change has continued since 1940 to add emphasis to the relationship between educational institutions and processes and the expectations of social groups. Racial and ethnic groups have joined the lower socio-economic groups of earlier debates – with education being called upon to contribute to their advancement, to the removal of economic, social and psychological obstacles. However difficult it has proved to be since 1940 in responding to such imperatives, it is as critical for education to do so as it is to respond to international economic competition and specific manpower needs for technology and trade. Unemployment and the differential distribution of unemployment impinge as directly on education as do national debates about the curriculum or new technology. The changing pattern of disadvantage makes it essential for us not to lose sight of the emphases we learned to place from the 1950s, as well as not to repeat some crucial weaknesses and mistakes. The time-scale has been incredibly too short for us to dwell on the disappointments.

To argue that education has not responded and therefore *cannot* and *should not* respond to the built-in social deficiencies of our society is to accept either that those deficiencies are inevitable and even necessary, or that there is nothing to be done but wait, whilst making more and more sophisticated revolutionary models for another day. The problem on which history most appropriately focuses is how in the past we have moved from one position to another, one structure to another, one dominant set of social values to another. It does not invite us to abandon models, but it does remind us that we have to live with realities, or with our perceptions of them. It reminds us of the need to grapple with the zigzags of social change and with the possibilities of planning so as to harness change or solve the problems it creates. In the decades since Clarke wrote his book, social and economic changes have been real and far-reaching, as has been the international condition in which our national problems have been increasingly defined. In setting out to adapt educational traditions to new circumstances we may not have profoundly altered either side of that equation, but neither have the relationship and the possibility been disproved. It has been a swiftly moving and busy period, and not least of its accomplishments may prove to have been simply that we learned to translate *some* of the empty educational rhetoric into the explicit politico-social terms which Clarke demanded. A quarter-century may yet look a short period of time in which to have recognized and explored the processes of social and economic disadvantage and to have developed a widespread commitment to tackling them. The ultra-conservative rejection of the realities of that condition or of any concern to engage with them, and the ultra-radical attack on reforming approaches to it, may both prove to have been historically trivial.

It is going to be difficult to find the right level of confidence to invest in our formal educational structures. The confidence of the 1950s and 1960s in the efficacy of schools has been seriously undermined in sections of the community where support for education has been traditionally strong. We need to weigh with care the evidence of what schools can and cannot do, and their ability to act as agencies of improvement. We need to be particularly careful about the judgements we make on the basis of those aspects of schooling and educational processes that appear to be measurable. American and British attempts to judge effectiveness on the basis of measurements of, for example, cognitive achievement and the impact of schools on social mobility have not carried us very far towards the kind of understandings under discussion here. They may even have taken us further away by focusing on narrow aspects of educational processes and pupil performance, leaving the central questions untouched. That is one level at which confidence has been undermined. At another it has been affected by the over-zealous positions adopted in the past two decades. The ways in which education has been used, especially in the 1960s and 1970s, in response to the most acute problems highlighted by rapid social change are typical of the occasional bursts of over-confidence that have marked the nineteenth and twentieth centuries. In turn, education has been urged as a bulwark against the influence of the French Revolution, the guardian of values disrupted by the Industrial Revolution, a cheaper form of police, a protection against mid nineteenth-century radicalism, the agent of industrial renewal in the face of late nineteenth-century German and American competition, a centre-piece of empire, and in this century just about everything – guardian of morals, restorer of authority, protector of health and of the consumer, and universal rescue agent.

Historians have not been as careful as they might have been in evaluating the outcomes of nineteenth- and twentieth-century educational programmes and policies, too often assuming that outcomes were what was intended, and only what was intended. Educational processes have become increasingly complex, and the 'clients' have not always been compliantly processed or 'socially controlled' in the ways for which schools and other institutions have been designed. The assumption has tended to be that the relationship between educational development and social outcomes is visible and even measurable when this has rarely been the case. In recent decades we have therefore – and we share this with the rest of the world – placed enormous confidence in the power of the school to effect change or to guard against it. Over-confidence in the school as a social agent has meant an underestimation of other agencies, and in some cases the emphasis on school reform *may* have been intended to divert attention from other necessary, fundamental, economic and social reforms. The confidence generated by the research, especially that of the sociologists, in the 1950s and 1960s, was too unguarded, and resulted in strategies that were too narrowly designed to achieve what was so broadly intended. If we have learned since Clarke neither to abandon confidence nor to misapply it in isolation, it is not going to be easy in the 1980s to operate on that basis. What our social condition requires is that we re-examine the meaning of our past confidence.

The prophets of retreat from the socio-educational emphases of the last quarter-century have become more strident and powerful. The balance needed will be to resist over-confidence but to rescue a sense of education as a necessary partner in improving the social condition. More than ever this century this will mean arguing through the nature of State intervention in critical areas of social experience – including education. Conservative and liberal theories of the State have emphasized either its neutrality or its danger to the rights and initiatives of the individual. Marxist and radical theories have emphasized its role as an instrument of a ruling class, its subservience to the centres of real power. Clarke did not confront these stances, and merely saw the State as a possible and necessary agency of major educational and social reform. We have in the past decades had considerable experience of the more active intervention of the State in matters of economic organization, welfare, education and a wide range of areas which directly and regularly affect our lives as citizens and individuals. Our history in this respect is difficult for Americans, for example, to grasp and sympathize with, even in the context of systematic attempts by American governments to move in some of these directions and of the recent history of substantially greater federal government involvement in education. Clarke's view was that State intervention to restructure and improve education would not result in uniformity or conformity. Clarke, like Beveridge, was defining a greater role for the State, at the end of the economic and social hazards of the 1930s, in conditions of war and the first formulations of ideals for the peace. Through increased State action lay the only path to reform.

We have developed hesitations of various kinds since then and seen some of the hopes of social renovation through State action disappointed or only partly fulfilled. We have developed various sorts of suspicion of action by State and public authorities, and critiques of the State from the political left and right. The Thatcher Government of 1979 was a beneficiary. None of this experience weakens the emphasis Clarke gave to the State's relationship to social and political reform. There are serious problems about the balance between central and local government, about the competing claims of 'government' and 'bureaucracy' and 'community', about the contexts in which government and its agencies operate and the nature of their accountability. That is where the battle begins – in the forums of public debate, directed towards the agencies of public provision. There is no way of seriously thinking about educational and social advance without an increased commitment to improving the provision and the social condition, and without as great a stress on local diversity within national State intervention as Clarke postulated in 1940.

The extended reference to Clarke's *Education and Social Change* is intended to indicate the strength of the tradition in which it is located, and the continued relevance of its argument. Clarke was hoping that greater clarity about the nineteenth century would help to situate more clearly the educational and social world as he witnessed it. Whilst we do not and cannot have definitive analyses of that history, it is possible to have what Matthew Arnold described and Clarke accepted as 'adequate' ones. We still live with many of those nineteenth-century contours, and the kinds of adaptations that Clarke advocated have indeed been begun, but perhaps only begun. Reflecting in the late 1940s about the origins and impact of *Education and Social Change*, Clarke considered the importance of the new awareness of social realities and difficulties, and the task of post-war reconstruction:

This heightened awareness of the social and cultural setting is of peculiar importance for the re-planning of English education. During the present century English theorizing about education had become much too speculative, too much bound to the findings of purely individual biology and psychology. So it tended to take for granted the actualities of society when it did not ignore them completely.[14]

It is still crucially important to be aware of this social and cultural setting and these actualities in thinking about and continuing to replan education. What we have done in the recent past is explore more fully how the school and the setting interlink, but also – and perhaps this will be more important for the future – we have begun to see, as Clarke urged, the social and cultural setting as itself an 'educative function'. The relationship does not end at the formal levels prescribed by institutions and policies. The adaptation of the nineteenth-century contours is not just a question of adapting the school – it is a question of incorporating into our understanding of education the whole social experience of our communities. The expectations of racial groups, disadvantage, the actualities of urban life – these are not 'factors' which impinge on education, they are not a context. They are part of that social condition which is integral to education, which *is* education. It is as important now as it was in 1940 to develop that understanding, and to act on it.

Our commitment to understanding the social as well as the individual condition has a longer history, but in the senses in which Clarke defined it the period since 1940 may be considered to have been the real start, and perhaps even a good start. An increased awareness of the relationship between education and the social condition may yet be seen to have been a major achievement of these past decades.

2 Education and social policy

Education has been used in this century as a vital instrument of social policy by governments of all kinds – with varying degrees of commitment or reluctance, and with different and conflicting intentions. The level of confidence in the instrument has been marked by spurts of expansion and contraction, investment and cuts, flurries of enquiry and policy-making, legislation and regulation, and the diversification of levels and types of provision. Whatever the other functions of the increasingly large and complex system of education, its history can be written in terms of social policy – the attempt to use education to solve social problems, to influence social structures, to improve one or more aspects of the social condition, to anticipate crisis. All schooling and all education have involved such 'social' dimensions, whether it be the medieval song or grammar school, the aristocratic 'grand tour', the eighteenth-century charity school or the nineteenth-century mutual improvement society of working men. It is only in this century, however, that an education system has been deliberately filled out, stage by stage, under a variety of pressures and with varying rhythms, to provide – through education – an elaborate social service, responding to expressed needs in child psychology, child development and child health; providing (or under the stronger pressures of economic policy, taking away) school meals and milk, medical inspection and dental treatment, open-air classrooms and playing fields, pre-school education, community schools and education for retirement. Although the criticism of educational isolation remains pertinent, educational policy has throughout this century been responsible (often slowly, reluctantly or half-heartedly, under threat, pressure or persuasion) to questions of health and welfare, to changes in employment or social structure, and to changing expectations by different social groups of access to education – and to privilege or power or anything else that education may imply.

Education-as-social-policy has in Britain meant overwhelmingly the State-provided and State-supported sector of education, subsuming but leaving intact the Churches' involvement in education from the 1902 Education Act onwards. It has imposed only marginal constraints on the independent, fee-paying sector of education. The English 'public school' has never become amenable to the pressures of national social policy-making, which is not, of course, to imply that it does not have social 'functions'. It was untouched by the Government-sponsored enquiries and reports during the Second World War and at the end of the 1960s.

To come closer to an appreciation of specific educational issues and roles it is important to establish the nature of the developments in education-as-social-policy, especially since the First World War. Socialist and radical pressures for health and welfare measures for schoolchildren emerged in the final decades of the nineteenth century, and school meals, medical care and other services began to appear systematically at the beginning of the twentieth century. The experience of the First World War was crucial in a number of respects. Education, wrote R. H. Tawney in 1917, was better understood to be worth sacrifices because 'the war has been itself an education'. The war would be judged by 'the kind of civilisation which arises from it'.[1] A quarter of a century and another world war later, Tawney was again looking at the chance of education contributing to the peace. The speed and energy with which Butler's promised education Bill was enacted and implemented by the Government, Tawney wrote in a pamphlet, 'will be generally and properly regarded as a test of its sincerity in the sphere, not only of education, but of social policy as a whole'.[2] Educational policy was, for Tawney, 'always social policy', and wartime awareness of this fact had to be exploited. The two education Acts of 1918 and 1944 are signposts not just of twentieth-century education, but also of twentieth-century social consciousness, as heightened by war and by anticipations of and planning for peace. If education before 1914 is most often viewed in the context of the increasingly powerful State, it emerges most clearly from the First World War and the inter-war years as an increasingly explicit instrument of social policy.

Education in all its forms, we have suggested, has always been a social instrument, and historians have constantly to evaluate the motives of the makers and users of the instrument. Its most recent declared purposes have included the protection of democracy and social values, the improvement of national efficiency and the protection of the nation. It has been seen both as a means of selecting and perpetuating elites, and as a means of promoting social justice and undermining elites. It is discussed in terms of class domination and social control, but also of social liberation and progress. In the twentieth century education has become more and more prominent in political manifestos and policies, economic calculations and family discussion, bookshops and the Press. It has also become international. It has universally become a major instrument of national policy. Educational systems and educationists have come together in education movements, professional conferences and attempts at educational policy at regional and supranational levels. Education has become one of the most sensitive national responses to international economic and political change. Finally, it has responded to threat – internally in the form of social conflict and internationally most directly in the form of war.

Pressures towards educational planning as part of national reconstruction strengthened in Britain in the latter part of the First World War, pointing, for example, towards post-war concerns with adult education and an emphasis on community and citizenship. A new concern with the concept of adolescence and its problems emerged in the war. Demands for a new deal in elementary education and for an expansion of secondary education were heard. A more humane view of education itself was being urged. The 1918 Education Act was a set of compromises enacted by a Liberal Government with cautious support from the parliamentary Labour Party, some opposition from industry, and reflecting widespread uncertainty and controversy about how far and in which directions and forms compulsory schooling ought to go. It laid down fourteen as the school leaving age, abolished fees for elementary education, and proposed part-time 'continuation schools' up to the age of sixteen – intended later to be raised to eighteen. In this and subsequent legislation attempts were made to extend the range of educational concerns beyond the immediate ones of the classroom: the Act was concerned with holiday camps, physical training and playing fields, 'facilities for social and physical training' and, in the case of nursery schools, arrangements for the 'health, nourishment, and physical welfare of children'.[3]

From 1920 the discussion of education was concerned with economic disaster, failures to implement the 1918 measures, and attempts to hold back an already impoverished elementary school system. The story is of education in terms of political and economic strategies, to be considered alongside the inter-war picture of economic decline and the profound conflicts symbolized by unemployment, the general strike, and the rise of European Fascism. All of those provide a frame in which to consider the explicit concern with the social dimensions of education.

In the 1920s, as always, the school was seen as a means of attacking social problems – though not within the same context of comprehensive planning as after the Second World War. Once concern was with the health as well as the academic accomplishments of children. The school, wrote Bolton King, a former Director of Education, 'has become one of the most hopeful of all fields for improving the national physique'.[4] The period before the war and during the war itself had sharpened the awareness of the extent of ill health, and the social distribution of disease and infant mortality. Reports on dental decay had produced 350 school dental clinics by 1918.[5] Not only had the child been 'discovered', and new concerns with the child's freedom to act and develop been underlined, but new emphases on the relationship between education and protection against ill health had come to play a prominent part in the literature of the 1920s and 1930s. Margaret Macmillan continued to thrust nursery schools, fresh air, children's health, into the public consciousness, and the labour movement increasingly linked education with demands for wider children's and welfare benefits.

A parallel concern with children's mental health was developing rapidly. The psychology of childhood and adolescence was becoming an important field of interest. By the beginning of the 1930s the concern with stages of mental development was reaching the official literature. Progressive educators like Percy Nunn were basing their work on new theories of intelligence (in 1932 Susan Isaacs discussed in *The Children We Teach* the contribution of intelligence testing to groupwork with children, enabling them to 'have the free activity which is their breath of life'[6]). As an indication of the contribution it was now believed child psychology could make to the problems of maladjustment, the first child guidance clinic was opened in Birmingham in 1932, and there were seventy-nine such clinics by 1945.[7] Campaigners like H. Crichton-Miller lectured and wrote on child and adolescent health and psychology, and the Tavistock Clinic (of which Miller became Honorary Director) was created in 1920 and opened a children's department in 1926.[8]

In Britain and the United States economic and social realities had 'created' the adolescent (or at least had brought the category to prominence as a social category), by reducing work opportunities for the older child, extending school life, producing a new set of definitions and anxieties. Britain's most characteristic document of the new concern was the Hadow report on *The Education of the Adolescent* in 1926, with its famous reference to the 'tide which begins to rise in the veins of youth at the age of eleven or twelve. It is called by the name of adolescence.' The report indicates 'the rising interest in the problem presented by children between 11 and 15 or 16'.[9] Structural changes in industry and commerce, the weakening of family controls in wartime, and developments in psychology, had produced a new educational and social 'problem'. Unemployment exacerbated it. The demand for secondary education as a right became entangled with the role of the school in keeping adolescents off the labour market. Attention began to focus on the education of the adolescent as a major feature of social policy.

The establishment of a minimum school leaving age and the provision of continuation schools in the 1918 Act (the latter measure never really implemented) were intended, among other things, to extend the provisions of the factory Acts. It ended the nineteenth-century half-time system which still existed in some industries. In 1915 it was estimated that over half a million children under the age of fourteen were in employment in England.[10] The 1918 measures were seen by Tawney and others as an advance but 'a makeshift'.[11] During the economic difficulties and conservative counter-attacks after 1920 (especially the cuts following the Geddes Committee of 1922) even these makeshifts proved vulnerable. In the social and ideological struggles of the 1920s and 1930s, however, education continued to be seen widely as an essential component of any strategy for social and democratic advance. Adult education is one example. A Ministry of Reconstruction committee on adult education in 1919 described it as a 'primary obligation' on the community. It was a product of the desire of individuals for 'opportunities of self-expression' and of 'the social aspirations of the democratic movements of the country'. It rested on the 'twin principles of personal development and social service'.[12] The co-operative movement, the Workers' Educational Association and other popular movements and organizations had pioneered such developments, but by 1933 it could be said that the adult education provided by local authorities had 'widened its scope to include all classes in the community and all kinds of demand'.[13] A second example would be the extensive concern with rural education. A chapter on rural schools was almost mandatory in any book on education. When the Board of Education in 1933 publicized a successful experiment in rural school reorganization (along lines proposed by the Hadow Committee in 1926), it emphasized the importance of school halls, for example, in rural communities as social centres, for 'what for want of a better term may be called "mass" instruction'.[14] Schools were seen as helping to break down rural isolation and combat the drift from the countryside. One of the most important and far-sighted of these developments between the wars was the creation of the Cambridgeshire village colleges by Henry Morris.

At the heart of educational, social and political policy lay tensions made increasingly visible by economic conditions. They were most acute and explicit in relation to secondary education. The debates about secondary education encompassed mainly its structure, access to it, the extension of the free place, special place or scholarship system, and financial support for children from poorer families. The division between working-class elementary education and middle-class secondary education was becoming, especially after Tawney's *Secondary Education for All* in 1922, increasingly intolerable to those sections of opinion that Clarke was later to represent in *Education and Social Change*. The existing system was seen by the labour movement and an increasing number of educationists as either unjust or inefficient or both. By the 1930s waste, maldistribution of resources and manpower needs had begun to join the political and social promotion of 'secondary education for all' as important themes in the discussion. Voices were also being raised in counter-attack. In the 1920s J. H. Garrett (in *Mass Education in England*) and M. Alderton Pink (in *Procrustes*), for instance, were attacking the 'cult' of education, faith in the 'fallacy' of educability, and over-enthusiasm for secondary education. What they thought most necessary was 'ordinary' education for 'ordinary' children, help towards earning a living – not in the schools, but on the job.[15] The clash of ideals and ideologies that was to become familiar in the comprehensive schools debate of the 1960s effectively begins here.

The focus of the debate nationally before the war was the Hadow report on *The Education of the Adolescent*, with its proposal that secondary or post-primary education should, for all children, succeed primary. Even those in the labour movement most vociferous in demanding such educational reconstruction were, however, uncertain about what this meant. The Labour Party and the TUC in the late 1920s were simply calling for some kind of secondary education for all. Although support was developing within the Labour Party for the 'multilateral' school, the alternatives of common diverse secondary schools remained confused, and the prevailing tone of discussion was one of uncertainty. It continued to be so into the interpretations of secondary education policy under the Labour Government after 1945.

If Labour was hesitant about the form of secondary schooling, it was equally ambiguous about the independent public schools. Tawney and other socialists attacked them vigorously for their social class exclusiveness. But should they be abolished, reformed, integrated into the State system, or what? The Workers' Educational Association in 1943 wanted a review of 'all independent and private schools with a view to their being included, if suitable, in the public system of education'[16] – a statement which reflects the ambiguities of the attack on the public schools. A Nuffield College report in 1943 (one of the signatories was socialist G. D. H. Cole) outlined two extremes of opinion: 'At one extreme . . . are those who hold that the public schools belong to a past age and that in a democracy there is no place for private expenditure on education.' At the other extreme were those who 'hold that any step taken to widen the entry to the public schools will destroy their character'. This report agreed with neither.[17] The Fleming Committee on the public schools, set up in 1942 and reporting two years later, recommended as a middle path the opening of the public schools to a proportion of children from local education authority schools. The fee-paying schools have continued ever since to exist on a borderline of discussion between the injustice of privilege and freedom in a democracy.

From 1926, in England and Wales, discussion – and action in the case of some local authorities – was directed primarily towards the possible reorganization of the system, the status of the various elements, and the rights and roles of the various partners, national and local government, and the Churches in particular. The 1936 Education Act was intended, among other things, to reintroduce building grants for the voluntary (Anglican, Catholic, and other) schools, to enable them to cope with the problems of reorgnization on the basis of a two-tier system of primary and secondary education. The reorganization was piecemeal, but by the outbreak of war over 60 per cent of pupils aged eleven and over were in schools that had been reorganized along Hadow lines. The intention to raise the school leaving age under the 1936 Act had to wait for implementation until after the Second World War.

The war produced a sustained and widespread discussion of every aspect of education, and a multitude of policies and plans for post-war educational reform. One central theme was summarized in a question at the start of a book by Sir Richard Livingstone in 1941: 'Why are we an uneducated nation and how can we become an educated one?'[18] The truth was, said the McNair Committee on teacher supply in 1944, that we had not yet 'emancipated ourselves from the tradition of educating our children on the cheap'.[19] A second, related theme was the relationship between education and welfare, especially a mounting wartime interest in nursery education, the home and child health. Beveridge's 1942 social insurance plan was conceived 'as part of a general programme of social policy'. The organization of social insurance was 'one part only of a comprehensive policy of social progress', and of the giants to be overcome on the road of reconstruction one was Ignorance.[20] Education was seen in wartime as being for health, for citizenship, for democracy. It was a 'primary duty of national education', said a Conservative Party report in 1942, 'to develop a strong sense of national obligation in the individual citizen, to encourage in him an ardent understanding of the State's needs'.[21] Planning was heavily influenced by the experience of evacuation. The health, education and behaviour of poor, urban evacuee children caused wide social ripples. A study of *Our Towns* between 1939 and 1943 concluded that the disclosures of evacuation produced 'such a degree of shock and scandal' because pre-war social legislation had led the 'ordinary citizen . . . to believe that all was well with our society'.[22] The experience with evacuees strengthened the demand for more interventionist policies. An evacuation survey conducted in Cambridge and edited by Susan Isaacs concluded that as a result of evacuation 'the health of the children has greatly improved, and this is ascribed to more sleep, more fresh air, better feeding, a quieter life, and less "potted amusement"'.[23] There are moral and cultural as well as social considerations here. The *Our Towns* report talks about 'cutting the slum mind off at the root and building the whole child while yet there is time'.[24]

The Education Act of 1944 was both a key outcome of the wartime demand for 'a comprehensive policy of social progress', and an attempt to complete the processes of reform struggled for between the wars. The American Commissioner of Education, referring particularly to the 1906–7 legislation on school meals and school medical inspection, had written in 1912 that in Britain 'the entire life of the children of the humbler classes has become a matter of public concern'.[25] Such concern had resulted between the wars in changes in the status of education in public debate, but a disappointing level of improvements. The anomaly was that improvements were not only planned, but also experienced, during the Second World War. As Sir Richard Livingstone put it in 1944: '. . . the clearest condemnation of our pre-war civilisation is that though the war has destroyed much of it, we have little to regret except some beautiful buildings, and are a better people leading better lives than in peace.'[26]

Under Butler's 1944 Act education was to be organized in three 'progressive stages to be known as primary education, secondary education, and further education'. Local educational authorities were to contribute to the spiritual, moral, mental and physical development of the community 'by providing efficient education at each of these stages'.[27] Schooling was to be compulsory to the age of fifteen and, as soon as practicable, sixteen. Authorities were to provide medical inspection and treatment, milk and meals, clothing grants, facilities for recreation and social and physical training, and other ancillary services. The Act was comprehensive, consolidating, and on almost all views, triumphant. All children were, under the Act, to receive free secondary education and, when the Act was implemented by the post-war Labour Government, a long-campaigned-for dream had come true. With the Education act, said Lady Simon, 'the process initiated by the Hadow Report in 1926 is completed'.[28] Lord Butler later reflected that in education and other fields of reconstruction the post-war Labour Government had 'only to complete work which the Coalition had begun and in some cases to bring forward Bills already drafted'.[29] The implementation of the Butler Act was part of that wide-ranging programme of post-war 'welfare state' construction that had its roots in pre-war social problems and conflict, earlier twentieth-century legislation, wartime coalition planning, and labour movement ideals and programmes. It flowed from the Beveridge-type commitment to social progress through 'co-operation between the State and the individual'.[30] Greater State intervention was a necessary part of the equation.

Progress through comprehensive community intervention was a feature of post-war social philosophy, much of it shared with the Labour Government by the bulk of Liberal and Conservative opinion. It was at its clearest in the welfare state and nationalization Acts of the first post-war Labour Government. The National Insurance Act of 1946, for example, declared that people 'shall become insured'.[31] The National Health Service Act of the same year introduced 'a comprehensive health service designed to secure improvement in the physical and mental health of the people'.[32] 'To ensure equality of opportunity,' wrote Ruth Glass in 1948, 'is no longer a planner's dream, it is now the duty of every local education authority.'[33] Reviewing the provisions of the 1944 Act the London County Council emphasized that 'it is now the duty of authorities to establish equality of opportunity for all children'.[34] Collectivist assumptions were dominant in all areas of social planning, and education was the first step towards Beveridge's 'comprehensive policy'. In England and Wales the local education authorities produced their plans and prepared to implement the Act as and when post-war economics allowed. Most local authorities opted for differentiated secondary (grammar and modern, and in some cases technical) schools. The authorities' plans provided for nursery and special schools. An emergency scheme to train the necessary teachers was launched. Although the 1945 Education (Scotland) Act pointed in the same directions, Scotland had an educational structure which had developed between the wars in ways similar to those foreshadowed for England and Wales in 1944.

The fulfilment of the plans fell short of the promise. Nursery schools and classes, for example, failed to keep pace with increasing expectations. In 1948 the National Union of Women Teachers thought there was 'general disillusionment'.[35] Investigations of secondary education from the early 1950s showed that the grammar schools had remained largely middle-class preserves. The sociology of education was in fact established in Britain in the 1950s primarily in order to describe and explain the continuing influence of social class on educational experience and achievement. The pattern of selection at eleven could be seen to be governed mainly by social class. The new secondary modern school did not have – as Clarke had warned – the hoped-for 'parity of esteem'. It was 'free' of the examination and other constraints on the grammar schools, and its main difference from other secondary schools, said the Ministry of Education in 1947, was 'its very broad outlook and objective'.[36] It was designed, according to H. C. Dent, to create and apply 'forms of secondary education appropriate to ordinary children'.[37] It was a predominantly working-class school. Discussions of education and reorganization in the 1960s were to be dominated by the realization that an old concept had been discovered to be present and basic in a new structure.

The comprehensive school was seen predominantly in the 1950s as a matter for experiment – as, for example, in London – and for areas such as Anglesey where it could be justified on grounds of convenience and economy in addition to or as well as social and educational policy. In 1950 John Newsom wrote that it was 'unlikely that any of the present children of my readers will go to comprehensive schools, because their construction during the next decade will, inevitably, be extremely limited'.[38] Governments hesitated over them. Economics seemed to prevent them, popular opinion seemed uncertain about them. Not until the mid-1950s did information about the nature and successes of the existing comprehensive schools begin to circulate and influence discussion. Extensive argument about the academic results of the comprehensive school continued in the columns of *The Times Educational Supplement* and elsewhere into the late 1960s.

More Labour-controlled authorities began to consider 'comprehensive reorganization'. Some produced schemes, often against strong local pro-grammar school opposition (occasionally involving public demonstrations, as for example in October 1964 when the Liverpool police dispersed a crowd of 400 grammar school pupils protesting against the scheme adopted by the city council that month[39]). Many local Labour parties were reluctant to abandon the grammar school, and local organizations of the National Union of Teachers and socialist teachers were often engaged in the mid-1960s in trying to persuade Labour councils to 'go comprehensive'. The policy on secondary education adopted by the Labour government elected in 1964 was to invite local authorities which had not yet done so to draw up comprehensive schemes. Circular 10/65, in requesting local authorities to do so, was intended as a first step towards the Government's declared objective 'to end selection at eleven plus and to eliminate separatism in secondary education'.[40] Reorganization was from this point to be a focus of educational debate within and between parties, and subject to the fluctuations of parliamentary and local authority control. Mrs Thatcher, as Conservative Secretary for Education, withdrew Circular 10/65 in 1970; Mrs Williams, as Secretary for Education in a Labour government, piloted the 1976 Education Act which gave the Government powers to move from requests to enforcement of comprehensive school policy. The election of the Conservative Government of 1979 swung the pendulum back in the other direction.

Whilst policy was in this period concerned mainly with the secondary school, sociologists extended their interests into more detailed studies of the mechanics of educational and social selection. The 1950s and 1960s had seen greater expenditure on educational resources, greater concern for the health and welfare of children, and the implementation of post-war schemes intended to improve social security. And yet, as Floud, Halsey and Martin discovered in 1956, Douglas in 1964, and many others in many ways at many points in time, the child's achievement in school continued to be defined largely by considerations of class, parental income, home background, and a large variety of related factors.[41] 'Separatism' between schools, it was also suggested with increasing vigour, was matched by separatism even within comprehensive schools, where streaming and the structure of the curriculum operated in similar ways against the working-class child. The outstanding educational literature of the 1960s and 1970s was concerned with attempts to understand this range of phenomena and to offer strategies to solve them. Interest in the relationships between education, social class and 'under-achievement' extended, especially in the 1960s and 1970s, in three important directions.

First, it underpinned crucial official or semi-official reports on education, ones which significantly influenced educational policy. In 1963, for example, the Newsom Committee reported, in *Half Our Future*, on 'the education of pupils aged 13 to 16 of average and less than average ability'. In the same year the Robbins Committee reported on *Higher Education*. Both reports discussed what Newsom called 'reserves of ability which can be tapped', and Robbins called 'reserves of untapped ability', especially in 'the poorer sections of the community'.[42] Whether discussed in terms of underprivilege or manpower, the message of educational and social injustice had been absorbed into national policy-making and planning. The trend was to be confirmed in 1967 with the report of the Plowden Committee on *Children and Their Primary Schools*, with its strong emphasis on links between social and educational deprivation. Its discussion was mainly in terms of resources: there were neighbourhoods 'starved of new schools, new houses and new investment of every kind', and the need was for 'a new distribution of educational resources'.[43] The designation of educational priority areas was the proposal, and the outcome. The EPA was a peak in post-war interventionist approaches to education, aiming to implement a strategy of what now became known as 'positive discrimination'. The greatest resources, the strongest incentives to teachers, the most extensive community support, were to be recruited for the schools in areas of greatest need. Research projects in a number of areas aimed to devise methods of improving the educational performances of children, the involvement of parents and links between the home and the school, pre-school programmes, and the development of 'community schools'. The awareness aroused in the 1950s had led to the identification of areas, schools and children with special needs, and the commitment to additional resources. Only in the 1970s did questions begin to be asked about the adequacy of a resource strategy related to schools in this way. British and American researchers began to look at the experience of the previous decade, and asked how far education – even with in-built positive discrimination – could mend the dislocations of society.

Higher education remained an important touchstone of the success of the policy. The Robbins Committee pointed to the tiny fraction of students in higher education who came from unskilled manual workers' families. The drop-out of school students from this social group had been a focus of attention since the early 1950s, especially in the *Early Leaving* report of 1954. The expansion of existing universities and the creation of new ones helped to increase overall numbers, but the problem of the under-representation of the lowest social group was not tackled. The Department of Education and Science expressed the hope in 1978, in *Higher Education into the 1990s*, that the future representation of this group in higher education might be affected by 'the gathering impact of policies in the fields of housing, health and the social services', as well as by educational policies as was already the case with comprehensive secondary school reorganization.[44] The failure of education to 'solve' the problems of access to higher education was no longer accepted as a problem solely for higher education or the education system. It was not local or private, but Labour Party and Labour Government, initiative which, in the 1960s, planned a 'university of the air' and produced the Open University.

The second extension of interest relates to public debate. By the 1960s all aspects of education had become the subject of intensive public attention and controversy. Pressure groups and campaigns (such as the Confederation for the Advancement of State Education) had become important features of the educational scene. More and more organizations were being drawn into the discussion of educational objectives and their relationship to social and economic change and stability. The whole position of education in the context of the discussion of social justice and economic planning was challenged in 1969 by the first of a series of *Black Papers*. It suggested that 'free play methods in primary schools, comprehensive schemes, the expansion of higher education, the experimental courses at new universities' were contributions to anarchy. All of these, and others, had arisen from social and political pressures summarized by Angus Maude in this first *Black Paper*: 'the most serious danger facing Britain is the threat to the *quality* of education at all levels. The motive force behind this threat is the ideology of egalitarianism.'[45] Ultimately, argued the authors of the *Black Papers*, education was about tried and tested standards, quality, the pursuit of rational educational goals, not experiments for purposes imposed on education from outside. The undermining of standards was a theme which continued to gain attention into the late 1970s. It was in part responsible for Prime Minister James Callaghan's speech at Ruskin College in October 1976 and the 'Great Debate' it inaugurated. The focus of educational discussion in the second half of the 1970s had moved towards standards and assessment, core curricula and preparation for working life.

The third direction was that of immigration and race. Not until after the middle of the 1960s was there any attempt to analyse the rapid recent developments, not as one writer described them in 1968 in terms of the 'touch of the exotic' that the new 'settlers'[46] brought to our drab cities, but as a significant extension of the problems of education especially in urban areas. Multi-racial dimensions of school experience, achievement and failure further compounded the familiar problems discussed in terms of social class. The map of educational and social disadvantage was having to be redrawn.

Education had in general by the 1960s become more visibly related to underlying social and economic needs and difficulties. Educational policy was increasingly identified with economic policy and fortunes. New thrusts in technical education, particularly from the mid-1950s, related to perceptions of national economic weakness. The development of higher technological education, including the designation of the colleges of advanced technology in 1956, was part of this response to international economic pressures. Anthony Crosland's 1965 policy for a 'binary' system in higher education was a similar reaction. Within two years a White Paper had been issued and the first set of new polytechnics had been designated, producing a 'public' higher education sector which, it was hoped, would be sensitive to the country's economic and industrial needs. The Green Paper of 1977 on *Education in Schools*, a contribution to the 'Great Debate', pointed in an early paragraph to the 'wide gap between the world of education and the world of work. Boys and girls are not sufficiently aware of the importance of industry to our society'.[47] At all levels, the relationship between educational policy-making and national needs reflected a widespread awareness of deep economic, social and political difficulties, and the need (yet again) to harness education for the solution of the problems.

The constant search for national patterns of educational development followed logically from the ideologies and structures of 1944 and after. National committees and commissions played an increasingly important role from the beginning of the 1960s. Educational priority areas and urban aid programmes were parts of national social strategies. The cutback in teacher education in the mid-1970s was based on national population and manpower forecasts. The 1977 Green Paper hoped that 'generally accepted principles' would be found, on which to base the secondary curriculum for all his pupils.[48] The Labour Government from 1974 moved to finalize a national pattern for comprehensive secondary education, and in 1975 issued regulations for phasing out the direct grant grammar schools. Postponements until 1973 in the raising of the school leaving age to sixteen related directly to national political and economic problems and national financial strategies, as did the Conservative cuts in the education service introduced in 1979.

A crucial feature of developments in education since 1944 has therefore been its treatment as an arm of national policy. The identification of areas of social difficulty and conflict increased the demands on education. It has been described as 'perhaps the most researched of all the social services'.[49] Parents, teachers, students, political parties and the nation at large have become involved in controversy which, if nothing else, has indicated near-universal agreement about the central importance of the educational system.

There was confidence, in the 1960s particularly, that educational expansion would itself overcome inequality and disadvantage, and growth was in fact considerable. A Fabian research pamphlet commented in 1970 that education had 'throughout the last 20 years, expanded faster than the national income, faster than private consumption expenditure and for most of the period faster than any other social service'.[50] From the mid-1970s education became vulnerable to a combination of economic pressures and cuts, and a prolonged fall in the birth rate. The integration of education into national economic policy and planning was apparent. Education was brought into the discussion of every conceivable social problem. A chief constable summarized a common view of the importance of education in 1978: 'Since educators, perhaps more than any other body, have been responsible for the defeat of authoritarianism, they have a primary responsibility for getting true authority into shape . . . we ask for energy and dedication towards the new social control.'[51] Education still remained a focus for almost everyone's grand design for social and economic solutions. Theorizing about education might still be what Clarke described as 'speculative', but it was inescapably subjected to the cross-fire of social, economic and political controversy and policy-making.

3 Equality of educational opportunity: the map of uncertainty

At the centre of the politico-social disputes over education has been the concept of equal opportunity – a concept handled so incautiously in the 1950s and 1960s and productive of so much uncertainty and disillusion in the 1970s. If the sociological research of the 1950s and 1960s fed into the social policy, the uncertainties of the 1970s fed into a retreat and the conservative backlash of the *Black Papers,* Rhodes Boyson and Mrs Thatcher. The concept of equal opportunity had for a long time attracted and held some of the political middle ground, but by the 1970s was crumbling somewhat in the hands of the hesitant left, abandoned by the middle as economic expansion turned to stagnation and decline, and attacked from the left flank as a concept incompatible with that of equality itself. It turned out by the end of the 1970s that people either did not understand it, had over-estimated it, had been disillusioned by the research or the rhetoric, could no longer wait for it, or did not want it.

Equal opportunity in or through education has been a popular if ambiguous slogan, and a much analysed perspective. Since inequality has been a continuous and tangible part of our experience, and at the heart of approaches to education-as-social-policy, the issue of equal opportunity is also crucial for our discussion of the social condition. It has been *the* educational issue of post-Second World War Britain, Europe the United States, and beyond. It is a concept with a litera- ture, a place in sociological (though not yet sufficiently in historical) textbooks, and an uncertain future. The vocabulary of discussion has changed from time to time in the past two decades, but on the whole it has been used confidently. In the conditions of the 1960s in particular we needed to be sure that education was contributing, or could contribute, to the more equitable distribution of resources, to a more just society. In the 1950s the sociologists had cleared a lot of ground – rediscovering the relationship between educational failure and social background, announcing that *educational* success and failure were *socially* distributed. 'Equal opportunity' had by the 1960s become a concept of paramount importance in social and educational debate, and carried with it messages of the fight against class barriers, against inequality. There was a confidence in the use of the phrase that was associated with a number of related aspects of confidence. We were beginning – it seemed certain – more seriously to identify the social causes of educational disadvantage, particularly features of class and family experience, the cultural poverty of the child's background, the cultural and linguistic advantages of the middle-class child in the school setting, and all those factors of home and social class analysed with increasing sophistication through Floud, Halsey and Martin in the 1950s, J. W. B. Douglas in the 1960s, and reaching its apogee perhaps in the report by Davie, Butler and Goldstein on *From Birth to Seven* in 1972. We were witnessing an increasingly clear interpreta- tion of how the machinery of social selection worked.

The vocabulary of class and disadvantage and opportunity was accompanied from the late 1960s (a long time ago seen from the receiving end but very recent seen historically) by the vocabulary of new educational policies. Secondary reorganization was in the 1950s and 1960s an increasing murmur, though its advocates, stressing efficiency, choice and advantages of scale, were profoundly reluctant to describe it for what it was – a strategy for improving social justice. The confident vocabulary of education as an interventionist instru- ment was most audible in the Plowden Report, which in 1967 pronounced the need for a new distribution of educational resources, the proposition that 'good schools should make up for a poor en- vironment', and the demand for 'positive discrimination' through educational priority areas.[1] EPAs and the use of urban aid funds in Britain, just like Title I, Head Start, Home Start, Middle Start and other interventionist schemes and experiments in the United States, all shared the intention to make education a more powerful instrument in achieving an education and a society that were more just and more fair. Positive discrimination and compensatory education indicated substantial levels of confidence in the promise of interventionist policies.

In spite of warning signals from the United States, the confidence remained reasonably buoyant in Britain well into the 1970s. There were, of course, controversies – not least about comprehensive schools. All was not well with Head Start. By 1970 Bernstein's widely quoted and discussed theories of working- and middle-class language codes were coming under serious criticism. By 1970 also Bernstein was influentially attacking the concept of compensatory education.[2] By 1972 Christopher Jencks and his colleagues in the United States had published, in that much-discussed and much-remaindered book *Inequality*, an account of research which seemed to show conclusively that schools had no visible impact on the distribution of economic and social rewards. 'The egalitarian trend in education', said Jencks emphatically, 'has not made the distribution of income or status appreciably more equal over the past 25 years.'[3] In England in 1975 the third volume of *Educational Priority*, reporting on the London EPA experience, offered a different view from A. H. Halsey's first report, and announced that it considered the concept of positive discrimination and of EPA to have failed: the disadvantaged had not been reached because 'the majority of disadvantaged children are not in disadvantaged areas, and the majority of children in disadvantaged areas are not disadvantaged'. To reduce inequalities in performance, it argued, 'more powerful policies than school reform' were needed.[4]

By the mid-1970s in both Britain and the United States, where educational strategies had been similar and for similar reasons, confidence had collapsed. The new literature abounded with analyses of what now seemed to have been fallacies. Newly explored dimensions of class, race, ethnicity and sex influenced the discussion. Halsey has interestingly reflected both on the relatively uncriticized social principles on which the Plowden Report rested, and on the intellectual confusion or uncertainty at the point of EPA take-off – one at which the advantage of innovatory, action-based projects with strong financial support outweighed the merits of delay to get the research principles straight.[5] Since the early to mid-1970s there has been a long transatlantic intake of breath, during which the uncertainties have gone deeper and conservative responses become more influential. Have schools failed? And in what respects? Does education matter? What is central and what is ancillary – and what, when the economy 'demands' it, should be pruned, cut, eliminated? Should we deschool ourselves? Should we really be talking about lifelong education? Is school, after all, merely the most available instrument of 'social control' – given the decline of the moral authority of the Church and the family – what Harry Rée so vividly described as 'The death of Dad'?[6]

It is important, before turning to recent British and American discussions, to emphasize how crucial to the confidence of the 1960s was the notion of expansion. At many points on the political spectrum the assumption in the 1960s was clearly that these interventionist policies could and would produce results. Economic expansion and expansionist educational policies – typified by the Robbins Report on higher education in 1963 – provided a reassuring context. The mid-1970s produced a fair crop of analyses of the expansionist background in which the previous decade of educational policy-making had taken place. In 1974, for example, the editor of a European collection of papers on compensatory education described the educational reform movement of the previous decade as having been 'coloured by an optimism that expansion of educational provision and reform of the educational system can produce both greater educational opportunity for the individual and greater social equality'.[7] British policies and experience had been similar to those in other European countries. An OECD conference at the beginning of 1975 reviewed the previous decade's belief in educational expansion as 'an extension of individual liberties' and also as a trigger for changing social structures and reducing inequalities of income.[8] President Lyndon Johnson is said to have commented, in the planning stage of the War on Poverty in the early 1960s, that 'this is going to be an education program. We are going to eliminate poverty with education, and I don't want anybody ever to mention income redistribution. This is not going to be a handout, this is going to be something where people are going to *learn* their way out of poverty.'[9] Much of the sociology of the 1950s and 1960s, and the policies that went with it, had in fact assumed a close correlation between educational expansion and greater equality. For sociologists like Jean Floud education pointed towards a more efficient *and* a more just society, and politicians listened carefully.[10]

But the faith crumbled in the 1970s. In the United States especially, in the conditions of the late 1960s and 1970s, there was a sense in many quarters that all educational expansion had done was to legitimize existing inequality. Nothing had changed except scale. The centre of the stage was vacated by the reforming egalitarian, and both here and in the United States two groups of would-be stars waited to be auditioned to occupy it.

First, there were the radical critics of schooling as a means of social control or manipulation, critics of the liberal or social-democratic assumptions of the previous decade, critics of the school as having allied itself with, become part of, or failed to see itself being used by, the ideological apparatus of the corporate state, critics of schooling in the service of capitalism. In the United States much of this analysis turned on indictments of America's past, including revisions of the historical role of American educational institutions. Colin Greer, for example, described 'the great school legend', the myth that the American public school was an 'agency for the amelioration of most social problems'. Its main role, he and other writers proclaimed, was to teach large numbers of children how to fail, by providing a 'learning experience precisely appropriate to the place assigned them and their families in the social order'.[11] In Britain the discussion was bound up with concepts of culture, knowledge and the discussion of control identified particularly with the volume on *Knowledge and Control* edited by Michael F. D. Young in 1971. On both sides of the Atlantic the critics labelled the school, its curriculum and all of its processes, as supportive of the existing social order. Society, they maintained, had in no way altered as a result of the discussion of and policies for greater educational opportunities.

The second claimant for the centre stage came from multiple points on the spectrum from liberal centre to right. In Britain, G. H. Bantock had consistently and unfashionably argued since the 1950s that equal opportunity was an irrelevant concept to the framing of an educational system – which was about education and culture, about appropriate levels of education and appropriate curricula, and not about social engineering. It was the social engineering aspirations of the comprehensive school, the expansion and experiments of higher education, and educational reform of many kinds, that to a large extent provoked the *Black Papers* from 1969 and through the 1970s. In the United States, Arthur R. Jensen and others cast doubt on the relevance of the equality debate, given what they saw as the failure of compensatory schemes. Jensen's argument about the genetic basis of differences in intelligence between social groups led to uproar in the academic community, and to Jensen and IQ testing being labelled as racist. As Carl Bereiter said: 'the movement to abolish the use of IQ tests is a further illustration of the urge to kill the messenger who brings bad news.'[12] Jensen's central point, however, was one that his critics could not refute, compensatory schemes had not materially affected the constituency at which they were aimed (the difference between Jensen and the critics related to whether such schemes *could* be influential). 'Thus far', said Jensen, 'no new instructional program has been discovered which, when applied on a large scale, has appreciably raised the scholastic achievement of disadvantaged children in relation to the majority of the school population.' He saw no reason to believe that 'equality of educational opportunity or equality of environmental advantages should necessarily lead to equality of performance.'[13] From these and other directions came a newly fashionable vocabulary of basics, standards and the like. It was not only from economic pressures that came the restrictive educational policies of the 1979 Conservative Government.

By the 1970s the concept of equal opportunity was seen to have many meanings, or none. Equal education, Americans were beginning to emphasize, does not mean the same education, but it does mean what someone called 'equal concern'.[14] Bantock uses the same phrase in the 1977 *Black Paper*, when he comments that 'equality of concern – which is acceptable – has been interpreted as requiring similarity or sameness of provision – which is not'.[15] But of course the problems of the very phrase 'equal opportunity' are enormous. The notion of positive discrimination itself revealed the problems by postulating the need for deliberately unequal opportunity, deliberately unequal provision, in order to counterbalance social handicaps. Mary Warnock has disentangled 'weak' and 'strong' meanings of the term 'equal opportunity', its decline as a rallying cry and its function as an ideal (reminding us that it is no argument against adopting an ideal to show that it is unattainable – which is what an ideal is for).[16] There is now an interesting literature of the history of the term and its meanings,[17] but out of that discussion two predominant views have emerged.

The first has been that equal opportunity implies equal opportunity to be unequal. Daniel Bell points out that 'the principle of equality of opportunity, even if fully realized on the basis of talent, simply re-creates inequality anew in each generation, and thus becomes a conservative force in society'.[18] The *Black Papers*, it should be noted, have argued in *support* of the principle of equal opportunity, and against that of equality. Just as in Britain Michael Young had previously suggested – in *The Rise of the Meritocracy* – Walter Feinberg has argued in the United States that 'if the goal of full equality of educational opportunity were actually achieved, if the instruments for identifying talent and the institutions for training it were perfected, then it is likely that the society would be even more unequal than it presently is'.[19] The *Black Papers*, as we shall see, did not argue that case, but they understood it.

The second view, particularly from the left, has been that the discussion of opportunity, access, meritocracy, and similar themes of the past decades, was either too narrow or too irrelevant. Torsten Husén has traced the transition in Europe from the concept of equal *exposure* to education in the post-war period, to one of seeking more equal *results*.[20] A. H. Halsey has expressed the view that 'socialists take the liberal idea of equality of opportunity seriously by measuring it in terms of outcome'.[21] The radical disillusion of the 1970s in the United States rested on the frustrations of seeing education having no impact in terms of social and economic outcomes, and at the same time of seeing no possibility of wider social interventions to achieve greater equality within the framework of capitalism and control by the corporations and the corporate state.

It would be helpful at this point to review some other features of debates about educational opportunity since the mid-1970s. There has been in this period some discussion about the rival concepts of equality and liberty, but it is important to underline how little serious debate there has been about the issue of the independent schools. There has been only the occasional ritual political gesture. The whole discussion about opportunity has continued to be about the State sector. The reports of the Public Schools Commission in 1968 and 1970 produced no more tremor than the eventual disappearance of the concept of direct-grant schools under a Labour government (and the election of a Conservative Government pledged to reintroduce them), and had no serious influence on the equality debate. The British public school is a contentious issue, but it manages to be kept under similar wraps to those which halt discussion of the monarchy. Yet the tension between the concepts of equality and liberty is important to any discussion of education: as Remi Clignet points out, liberty is often acquired 'at the expense of other segments of society, it stimulates the perpetuation or the systematization of inequalities', and the pursuit of greater equality often entails increased centralization and a decline in 'the educational liberty of various groups'.[22] We have as in previous decades managed to evade the disputes implied by such formulations.

In Britain the most recent extensions of the opportunity discussion have been mainly in attempts to review the position after the mid-decade uncertainties. The cultural deprivation discussion, for example, seems to be still in a position of effective stalemate. Chazan and others had pointed from the end of the 1960s to the effects of 'material and cultural deprivation on children's educational progress and emotional development in the infant school years'. They had defined material deprivation as including 'poverty, overcrowding, ill health in parents, child neglect and lack of basic amenities in home and neighbourhood'. They had defined cultural deprivation as a situation in which parents provide a child with 'little in the way of linguistic stimulation and take minimal interest in his education, and when he has very limited opportunity for play or other experiences which are helpful to his intellectual development – in short when his environment is barren and unstimulating'.[23] The point about such quotations is that almost every concept and formulation they contain has been rejected in discussions inaugurated in this country by *Knowledge and Control* and especially by Nell Keddie's little collection, *Tinker, Tailor . . . The Myth of Cultural Deprivation*, published in 1973. The rejection was based on arguments already familiar in the United States. Indeed, the strongest piece in Keddie's collection was an essay on the American experience by William Labov, in which he summarized his central argument by saying of the Head Start programme that it was 'designed to repair the child, rather than the school; to the extent that it is based upon this inverted logic, it is bound to fail'.[24] On the left of the academic debate there has emerged the firmly held view that the whole stress on linguistic or cultural deficit and deprivation, and the related 'compensation' schemes, have been an assault on the working class and its culture, on the working-class family and its values. The attempt has therefore been to argue that the deficit lies in the school and the system, in *its* values, in the *teachers'* values, in school structures and curriculum patterns which *cause* working-class children to fail. With one or two notable exceptions (for example, Harold Entwistle's analysis in *Class, Culture and Education*) the discussion has remained too much at the level of assertion, and too little at a level where any kind of real debate about the concepts and about class experience can take place.

The same, in Britain, applies to the relationship between any concept containing the word equality and the curriculum. For all that has been written about the curriculum in recent years, the questions of common, core, standard, diverse, optional and other curricula still seem too much at the level of manifestos and hunch. There is a sharp analysis of this set of issues in Mary Warnock's *Schools of Thought:*

> If we are agreed that children have a right to be taught (an equal right to education) and if we can go further and think in terms of educating children according to their needs, then the question arises whether this is to be done by providing a common curriculum for everyone, or whether, as their needs are thought to be different, different children should be taught according to different curricula. The issue can be put quite crudely. Does equality in the distribution of education, or even equality of educational opportunity, mean everyone being 'introduced' to a common culture, or does it mean everyone participating in the culture in which he will in fact flourish . . .?[25]

Eric Midwinter and Geoffrey Bantock have, from totally different standpoints, argued versions of one theme – rejecting the common curriculum and the common culture that lies somewhere behind it. The discussion in Britain, one that underlay the Great Debate, the Green Paper and much else that happened after James Callaghan visited Ruskin College in 1976, relates to the problems or desirability of moving towards a curriculum which can in any sense, especially at the secondary level, be called common. The discussion in America has contained an element of a desire to *return* to a common curriculum. A number of American historians, including Lazerson and Violas, have traced the differentiation of American school curricula from the 1890s, though their analysis has contained a hint of a golden-age view of nineteenth-century American common school curricula. Industrial and vocational training for working-class children, they have argued, turned what had been a concept of equal opportunity into one based on segregation by class, curriculum and projected vocation.[26] In the 1970s American sociologists could assert that differentiated curricula and the 'individuation' of learning militated against equal opportunities.[27] In Britain we do not have even the rhetoric of a past common school, common curriculum and common culture against which to measure our present dilemmas.

There is, however, a vocabulary of ideological analysis that is as available in Britain as it has been in the United States. One indictment of Labour's failure to come to grips with class hegemony and dominant ideologies points to a tightening relationship between social-democratic educational policy and corporate capitalism: '. . . the collective interest is now defined . . . less in Labour's old terms of a "more equal society", but more in terms of the survival of a capitalist economy.'[28] What this kind of analysis does not do is suggest whether the trend is reversible, and what kind of educational policies might now be able to contribute to 'a more equal society'. There is a point beyond which such analysis – and the same is true of Bowles and Gintis's book on *Schooling in Capitalist America* – actually prevents discussion of education, simply confirming the uncertainties in which we are steeped. A related though entirely different kind of analysis is Paul Willis's *Learning to Labour*, which contains an extensive presentation of the nature of the 'counter-school culture' in urban, working-class schools, and its similarity to the shop-floor culture for which most of the pupils are destined. The book provides an important contact with experience which enables concepts to become useful. 'In contradictory and unintended ways', Willis persuasively argues, 'the counter-school culture actually achieves for education one of its main though unrecognised objectives – the direction of a proportion of working kids "voluntarily" to skilled, semi-skilled and unskilled manual work.'[29] Studies of this kind, as in a different way Sharp and Green's *Education and Social Control*, help to root analysis in something other than conjecture.

In their American setting many of these issues have quite different profiles and dimensions. But there are important similarities. John Rawls's *A Theory of Justice* has stiffened the American discussion of the concepts of equality, fairness and the distribution of social benefits since the beginning of the decade.[30] Jencks's *Inequality* caused widespread debate about what he and his colleagues had measured in terms of school achievement and social mobility, including controversy about whether the narrowness of his definitions and his methods had trivialized the concepts.[31] Jensen's discussion of genetics led him to conclusions similar to those of Bantock in Britain about the possibilities of diverse curricula.[32] The same debates have continued to take place in the United States around what two writers on higher education in 1978 called 'the ubiquitous pull between equality and excellence'.[33] Bowles and Gintis in 1976 dismissed past attempts at educational reform as irrelevant to the basic economic realities. For them the educational system merely legitimized inequality: schools had for the past century helped to reproduce the social relations of production by virtue of the correspondence between school and social class.[34] In both countries there have in the recent past been voices to argue that equal opportunity as a concept and as a strategy for educational action had done nothing for the poor, the black, the exploited.

Within these multiple uncertainties and controversies it is difficult to see the directions in which the discussion of educational opportunity is going or can most usefully go. It is clear that education, or at least schooling, has too often in nineteenth- and twentieth-century America and Europe been allocated an exaggerated or 'mythological status'.[35] It has claimed or been ascribed powers far beyond its capacities, often resulting in dashed hopes and cynical responses.[36] It is also clear that much of the research has offered the appearance of certainty when its messages might have been conveyed in more modest and guarded terms. If measurement-based research like that of Jencks has a tendency to 'trivialize far-reaching, deeply significant concepts for the sake of measurement',[37] it even less helpfully confuses meanings. It is vitally important to us to know the limits within which measurements are made, the complexities into which they dip, and the elusiveness of the concepts that surround them.

Rutter and Madge's 1976 book on *Cycles of Disadvantage* contained some useful messages. It reminded us of the breadth and the intricacy of the context in which educational disadvantage has to be seen. They took Sir Keith Joseph's 'cycle of transmitted deprivation' and made it into a more complex and usable concept, surveying its literature and dimensions. They raised sharp questions about the research and its implications, including how schools might be most able to influence educational progress, and in what sense compensatory education could be judged to have failed. They reminded us, equally usefully, of the futility of 'a search for a basic cause'.[38] The subsequent research on secondary schools, their differences and their effects, by Rutter and his colleagues (published in *Fifteen Thousand Hours* in 1979) pointed in some further important directions. They concluded – and in this went beyond much earlier British and American research – that children from quite similar family backgrounds and with similar personality characteristics performed differently in different schools. The differences, they concluded, were not concerned with physical factors, such as size of school, nor with broad administrative or organizational differences. The differences were related 'to their characteristics as social institutions'. They were confident enough to postulate a causal relationship between school process and outcome: 'In other words, to an appreciable extent children's behaviour and attitudes are shaped and influenced by their experiences at school and, in particular, by the qualities of the school as a social institution.'[39] There is nothing definitive about this research but it provides a stern reminder of the flimsy basis on which the schools-make-no-difference models of the 1970s had been constructed. For all the work that has been done in the past two decades we are still in a rudimentary stage of trying to understand educational processes and their wider relationships. 'A limitation of social science, as it has come to be defined,' says Christopher Lasch in a review of Jencks, 'is that it simply ignores what it cannot measure.'[40] This is an important warning when it comes to re-evaluating, as we must, our experience of the 1950s and 1960s.

We need to be warned especially against the dangers of seeking simple, single causes. We need to examine carefully what is offered for remedies, for improvements. In the United States it is now widely argued on all sides that more comprehensive strategies than educational ones are needed if there is to be any advance towards equality of opportunity or of outcome. Jencks turns attention to those outcomes that we may wish to influence: '. . . if we want to equalize the distribution of income, then, we need a more direct approach.'[41] Lyndon Johnson's 'people are going to *learn* their way out of poverty' already had a musty smell about it a decade later. Other Americans are underlining the need, not for the 'abandonment of the notion of equal opportunity but special steps to mitigate the failings of the system such as the establishment of a variety of income-maintenance programs like social security, welfare, and food and housing programs.'[42] An American analysis of the process of cycles of inequality concluded that 'only by attacking poverty directly at its source, the family . . . can the nation hope to short-circuit the process that results in the replication of unequal distribution from one generation to the next'.[43]

In Britain, Jack Barnes's report on London EPA experience concluded, as we have seen, that 'if what is desired is to reduce inequalities in performance between all children then . . . on this evidence, more powerful policies than school reform will be needed'.[44] Robert Thornbury, in his infuriatingly provocative and useful book *The Changing Urban School* argued that with the arrival in

1977 of a Government policy for the inner city, 'now it was up to educationists, especially teachers, to enlarge their vision and actively campaign for the urban strategy that was proposed'.[45] With the arrival two years later of a Government committed to educational de-reform and the abandonment of major government strategies except for retrenchment, Thornbury's appeal became all the more cogent. There are a number of things you can do in a situation of uncertainty, shaken confidence and educational retreat. A careful reappraisal of earlier confidence and values is one. Enlarging the vision is another.

4 Schools, social change and standards

Rapid change has made consensus difficult to attain, as established values have been threatened, challenged, defended. Economic expansion has made it easier to establish new and often apparently radical goals, and even orthodoxies. Economic difficulties have made it difficult to keep educational discussion and action at the level of principles, and policy above that of immediate need and expediency. These have been three interlocking trends – and occasionally discrete phases – since the 1950s. Social change has been neither steady nor uniform. In spite of continuous policies, aims, priorities and commitments, the discussion of the educational and social condition has been compelled to respond to basic and sudden changes of contour. The question of education's relationship to the social changes of recent decades ought really to be approached in the plural, in order to reflect the complexities: how do 'educations' respond to and influence social 'changes' and 'conditions'? There is no difficulty in locating sudden changes of social actuality or mood – though 'sudden' may, of course, seem much more abrupt in historical and sociological analysis than it did to the participants. Post-war optimism to cold war; economic planning and expansion to economic drift and recession; imperial leader to commonwealth member; apparent national consensus to protest and confrontation; images of social stability to images of racial tension and conflict; education as a feature of 'progress' to education as a contributor to 'disaster' – these have been only some of the movements of the kaleidoscope.

From the largest historico-political perspective, change is difficult to find, and the forces of change are long-term and over-arching as defined by Marx and by generations of Marxists. The history of education, in its concern with minutiae, has in Britain not engaged too directly with such large-scale analysis, though Marxism has not been without its influence. The question of change implies important historical value judgements and is at its sharpest in the form: how significant is change on the longer historical view? Marxist, and not only Marxist, historical analysis diminishes the relevance of the shorter term, smaller-scale perception of change unless it confirms or illustrates the larger historical sweep. The centre-piece of Marxist historical analysis is the dynamic of class relationships, the underlying tendencies of capitalist economic structures, the subservience of social agencies to class hegemony and control. The interpretation and the methodology are not uniform even within Marxist approaches to history, but in general the nature of social change is contained in such approaches within the structures imposed by capitalist society. Capitalism, it is argued, reacts to internal tensions or 'contradictions' by adjustments, adaptations, reforms aimed at its own self-protection and perpetuation. Change and reactions to change are therefore presented as misleading, exaggerated, superficial, peripheral.

What has irritated some Marxists about the Marxist historical interpretations of Edward Thompson, for example, has been his accent on the historically visible relationships of class, on social experience, on the smaller scale of historical processes within the larger canvas, on the admissible evidence of the changing social perspectives and political efforts of the actors in the process.[1] What has irritated many Marxist historians – including Thompson – about sociology has been its concern with generalized patterns and structures, and its neglect of human agency and historical vagaries in the process of change. What irritated social historians in the 1960s and 1970s about the established economic history from which they sought to break loose was its apparent commitment to a model in which human intervention counted for little against the backcloth of underlying economic forces. One of the most illuminating texts of the history of late nineteenth- and twentieth-century change in the United States has been David Noble's *America by Design,* which reveals the human face of technology, the social and political intentions of the engineer, the deliberate construction of a capitalist ethic of production, research and technological progress by emergent groups of professional technologists. It is a story of social agency, not the inevitable, relentless, disembodied processes often considered to be 'technology'. It is a crucially important message: men make and remake their society (even what *appear* to be the most autonomous parts of it) at the same time as they are socialized into it.[2] The Marxism which makes theoretical models and rejects 'experience' as a focus of historical presentation drives all argument away from change, from issues, from 'actualities' towards the upper strata of anti-historical logic. On the other hand, conservative or anti-Marxist or empirical concerns with short-term, small-scale social and economic changes without regard to substantial, long-term forces of change, are unable to suggest usable explanations. The balance lies between a preoccupation with the 'underlying forces' and a sensitivity to socially recognizable changes in structures, relationships and undertakings.

It is the difficulty of establishing this balance and of abandoning an attempted monopoly of the one or the other that suggests the nature of the failures to interpret the relationships between education and social change that were attempted in the 1970s. Of all the failures the most total was that of the conservative response, expressed most vividly in the *Black Papers* between 1969 and 1977. The first three were published between 1969 and 1972 as a campaign against every aspect of 'progressive' and socially motivated ('conservative' being excluded from the *Black Paper* definition) educational development. The fourth, *Black Paper 1975: The Fight for Education*, is worth some attention here, not just because its message was, as one reviewer described it, 'more constructive than that of earlier papers',[3] but also because it sought emphatically to divorce education from social change, from the commitments of the 1960s and early 1970s to linking education and the social condition. Like its predecessors, the attack was concentrated on the 'progressives', or what it preferred to call the 'experimentalists', because in the view of the editors and the writers the new structures and new emphases meant the lowering of standards, the 'academic ineffectiveness' of the comprehensive school, and the distortion of schooling by its attempts to take account of social conditions and their influence. The key editorial paragraph of *Black Paper 1975* reads:

Teachers should be teachers again and not social workers. Deprived children are not deprived unless they feel deprived; school should be the one place where they are treated as normal children and not social curiosities. Poor home conditions, parental neglect and even malnutrition and ill-treatment have always existed, but the traditional teacher by treating the pupils as pupils has opened the eyes of children to a new world of exciting and liberating learning. The teacher who uses poor social conditions as an excuse for poor teaching is the cause of greater deprivation than the home background itself. At a time of rising living standards since World War II the teacher by becoming a second-grade social worker has become a third-grade teacher. It is far easier to blame the lack of an internal water closet for the failure of a pupil to read than to slog at teaching that pupil to read.[4]

It is not so much the polemic of this central argument that is important here as its relationship to a concern with the social condition and the historical framework we have tried to suggest. The derogatory references to teachers as social workers denies the concern of the twentieth century to *understand* the social processes which are co-terminous with education. The strong dichotomy expressed between social handicaps and learning denies the concern of recent decades to account for the *failure* of large numbers of working-class pupils to find school 'exciting and liberating'. The allegation that awareness of poor social conditions becomes an excuse for poor teaching denies the concern of educationists and teachers in this century to make such an awareness the basis of more effective teaching. The counterposing of water closets and slog at teaching denies the thrust of generations of criticism directed to act on greater understanding of the constraints of social conditions, and of the educational and social limitations of slog. The argument of *Black Paper 1975* is in general levelled against the mounting twentieth-century interpretation of education as social policy, and the related exploration of the society–education interconnections.

The editorial analysis in *Black Paper 1975* is prefaced by a ten-point manifesto entitled 'Black Paper Basics' which contains among its points:

- Schools are for schooling, not social engineering.
- The best way to help children in deprived areas is to teach them to be literate and numerate, and to develop all their potential abilities.
- Without selection the clever working-class child in a deprived area stands little chance of a real academic education.

– You can have equality or equality of opportunity; you cannot have both. Equality will mean the holding back (or the new deprivation) of the brighter children.[5]

The concern is explicitly with the clever and the bright, with no acknowledgement that these concepts have in past decades been closely scrutinized for their socially and politically determined ingredients. The manifesto makes proclamations about schooling, literacy, potential abilities and selection as if these phrases were entirely neutral, had no recent history, and were immune in their common sense usage from the controversies and confusions of past debate. The attempt to lift the subject and its various elements 'above' social engineering becomes a more advanced form of social engineering. There could be no clearer example than this of Clarke's warning about the ingenuous use of 'politico-social ideals' as if they were 'pure educational theory'.

At the heart of the comprehensive school dilemma, writes G. H. Bantock in *Black Paper 1975*, is the confusion which results from

an unwillingness to face up to the fact that education, *by its very nature, is socially divise*. To educate is to transmit meaning; and the development of meaning implies the ability to make finer and finer discriminations in a language of ever-increasing complexity and precision. For whatever reason (historical or genetic) only some can grasp this refined meaning; and *neither genetic make-up nor history can be much transcended* . . .[6]

History enters this picture only to be dismissed. The categories are apparently fixed. In less crude terms than those of the editors Bantock manipulates concepts like meaning, discrimination, complexity and precision as though they are immutably established at a level to which some may climb and some may not. If the debates of the 1950s and after indicated anything it was that the levels and the climb, and the nature of the climbers and their ability to climb, are not fixed and permanent. At every stage of the process – the selection of the climbers, the interpretation and presentation of the task, the variable rates of progress, the changing relationship between the task and the level to be reached – the whole exercise is repeatedly called into question. When nothing can be transcended there is no problem to solve, the present remains intact, history can be disposed of, and the future is assured. A new form of social engineering is invented – one which is designed to ensure that nothing changes.

The logic of the situation as Bantock analyses it (here and elsewhere in his work) is one which presents the aims of the comprehensive school as inevitably confused, especially with regard to values and culture. The confusion leads its sociologically and politically minded proponents to make a misguided attack on 'middle-class culture', and an equally misguided attempt to build school curricula on 'working-class culture'. It leads to an all-round impoverishment of education which puts at risk the 'ablest' and the 'lowest achievers', and 'mediocratizes still further the mediocre': 'The schools currently reflect an . . . impoverishment as a result of the impact of progressivism – which is, after all, only the pedagogic manifestation of a general cultural debilitation.' We are faced with what Bantock calls 'a general movement towards reductionism and homogenization which constitute the present threat to the future of European culture in a mass age'.[7] Given such arguments, and as a way out (or back), the *Black Papers* attempt to colonize the concept of equal opportunity – using it entirely to mean choice, selection, and the 'hardest' competitive interpretation.[8] This obviously goes hand in hand with the rejection of 'social engineering', and again simply conjures away the debates and experience of previous decades.

Whatever the weaknesses and confusions of the concerns of the 1950s and 1960s, the concept of equal opportunity was generally interpreted to mean equality of access to a system, to levels of education, to knowledge, to educational experience, to facilities, to encouragement to create and to investigate and to learn. As a result of all of these it implied equal possibility of entry to occupations and participation in society's resources and rewards. We have discussed the limitations of this vision and of the accompanying strategies, but it is important to emphasize that the *Black Paper* borrowed for its own purposes the concept of equal opportunity and attributed to the 'experimentalists' and 'social engineers' a concept of equality as an educational goal, one which they have not normally claimed. What they have, in fact, claimed from Tawney to the E P A projects is that children should start and continue the educational process without dispensable handicaps. How far education can be an instrument in overcoming the various kinds of handicaps is, as we have seen, far from clear. The point here is simply that in the past the structures of the educational system and of schools, the organization of curricula and examinations, assumed the *inevitability* of certain kinds of social, cultural and educational handicaps. They did not allow for changing definitions of education itself, or the educational roles of schools and other institutions. They assumed a static or near-motionless concept of the child in society, the child in the school, and the very notion of child and pupil and student. This continued very largely to be the case half a century after Dewey and Freud, and through the decades of debate and attempted innovation that followed. Through most of the twentieth century, secondary education remained adjusted to static models.

Behind the comprehensive school movement was an attempt to remove or diminish identifiable handicaps – or at least to provide a situation in which they were minimized. 'Forcing' all children into comprehensive primary or comprehensive secondary schools was aimed – for most of those concerned – not at an illusory 'equality' but at a greater measure, for a longer period of time, of opportunity to develop *without handicap*. If there have been socialists, or radicals, or progressives, or whatever, who have argued for 'equality', their messages have been in the main guarded or confused and have been only erratically and intermittently argued. The *Black Paper* distinction was designed to confuse that issue.

What the authors of the *Black Paper* did not understand, accept or notice was the necessary relationship in Britain between the principle of common schooling and that of diversity in learning and experience. The twentieth-century history to which we have referred, and that to which we shall draw attention in a discussion of accountability, make the charges of uniformity and conformity unlikely to stick in British educational experience. The comprehensive school is no less amenable to pressures for diversity in curricula and teaching styles, to conservative, radical and innovatory pressures, than are administratively separate non-comprehensive schools – a fact which underlay the difficulty of defining common curricula or common cores in the late 1970s. Among the supporters of and teachers in the comprehensive schools there are profound differences of view about the content, structure and processes (not to mention aims) of the schools. Does equal opportunity imply at least a common core of school experience for all children within a school, and – a more difficult question – across schools? Does mixed ability teaching lend itself more to one area of the curriculum than another, and do the differences derive from the subjects or the teachers? When can and should options be introduced to service the diverse abilities and goals of pupils? How far do American attempts to reconcile the rival concepts of integrated schools (and busing) and neighbourhood, community schools, relate to British experience? How is the question of the tension between autonomy and accountability – within the school and between the school and its outside controllers and partners – best approached and resolved? The discussion of opportunity has needed to turn more towards these and related questions, and to a degree has done so, but in over-simplifying the issues the *Black Papers* have offered crude *a priori* and anti-historical assumptions. Answers to all such questions lie in a profound sense of social and cultural change and its meaning for authority, for educational processes, for the whole vocabulary used so statically by the *Black Papers*, including the vocabulary of 'secondary', 'pupil', 'learning' and 'education' itself.

Underlying the discussion in all of the *Black Papers*, and in much of the public discussion in the 'great debate' of the late 1970s, has been the question of 'standards'. One of the points in the *Black Paper 1975* manifesto was that 'We have sacrificed quality for numbers, and the result has been a lowering of standards.'[9] The attempts to substantiate such an assertion have been signally unsuccessful, and the discussion of standards has in general been more strident than the contributory concepts and data should have allowed. There are historical, caution-ary tales to tell in this respect, not in order to dismiss as irrelevant the discussion of standards, but in order to place it in a wider setting than is provided by much of the *Black Paper* and other recent discussion.

'There is no acquirement to which Her Majesty's Inspectors attri-bute more importance, and none which they find more deficient in the Training Colleges, than good reading.' There was, agreed the Rev Derwent Coleridge, Principal of St Mark's College, Chelsea, room for improvement in the teachers and the taught. Coleridge was writing in 1862 and he was attacking the Revised Code of that year, which ushered in payment by results in elementary education. Good teachers of reading, he emphasized, needed a high 'standard of mental cultivation'. They had to be educated to the full, so that better teachers could make better pupils, improvement coming as the 'cycle of instruction' went round. For the teacher to impart 'the barest elements' was not enough – wider, higher standards of culture were demanded, and needed.[10] Standards, for Derwent Coleridge, were complex matters that could not be pinned down by an inspector's 'reading test'.

In the previous year the Newcastle Commission on elementary education, godparents of payment by results, had expressed quite different assumptions and conclusions. It had been considering 'the extension of sound and cheap elementary instruction', and the Commission and its witnesses had discussed standards in elementary education at some length. Inspectors, the Commission pointed out, described schools as 'excellent', 'good' or 'fair', but 'what do these words mean? What is the standard by which an inspector judges a school?' One inspector had told the Commission that a 'fair school' would have a top class which could 'read a page of natural history – about an elephant, a cotton tree, or a crocodile – with tolerable fluency'. They would know the distribution of land and water over the surface of the globe, would know the English counties, be able to describe a familiar object, know the leading incidents of Genesis and the Gospels, and match some similar precise criteria. The Commission decided that school work was in general too superficial and too ambitious, and that more attention to reading was needed. The humanizing influence of a school was important, but it should not evade the 'necessary drudgery' by which teachers taught the basic and 'indispensable elements of knowledge'. Payment by results would compel the teachers to undertake the drudgery. There was a danger, the Commission believed, that teaching children to read and spell was becoming connected with 'elaborate theories of various kinds', concealing the fact that 'after all there is no profound mystery in teaching children to read, write, and cypher'.[11]

The contours of the discussion are extraordinarily familiar. Disputes over standards, over breadth and basics, have not diminished in the past century, and have been present in every controversy about education in the recent past. The 1970s were merely repeating yet again perceptions about reading standards that had been voiced for generations. There is nothing surprising in a flurry of concern about standards in education. Since education contributes to nations' economic, social, political and cultural purposes, they blunder into periods of uncertainty about the effectiveness or rightness of their educational machinery. Provocations to reassess or realign education come from the left and the right and the uncommitted. Change is seen at one and the same time as being needed or as having already gone too far. Central to the search for standards is a continuing dispute about what they are. Standards of what? Whose standards? Standards for whom? Measured how?

Such flurries of concern have accompanied economic spurts and dislocations, crises of social and political change, moments of national alarm. When schools, their curricula and their teachers are under attack the explanations lie at least partly in the political, social or economic crisis. Education in the 1860s and 1870s was central to sharp political and social change. The comprehensive school debates, the *Black Paper* attack on the 'experimentalists' and the clamour about standards, are political – as directly political as support for the independent schools or cuts in higher education. Education is an instrument of society, society orders itself politically, politics is conflict, education is political conflict – including the concept of standards.

In the 1860s and 1870s the development of a national system of elementary education was accompanied by serious concern about standards, not only in relation to payment by results. It was no good expanding the system, Lyon Playfair told the Social Science Association in 1870, without 'discussing the subject of quality in our schools' – which he considered to be abysmal. The education of the country was 'in a truly melancholy state', and the 1870 Act had dealt 'with the quantity of education, but not with its quality'.[12] Liberals and radicals were at the same time attacking the low standards of the Church and voluntary schools. John Morley expressed their views three years after the 1870 Act. The instruction 'which is given in the denominational schools has been almost worthless . . . Two-thirds of the children turned out by them come out in a condition of ignorance practically unbroken.' Politicians arguing for compulsory education 'seem never to think it of any importance whether the education is good or bad. They deafen you with the statistics of increased attendances . . . Yet a mere mouse comes forth from this labouring mountain.' Children were being compelled to partake of fare of 'beggarly and innutritious quality'.[13] Rival notions of standards, and political motives in propounding them, were at work then as now. Middle-class education assumed that even at its worst it contributed to a certain standard of gentlemanly behaviour. Even the mediocre private school offered a middle-class code of conduct which did not (and still does not) fail to attract customers – not only, but to a considerable extent, for that reason. The good public and grammar schools offered the classical culture identified with the ideals of a national elite. But even here there were social and political tensions, over proposed reforms and over the content of the curriculum. The middle-class proprietary school rivalled the grammar school, offering a more utilitarian curriculum suited to a different concept of middle-class needs. Matthew Arnold's middle-class Philistines did not all accept the aristocratic Barbarians' view of the curriculum, and pursued standards of different kinds.

In elementary education discussion easily polarized into conceptions of breadth and narrowness. For Derwent Coleridge the training of elementary teachers meant 'educating men, not forming machines', because the population was demanding 'ever more and more', and the 'plain household bread of intellectual life' was no longer enough.[14] The Newcastle Commission, on the other hand, had different priorities: 'The object is to find some constant and stringent motive to induce (teachers) to that part of their duty which is at once most unpleasant and most important' – to improve training in basic skills.[15] ('Slog' in *Black Paper* terms.) Payment by results set out to provide the stringent motive. It offered an either/or ideal, divorcing skill from culture, concentrating on standards in a narrow area of the curriculum, giving teachers the motive to pursue the 'unpleasant' – teaching children to read, write, and cypher. School log-books show how stringently the motive did, in fact, operate. The writings of the critics of payment by results reveal an alternative, perhaps less tangible, approach to the purposes of elementary schooling. The debate polarized into concerns about something broad or narrow, about the quality of schools or of reading tests, about culture or skills. The nature of standards was as elusive in the 1860s – as the Newcastle Commission and Coleridge were aware – as it is today. And it was as much identified then as it is now with interpretations of the educational and social condition and the political answers to its dilemmas.

The history of the past hundred years contains a continuing tension between broad and narrow conceptions of education, each of which is associated with an identifiable view, not only of the purposes of education, but also of the future of society. The poles have apparently come closer in recent decades, especially with the growth of examinations, at the secondary level in particular. The discussion of examinations, whether for the civil service in the nineteenth century, or through the School Certificate, General Certificate of Education or Certificate of Secondary Education and other examinations in the twentieth century, has invariably reflected the nineteenth-century view that an examination was to the student what the target was to the rifleman. There could be neither aim nor training without it. Examinations have embodied a confident concern for standards, confidence which has been disturbed, especially in the recent past, by curriculum reform, the development of new teaching methods and techniques, integrated and project work, and attention to creative and affective education. In *Black Paper 1975* C. B. Cox, one of the editors, offered seven questions which he considered opponents of public examinations needed to answer, questions which suggested, for example, that the average adolescent would not work hard at school at difficult subjects 'without the incentive of examinations', and that parents and the professions would be without protection against low standards if there were no public examinations. One of Cox's questions was: 'Without public exams, what control is left over the subjects taught in schools?', and his answer read:

> Today many secondary schools are offering children a mish-mash of sociology and politics instead of traditional study of past history and literature. These 'inter-disciplinary', 'relevant' courses are often heavily influenced by the teachers' own opinions. Teachers do not say 'Vote Communist or International Socialist' in their lessons, but they do suggest that capitalism and competition are evil. Public examinations force teachers to cover areas of study which general educated opinion in Britain believes appropriate for children. If there are no syllabuses laid down by the needs of public exams, children may be submitted to all kinds of eccentric courses, and parents will find out too late.[16]

The appeal to the teaching of history as a discrete subject does not protect the passage against the charge of being ahistorical. Again, leaving aside the obvious grounds here for polemic, the central point is its sense of a fixed, agreed set of criteria for judging curricula – and by implication standards. The history of the past century, and of the most recent decades, does not uphold the existence of a coherent 'general educated opinion', unless those sections of opinion which do not accept the *Black Paper* view are dismissed as *by definition* eccentric or uneducated. New curricula, new teaching styles, new forms of assessment, have emerged in times of uncertainty and change in order to test out what the response of 'general educated opinion' ought to be in times of uncertainty and change. The *Black Papers* suggest a certainty that does not exist. As an American historian has reminded us in writing about the contribution of William James to psychology: 'Of the many implications to be drawn from James's imagery, the most revolutionary was that certainty was a temporary halt in a thinking process whose one constant was change.'[17]

To assume, for example, that the new science curricula in Britain and the United States in the 1960s and 1970s could be rejected by 'general educated opinion' as unnecessary at best and eccentric at worst would be to deny the realities of economic and technological change and the responsibilities of the educational system in relation to such change. To assume that the new classroom and laboratory processes that are implied, and new forms of assessment developed, deprive the public of 'guarantees' as to content and to standards, is to reject any sense of organic relationships in education, and to see both schools and the outside world as ossified. Those, precisely, were the assumptions of the *Black Papers,* and the fundamental point at issue here is not the *educational* direction of their attack, but their expression of a philosophy of a static society, of static models of social organization, of static models of schooling, and of a model which implies no relationships between education and society, either in a situation of change or at rest.

The comprehensive school has suffered most from failures to determine these relationships. It has been torn between rival interpretations of its role and of its standards. Its aims were related to social purposes, but ones which – its supporters have argued – could be achieved without sacrificing academic standards. Robin Pedley, for example, in the 1950s and 1960s started the process of collecting evidence of examination successes in the comprehensive schools, suggesting that GCE attainment was at least as good in the comprehensive as in separate schools. The educational press offered evidence and counter-evidence, opinion and counter-evidence, opinion and counter-opinion, around this argument. Critics believed that conventional, measurable standards would be eroded in the comprehensive school, which, as G. H. Bantock put it in a letter to the *Times Educational Supplement* in 1965, thought of children 'as sociopolitical abstractions, simply as means to a more equal society'. Schools, Bantock argued, were not 'instruments for bringing about a social and political revolution, but cultural agencies for the performance of certain specific and limited tasks'.[18] Questions of standards were enmeshed with discussions about the structures of schools and about the purposes of schooling itself.

Among other things, the question produced a kind of minuet between British and American education. Early Soviet superiority in space was attributed, on the American right, to failure in American education. One of the leading critics of 'progressive' education, Admiral Rickover, attacked the 'mediocre scholastic standards of American education', identifying as one of the main factors the commitment to progressive educational methods. Rickover attacked the American comprehensive high school, and in the Britain of the early 1960s he saw selection at eleven as the explanation of the high standards of British education.[19] By the end of the 1960s the *Black Paper* editors in Britain were able to argue that the American reaction had led to greater emphasis on reading, and more structured programmes. The Executive Director of the US Council for Basic Education, writing in *Black Paper 1975*, described how the teaching of reading had been returning to a phonics-based approach since the mid-1950s: 'the outlook is for a continued drift toward more phonics and more use of phonics-approach programmes. Perhaps ten years from now, almost all schools will be using phonics-approach programmes and the cycle of change will be complete.'[20] While this 'advanced work' was preceeding in the United States, said the *Black Papers*, 'we in Britain invest our capital in out-of-date play-way and open plan types of junior school'.[21] Researchers and teachers are still, however, unable to make confident pronouncements about what is 'advanced' and what is 'out-of-date'.

Polarization has been considerable since the 1960s, including over the very concept of standards. The Plowden Report on the primary schools in 1967 concluded that 'it is not possible to describe a standard of attainment that should be reached by all or most children. Any set standard would seriously limit the bright child and be impossibly high for the dull'.[22] The Bullock Report, *A Language for Life*, in 1975, received evidence that standards of literacy had fallen, but pointed to the difficulty of defining literacy and illiteracy: 'there is a good deal of emotion adhering to the terms'.[23] Ray Hopkins, a former HMI, writing in the *Times Educational Supplement* in 1976, thought that 'the validity of this concept of standards is questionable . . . It is obscure, imprecise, muddled and misleading when applied to the academic performance of children . . . To assert that educational standards have fallen is meaningless, pompous and irresponsible.'[24] The *Black Papers* recruited Sir Cyril Burt to demonstrate that measured standards had fallen, on the basis of statistics which it has since been suggested he did not possess.

There has been frequent reference to and discussion of employers' complaints about the low standards of school leavers – complaints which have been made throughout this century. The *Black Papers* argued for a return to understood standards as measured by the only known reliable guide – examinations. As Angus Maude put it: 'There are certain standards of quality which are essential to the survival of civilisation, and they cannot be achieved and preserved except by rigorous and applied effort.' In terms of post-school education, he wrote, 'whatever you may *call* a technical college – and even if you install a department of social science in it – it is *not* the same as a university'.[25] The great public and direct grant grammar schools, wrote the editors, 'set a standard of achievement which is internationally recognised . . . They stand in relation to other secondary schools as Oxford and Cambridge stand to the newer universities.'[26] Close the grammar and public schools, wrote Richard Lynn, and Cambridge graduates will stop going into teaching.[27] Return, suggested S. H. Froome, to sum-books 'full of gloriously correct examples', and abandon unproven activity methods for the old elementary school virtues of 'discipline, quiet and hard work'.[28]

The political right, in the United States from the 1950s and in Britain mainly in the 1970s, set out to capture for itself a wide-ranging concern with standards. Setting aside any discussion about the league tables involved in the *Black Paper* quotations above (including the dismissal of the qualities of, say, Sussex University, and the ambiguity created by the absorption of Homerton College into Cambridge University and by the university status of some former 'technical colleges') we can see how the polarization reflects a continuing concern with standards. The concept has visible historical and social dimensions, and is not a pure instrument of pure theory. The Newcastle Commission could talk about the 'indispensable elements of knowledge' because there *was* wide agreement about those elements. Separate concern with the narrow classical curriculum of middle-class education, and with the skills and attitudes provided for what Eric Eaglesham called 'followership',[29] was part of a relatively unchallenged educational divide. The *Black Paper* search for standards uses an old, impure instrument in a world without consensus, and without the same tolerance of divides as in the world whose passing Clarke attempted to signal in 1940.

The late 1970s search for a 'core curriculum', for 'quality', for 'standards', continued the familiar tension between alternative approaches. There was a tendency both in the 1860s and in the 1970s to identify standards with a basic curriculum. James Callaghan, in his Ruskin speech, took care to point out that 'life at school is far more full and creative than it was many years ago'. He rejected *Black Paper* prejudices ('those who claim to defend standards but who in reality are simply seeking to defend old privileges and inequalities'), but wanted everyone to play a part in 'expressing the purpose of education and the standards that we need'.[30] There was, however, a temptation and a danger in his proposal for 'a basic curriculum with universal standards', failing to recognize that these were as elusive and as politically sensitive as they were a century before. It is still too easy to imagine that such a curriculum and such standards are, as in *Black Paper* reasoning, fixed and definable categories. Neville Bennett and Noel Entwistle pointed out that the research on formal and informal teaching published in 1976 in Bennett's *Teaching Styles and Pupil Progress* offered evidence of only one effect of informal methods: 'basic skills are not the only criterion of success in primary teaching.'[31] The Bullock Report, like Derwent Coleridge, realized that raising standards was not a question of some simple technique or device. Reaching a target is more complex than some participants in great debates and national alarms may suspect. When Callaghan talked about life at school being more 'full and creative' he echoed the Plowden Report's comment on infant schools as conducive to warm relationships: 'the achievement of many infant schools has been to build on and to extend children's experiences.'[32] Research such as Neville Bennett's has been aware that such characteristics of education cannot be measured, and it may therefore be assumed by some that education should concentrate purely on what can be measured – one of the difficulties underlying attempts in Britain and the United States to develop measures of educational performance. When Prime Ministers are aware both of the creative dimension of schooling and of employers' complaints about standards, it is assumed by some that those 'standards' are the more tangible of the two, and in times of stress the only category of importance. Shirley Williams usefully illustrated the difficulties of discussing standards when she referred in January 1977 to industry's complaints. Their conception of a decline in apprentice standards may in fact indicate a rise in educational standards: 'many of those who would once have been apprentices now take degrees at the universities and polytechnics, so that industry is selecting from a group of school leavers that has been much more highly creamed than was true a generation ago.'[33]

The point is fundamental. There are no universal standards, there are only perceptions of standards, and the factors involved in change and in attempts at measurement and comparisons are more complex than a Newcastle Commission or *Black Paper* pronouncement suggests. It may be possible to bring together polarized views of narrowness and breadth, basics and the creative child. But that is not purely an educational discussion: the search for consensus or understanding about standards is now, as in the nineteenth century, a political and social battleground. The central accusation against the *Black Paper* writers is not that they are misinformed, or wrong, but that they constitute a collective flight from reality. Their recipes are not as bland and commonsensical as their authors like to present them – they are recipes for conflict in that they pit old values against the process of change itself. That is now a fundamental feature of the conservative (and Conservative) educational and social legacy that is being carried into the 1980s.

The weaknesses to which we have pointed in the 1960s and 1970s opportunity arguments and strategies, and the naive assumptions that often accompanied restructuring processes like those involving the comprehensive school, must be accompanied by the even more stringent exposure of the conservative positions discussed in this chapter. Both must be related to the nature and difficulties of social change and responses to it. The comprehensive school was not an accommodation to reality but one attempt to master it. Progressive educators have in the past attempted to understand the relationship between educational practice and the inevitability or desirability of change. Throughout this century there has been a tradition – reflected in the attitude and policy changes previously discussed – of an analysis of education in relation to the environment, to democratic community relationships, to crises of the individual, of social groups and society, of the nation. It has involved responses to change in technology and international economics, in class and race relations, and in the educational aspirations of sections of the community not included in the *Black Paper's* 'general educated opinion'. The whole tradition has reacted, in fact, against any such established commodity.

The discussion of Clarke's *Education and Social Change*, of social policy and of the opportunity debates, was intended to illustrate some of the strengths and weaknesses of this tradition. The implication is that educational and social processes need to be subjected to sustained scrutiny in order constantly to re-evaluate how the maximum cultural, social and intellectual experience can be made available to all children – in what forms, and on what bases the processes of change can be envisaged and accomplished. There are, of course, major educational, social and political obstacles, and the defences built round old categories and values by the *Black Papers* represent one of them. Their translation into revived traditional institutions and practices is another. But there are obstacles and weaknesses of a different kind. The comprehensive school movement, for example, has been – naturally enough – preoccupied with technical and structural aspects of educational change, with establishing new bases in often hostile environments. They have been too little concerned with the realities of the arguments that surround them about social advance, with what they contribute, with what they are to become. The discussion of authority and decision-making in schools has been alive for a quarter of a century without producing real, energetic debate that goes beyond political rituals, uninfluential research and ready-made professional and trade union attitudes. Relationships between teacher education and social change, the varieties of home–school relationships, and a range of similar questions, have been present in some of the debate and policy discussion of past decades, but have either slipped away in the sand or failed to attract sustained evaluation.

There are many teachers who grasp and can respond to the changes but who are often frustrated by constraints placed upon them which they are unable to influence. There are many schools where response to the subtleties of change does have meaning to those who are involved. There are aspects of the tradition of concern for the social condition which have positive messages for people involved in all aspects of education. The *Black Papers* and the conservative reaction have made it difficult for these teachers, these schools, these participants in education, to break through the perplexities engendered increasingly through the 1970s. The function of the *Black Papers* was to sloganize against educational responses to change, against a concern with the nature of the social condition and with changes that might improve it, and therefore against change itself. Any return to confidence in educational improvement must be based on a more extensive, more committed and more satisfactory understanding and restoration of the relationships that the *Black Papers* set out to break.

5 Public control, choice and the State

The provision of education raises constant questions of diversity. Problems of community participation in education include the important one of choice. Both – and indeed all our discussion – suggest questions about the State, about which theoretical controversies have mounted in Europe and the United States in the 1960s and 1970s. We shall return to issues directly involving politics and the State, but for the moment it is necessary to underline that in the struggle to define diversity and choice and to identify common educational experiences and curricula we are increasingly confronted with United States models. Much of the literature of alternative schooling, for example, is American – though not all from the United States. Some of the best known educational experiments, successes and difficulties in recent years have been connected with places like Philadelphia and Boston and New York. Some of the most interesting analyses of the purposes of secondary education, and the frontiers of secondary schooling, are contained in publications like the Kettering Foundation Report on *The Reform of Secondary Education*, published in the United States in 1973, with its emphasis on 'a wide variety of paths leading to completion of requirements for graduation from high school'.[1] In this report and elsewhere, as David Tyack pointed out in 1977, the accent has been on finding new forms of compulsory education or experience outside school (and of finding work to substitute for schooling beyond a given age).[2]

Discussions of voucher systems have focused on the main existing experience, that of Alum Rock, California. Discussions of curriculum reform have hovered between models such as those of Sweden, where democratic schooling has been taken to imply a high degree of uniform access to the same knowledge and experience, and those of the United States, where democratic schooling has in recent years often meant the widest range of alternative schools and curricula, some sponsored and funded by government agencies. All our discussions of priority areas and compensatory programmes, equal opportunities and equal outcomes, the community school and lifelong education, seem to be measured against what the Americans have already done, learned and often forgotten or rejected. Much of the vocabulary and many of the concepts were reared in the United States. Levels of confidence and uncertainty have radiated from the United States. The provocation has often been helpful and salutory, but in the field of public control of education, and the nature of educational choice, the dangers of toying with the American experience are great.

To begin with, the structures are profoundly different, and they have been interpreted differently in the United States in attempts to Americanize and homogenize immigrant and minority cultures, at points in historical development which have no simple British parallels – although the periods of continental immigration to Britain, and immigration to England from other parts of the United Kingdom, still require serious historical analysis in relation to education. Second, the American private school, college and university are at many levels quite different from what seem their English counterparts. A Black Baptist college in Ohio, a private, radical graduate college in Massachusetts and a denominational high-quality private college of education in Pennsylvania, have no direct parallels in Britain – especially when their sources of funding and students are examined closely. The traditions of local and national, religious and political, private and public control, cannot easily be compared.

Third, the political line-up when it comes to alternatives to the predominant system is quite different. Their base is different. The ways in which important school authorities, such as Boston, adopted a model of alternative curricula within the public system of education in the 1960s and 1970s reflects a level and style of response to inner-city educational and social problems which cannot be matched in Britain – in part because the schools themselves reflect such different historical structures. Alternative schooling was an enormous and bewildering feature of the 1960s and 1970s in the United States, unlike the marginal nature of its British counterpart. Universities and colleges have become involved with schools in the United States in the construction of alternative school programmes and in curriculum development in ways totally different from apparently equivalent processes in Britain. Alternative schools offering *traditional* programmes began to appear in the United States in the 1970s, unlike anything in the British scene. The range of political and cultural commitments of the advocates of alternatives has been wide, though it has clustered mostly on the left of the American political spectrum. Although there are parallels in Britain to the emergent relationship in the United States from the 1960s of innovation, local initiative, grants in support from private foundations and corporations, and federal funding, the resulting complex patterns and tensions have been uniquely American. The enormous educational commitments of the American anti-poverty programmes of the 1960s and 1970s became internationally known, influential and copied, but the intricate web of compensatory programmes, interventionist schemes and affirmative action was different in many basic respects from the similar patterns sought in other countries, including Britain.

The traditions to which our discussions of Clarke and social policy have pointed have not been significant American traditions, and the American educational past came under strong scrutiny in the 1960s and 1970s, at the same time as the new educational approaches were being developed, in an intensely bitter and confused national political situation which – again with international parallels and reverberations – was more complex and sustained than in similar situations elsewhere. Against that background, doubt about the virtues of public education in the United States can be seen to have profoundly different sources from those discernible in Britain. Recent approaches to the history of American public education have stressed in enormously varied ways, for example, that it has disadvantaged the Catholic parochial school as well as racial minorities, that the growth of strong educational systems and bureaucracies has been at the expense of local and ethnic control and participation. Awareness of such historical, recent and present features of American education result in educational pressures which may bear any and every political label. In the United States right and left share opposition to the State and to the working of public authorities (and the range of support for various kinds of voucher scheme has illustrated this). While the two wings in Britain may occasionally share an anti-liberal stance, the extent and seriousness of the shared ground are nothing like the same.

The educational argument in the United States has turned in the 1970s towards questions of decentralization and cultural pluralism, and in American terms that may in fact mean widespread opposition to the structures that have grown up since the late nineteenth century in American states and cities. It may also mean opposition to national decision and policy-making, even though the nationally centralized machinery may seem weaker than it is in Britain. How strong this opposition can be is seen in one of the most interesting reports on teacher education – and by implication on education in general – to come out of the United States in recent years, a report by the Study Commission on Undergraduate Teachers and the Education of Teachers entitled *Teacher Education in the United States: The Responsibility Gap*, issued in 1976. Officially sponsored, nationally prepared, with strong minority and 'alternative' representation on working groups of the Commission (one of which was on 'cultural pluralism'), it held conferences, published, drafted and redrafted as it went along, after being called into existence under a U S Office of Education grant in 1972. Its findings and recommendations were crisp and sharp. Its basic tenet was that 'it is clear that our American society does not share a common image of the future, common goals, or a common culture'. Its basic historical message was that the vision of the good society in America had come to mean centralization of political power and of educational policy: 'the control of American education by national educational and professional societies, and the effective control of schools by the white middle-class majority are part of the fulfilment of that vision.' There is now a whole armoury of historical analysis intended to show how this came about within American communities, within towns and states, and nationally – and this commission felt as at home drawing on conservative E. G. West in support of its arguments as in drawing on Ivan Illich and the deschoolers. The message of the Commission was clear: decentralize and encourage diversity and alternatives. Educational authorities 'should foster a multitude of alternatives in and out of the public schools which can be recognized as counting towards a student's education'. Long-standing national pressures towards assimilation should be replaced by a national strategy for decentralization and cultural diversity: '. . . all teacher education programs should exist in a culturally-pluralistic atmos-

phere – that is in a system which accepts and encourages differences.'
The crucial word is 'encourages'.

The Report ended in fact with a 'definition of cultural pluralism' –
one which was drawn up in 1972 and guided the work of the
Commission from the beginning. It postulated that 'the educational
system of this country fails to educate all its students, especially
non-white students', and has used a model of the 'preferred American' in order to assimilate the variety of peoples and cultures to it. The
definition is directed towards 'meaningful pluralism'.[3]

The historical case, the political context, the very nature of the
attack on centralization and public control in its existing forms
involve discussions, issues and realities of a different order from those
familiar in the British discussion of the State, local authorities, control
and choice – though this is not to argue that they cannot become
important in the British situation, or that some of the concepts and
problems do not already feature in the British analysis. The question
of control and choice does not, however, easily benefit from the
American discussion. Cultural pluralism, the deprivation of
minorities, the use of 'preferred models' of citizenship – these are
indeed directly relevant to the British experience – but the American
deductions and implications are deceptively attractive. The historical
experience of the British State and its agencies, as well as the historical
commitments of British political and social movements, suggest
propositions that are probably unacceptable to most of the protagon-
ists in the United States. The critical American debates took place in
the 1960s and 1970s in a situation in which the accepted accounts of
the American educational past were being overturned, under the
impact of new political tensions, and the emergence of new American
radicalisms. The discussion of American educational history in terms
of social class, the capitalist state, social deprivation and disadvantage, and the newly found vocabulary of manipulation and social
control, was a creation of the changed political climate of the United
States in a period of struggle for civil rights, the war in Vietnam and
the first widespread articulation of Marxist and radical explanations.

The history of the search for these explanations in Britain is
different, given the long and influential presence of Marxist, socialist,
Fabian and radical analyses in social and educational history, and
given the long political debates about the British State, its agencies, its
educational system, the British class structure, the socially divided
and divisive education of which Clarke's *Education and Social Change*

was one, albeit a vital, critique. The struggles for and around education in Britain have, certainly since the last decades of the nineteenth
century, been centrally concerned with the possibilities, the potential,
the duties, of a developing State machine with its local and national
balances – all taken so easily for granted by Clarke. 'Alternatives', in
British terms, are inevitably marginal to the central issues and
problems of education. The need is not to undermine or evade, but to
strengthen and adapt, the public machinery for the provision of
education. In Britain 'alternatives' too often end up as provision for
children from higher income groups, and a diversion of resources and
effort from the places where most of the children are – as the history of
'progressive' education in the twentieth century demonstrates. To
Americans, whose campus bookshops suggest that the only Briton
writing about education this century was A. S. Neill, it appears that
Summerhill has something important to do with the history of British
education.

The private sector of education in Britain is more exclusive and
elitist than it is in the United States – which does, of course, have its
exclusive and elitist institutions. Public education has not been used
in Britain to 'defeat' religious groups and minorities in the same way
as in the United States. Indeed, it can be argued that British legislation and Government action since 1902 (perhaps since 1870) have
always *strengthened* voluntary participation in the system at large, by
rescuing financially unviable voluntary schools and perpetuating a
'dual system', down to the protection of the voluntary colleges in the
reorganization of teacher education in the late 1970s. Although
nonconformists have sometimes – especially after the 1902 Education
Act – felt grievance at being called upon to subsidize Church education from the rates, neither they nor anyone else have had to construct
a counter-system in opposition to the public one without public
finance and support. One feature of the British system (excluding the
independent fee-paying schools, which may one day become the
subject of serious discussion) is that it has incorporated the religious
alternatives, left them some room for manoeuvre, and made them as
publicly accountable as other 'public sector' schools. While the same
concept of the State may be used to embrace the British and American
versions, the differences are wide enough to demand quite different
historical and contemporary analyses.

The implications for Britain of American attempts at cultural
pluralism and decentralized decision and policy-making lie not in the

search for alternative, opposition forms of education, but in the work of the local authorities and their schools, public solutions to multi-racial and multi-ethnic educational issues, and nation-wide reconsideration of all the assumptions which underlay the research, policies and controversies of the past decades. The implications lie in the nature of the provision, in the structures and curricula of the schools themselves, in the nature of the services and para-educational machinery that the local authorities provide. The implications are to be sought in experiment and innovation within, by and for the educational system publicly provided. The strategy implied for Britain is that of enabling the machinery of public education to be diverse and to be equipped to cater for diversity – because in Britain disparities between State-supported and privately supported institutions now necessarily mean an exacerbation of social, class-based divisions. However crude Clarke's view of the State, it recognized that attempts to find solutions outside it would not be directed towards a lessening of government of the majority by a minority educated and 'advancing by a quite separate and more favoured path'. Criticisms of curricula and quality, problems of truancy and drop-outs, difficulties over cultural and racial diversity, hostility to repressive and authoritarian methods in schools, concern about favoured models of learning and behaviour and worries of every kind about the content and approaches of British schools, all still point to the need for strategies that will strengthen understanding and action in and around the public system.

Another feature of the British system is that it took the public authorities until very recent decades to tackle many of the structural diversities that have not explicitly plagued the more open American society to the same extent since the nineteenth century – diversities which are in fact structural inequalities. The Americans have not been without their inequalities, but these have not been contained within such stringent institutional definitions as their British counterparts. Since national and local authorities have become involved in Britain in modernizing the structure, the central argument has become how to get that right, how to get the balance of local and national control right, how to get the balance of the partners within the enterprise locally and nationally right, how to envisage public control in terms which do not conflict with and in fact encourage community participation or control. There is room within that argument for a range of opinions and practices, but the structures and processes of control –

and therefore of choice – cannot be easily illuminated in Britain by reference to American criteria. Education is, of course, about more than structure and control. It is about knowledge and curricula, commonalities and options, experiment and innovation, cultural diversity and an enormous variety of social differences. It is possible, however, to confront all of these more directly in Britain by accepting and strengthening public control – based on a balance of national, local and community participation which is profoundly different from that of the United States, and all the elements of which are open to and demand reinterpretation. Phrases like cultural pluralism, educational choice and community point backwards and forwards to different styles and forms of involvement and decision-making by national and local government in the two countries. The 'State' in British terms implies a different balance of involvements, even if there are similar underlying dangers. The radical view in Britain at this moment in history means not a search for alternatives or an attack on the intervention of the State, but a commitment to adapt and strengthen state involvement for more clearly understood purposes.

It is useful at this point to consider how the argument has been conducted historically in relation to American education, given the agonies of the reinterpretation that took place amidst the bitter controversies of the 1960s and 1970s. It is now impossible to evaluate the meaning of past educational experience without taking account of the American dialogues of the past two decades. Our concern with the State makes this all the more necessary. Such a concern must point towards political theory or towards history, and at this stage of the argument the latter offers the most essential clues to the value of the organizing concepts that we have used in the recent past to explain educational and social processes.

American confidence and disillusion about education have been directly related to a series of organizing concepts, and since the American pulse has been internationally amplified in the 1960s and 1970s it will be helpful to approach the historical framework within which the understandings have been sought. American 'revisionist' history of education in the 1960s and 1970s has become internationally familiar since the impact of Bernard Bailyn – and Lawrence Cremin in particular at the beginning of the 1960s, and the second wave of radical, revisionism that followed – including the work of Michael Katz, David Tyack, Marvin Lazerson and Carl Kaestle. Not all of this work has been as well known in Britain as it might have been

– and neither has that of the more ideologically committed writings of historians like Clarence Karier, Joel Spring and Walter Feinberg (though Samuel Bowles's and Herbert Gintis's *Schooling in Capitalist America* has gained some notoriety and distinction). The ideology and directions of attention have, of course, in the United States, related to the context of the reappraisal. This included an existing basis of reinterpretation of historical motive, a developing involvement with the history of other and related institutions, and the growing awareness of 'presentism' – the reading backwards into history of contemporary meanings and emphases. Above all, there was the search for historical 'fallacies' under the inescapable new political pressures to which we have referred – the civil rights movement, Vietnam, resistance to the corporate state, and new anti-poverty, campus, racial, ethnic, and feminist militancies of the 1960s and 1970s. The literature of the history of education generated in these United States contexts across two decades was enormous and exciting, and it has become conventional wisdom in the United States to suggest that the historians involved – 'radical' or 'revisionist' or whatever – asked crucial new questions, even if the answers were sometimes shrill, or premature, or wrong. By the end of the 1970s a kind of between-world feeling about the American scene had developed in the history of education, and a good deal of re-re-reassessment had been taking place.

The obvious question is – what had the history of education in the United States come to be *about?* In a review of two books by Lawrence Cremin in 1978, Jennings Wagoner explained that 'traditional assumptions about the "boundaries" of history of education have been cast aside as historians . . . have approached the study of education with revised agendas'.[4] Their agendas have, in fact, been endlessly revised, and there is no apparent end to the re-revisions and re-definings of the territory. There is a strong relationship between the range of subject and the conceptual machineries adopted. In 'The History of Education in *Past and Present*', Joan Simon talks about the changing subject preoccupations of British historians of education, their changing definitions of the territory. 'There remains,' she says, 'the problem of finding the proper way to focus on the matter.'[5] Her 'focus on the matter' and Wagoner's 'revised agendas' indicate the uncertain territory within which historical portraits of education need to be seen.

For Bailyn and Cremin what was mainly wrong with the pre-1960s

American history of education was its focus on the US public school triumphant. The account of its contribution to the modern, liberal, democratic, industrial state had been, it was claimed, apologetic, laudatory and restrictive. Later critics of the corporate capitalist state went further in their condemnations, but all were agreed that the narrow focus on the institutional development of public schools (opposite in meaning, of course, to the British counterpart) had by definition meant an underestimating and ignoring of other educational institutions and processes. The narrowness of range had meant a distorted picture and distorted explanations. Bailyn in 1960 moved the discussion out into the family, apprenticeship and other aspects of a wider, quasi-anthropological definition of education.[6] Cremin in 1965, whilst continuing to identify education with conscious ideals, talked of projecting historical concerns 'beyond the schools to a host of other institutions that educate: families, churches, libraries, museums, publishers, benevolent societies, youth groups, agricultural fairs, radio networks, military organisations, and research institutes', enabling historians to encompass 'such historical phenomena as the rise of newspapers in the eighteenth century, of social settlements in the nineteenth, and of mass television in the twentieth'.[7] From there Cremin went on to engage with what he later called 'configurations of educational institutions' and influences, the whole 'ecology' of education – the relation of educational interactions and institutions to one another and to society at large.[8] What all of this did was not only to turn American attention from a simplistic concern with the public schools and formal institutions, but also from assumptions about the *rightness* of those institutions. Questioning their centrality meant questioning the concepts which underlay the historical explanations.

The established themes of schools as basic contributors to American 'democratization' or 'modernization' suddenly became weakened and vulnerable. As Joan Simon makes clear in her article on *Past and Present*, such vocabulary is in fact an ideological machinery, and the over-simplified over-generalized use of concepts like 'industrialization' and 'modernization' have also in their British context become suspect as organizing concepts for historical description and explanation.[9] This issue of the use of terms and concepts is crucial, and can be approached through a rough categorization of the main work in the history of education following these diverse revisionist approaches – suggesting both ways of thinking about the American experience and the implications of its concepts and categories for analysing education in Britain.

A large amount of American work has related to schools and school systems, to reinterpreting the institutional past in the new, wider contexts. The main focus has been on urban Massachusetts and New York City, with isolated local studies of a small number of other communities, including St Louis and Chicago.[10] Central to the American history of this kind is the growth of the city system, and the work of Katz, Tyack, Lazerson and Stanley Schultz[11] in particular has re-examined the reforming zeal that produced these systems. They have described the 'elite bureaucratic'[12] nature of the late nineteenth-century and early twentieth-century 'progressive' reforms. This new autocracy, or what Schultz calls 'democratic coercion',[13] was – they underline – a means of undermining popular community control, and was therefore often anti-ethnic and anti-immigrant. The centralizing tendency of this system-making was not only, in this picture, bureaucratic and geared to efficiency, it was often much more sinister. Tyack and Lloyd Jorgensen, for example, have analysed the success-ful proposition that was carried state-wide in Oregon in 1920 to make public education obligatory for all children, and they have shown how the move was directed against Catholics, Jews and other minorities, and was sponsored mainly by the Freemasons and the Ku-Klux-Klan.[14]

The important interpretation in these studies of school systems is, therefore, one of bureaucratic reform as an attempt to regulate and standardize behaviour, a shift in the relationship of school and community. It suggests a search for stability through standardization, compulsory school attendance and the destruction of local, commun-ity and especially ethnic minority control over local schools. The concepts most in use to organize these descriptions and analyses are those of bureaucratization and centralization, both of which are vital to the work of the authors mentioned in the 1970s (including Tyack up to the publication of his *One Best System* in 1974). The equation of centralization with elite reform remained intact, but Tyack and colleagues went on to question the importance placed on these concepts in the urban–industrial explanations of mass education. None of these, they suggested, was a pre-requisite for mass education as it appeared in the United States, and they explored in particular the steep, prior climb in enrolments in nineteenth-century *rural* America. They indicated that urbanization was a key factor in explaining longer schooling and higher expenditure, but not the initial take-off.[15] As Tyack pointed out, there was a big question unanswered about how widely different non-urban communities in nineteenth-century America produced similar schools on an enormous scale before the urban, bureaucratic models became relevant.[16]

The concepts in use are often self-conscious pieces of organizing machinery, and historians have defended their usage. Katz, for example, in the second edition of *Class, Bureaucracy, and Schools*, defended himself against the charge that his perspectives on contemporary affairs had distorted his interpretation of the past. Katz had relied heavily on a view – which he made explicit and justified – of bureaucracy against which he measured historical processes, and which reflected his basic position – that the purposes for which school systems were reformed from the late nineteenth century were those of corporate capitalism. He asked the question: 'Can a structure be made to serve very different goals from those that it was constructed, successfully, to teach?' He inclined 'to answer it pessimistically; but I would be, and in this would be happy to be, wrong'.[17] The argument runs from a picture of schools as 'alien institutions' in the preface to the first edition, to this hesitant position at the end of the second. Via his conceptual machinery Katz asked some fundamental questions, but there have remained substantial questions to ask about the tension between the 'strong' use of concepts like bureaucratization and the processes it was intended to subsume.

With less explicit use of this conceptual machinery, some subsequent American work went on nevertheless to explore it. Tyack in the late 1970s wrote on the history of truant officers and school superintendents.[18] Don Warren, in *To Enforce Education* – which he felt obliged to explain was not 'strictly speaking a revisionist history' – examined the early years of the US Office of Education.[19] Clarence Karier's work on testing as a response to the 'sorting' needs of bureaucratic capitalism was followed by that of others, exploring, for example, the use of tests to solve the various administrative problems associated with immigration, and demographic and economic changes.[20] The framework of these explorations had been established largely by Katz, though the ideologies and end points of the researchers varied. Tyack and others had provided, and went on to provide, important points of departure for further analysis around these categories of explanation.[21]

These concepts and the work which embodied them interlocked

with other areas of interest. One of these was the development of the specialist, the expert, the profession, and related to these, their increasing operation in specialized institutions and departments, in complex structures. Much of the interesting work of the 1970s particularly was concerned with institutional specialization and the transition within those institutions from more idealistic or 'caring' roles to more bureaucratic or 'custodial' ones, the most seminal book in this area being David Rothman's *The Discovery of the Asylum*.[22] In *The Irony of Early School Reform* Katz had produced a case study of a reform school, and the analysis of institutional diversification accelerated during the 1970s to include delinquency and juvenile courts, institutional amenities for young workers in commerce, and the first reform school for girls.[23] These and others were in the same tradition and generated a considerable discussion of the purposes and meanings of these specializations – what Katz in an article in *Marxist Perspectives* called the 'institutional state' that was a feature of early industrial capitalism.[24] Since Christopher Lasch's work on asylums in the 1960s the school had been under discussion as one of them.[25]

The interest in institutional diversity and specialization and their specific American characteristics was also prominent in the history of higher education. The foundation work of Laurence Veysey and Frederick Rudolph in the 1960s on the history of the US colleges and universities was followed in the late 1970s by Rudolph's history of the American higher education curriculum,[26] a growing literature on the diversification of academic disciplines – especially in the social sciences from the 1880s,[27] and the historically informed analysis of diversification in higher education in which David Riesman and Martin Trow were key figures.[28] In the absence of centralized federal control over such developments this institutional picture was taken to reflect the increasing complexity of late nineteenth-century capitalist society, reaching critical tensions at various levels with the rapid growth of corporate business and the corporate state at the end of the century. Thomas Haskell, in a book on the emergence of the academic social sciences in the final decades of the century, organizes his analysis within the controlling concept of increasing 'interdependence'.[29] Within this development specialist expertise becomes accepted as necessary and is legitimized in and by newly created professional organizations, academic departments, learned journals, specialist publishing presses and changes in the structure of careers. The related concept is therefore that of professionalization. Mary Furner's *Advo-*

cacy and Objectivity analysed the career patterns involved in the emergent economic science, busy purifying itself from the comprehensive, pre-professional social science of earlier decades.[30] Carol Gruber's *Mars and Minerva* studied academics in the First World War, describing their search for legitimacy, their attempts to 'prove' themselves in the service of the State, their attempts to acquire status and power – all coming to a head over the issue of academic freedom.[31] The professionalization of the school superintendent, the university president, the administrator and the school-teacher has been of growing interest to historians – although it has been understood that the concept raises difficulties.

The book that most directly and fully tackled this part of the discussion was Burton Bledstein's *Culture of Professionalism*, which analysed above all the relationship between the search for middle-class professionalism, the growth of specialization, and consequent changes in higher education. Central to this analysis is his stress on the deliberate promotion of the authority of the 'expert', the sponsoring of faith in professional persons, in the 'magical role of expertise', forcing the client into dependence, creating new career structures (what he calls 'vertical vision').[32] Just as Katz saw bureaucratization as the victorious but by no means only available nineteenth-century option, so have historians come to question the 'inevitability' of professionalism, its role in reducing personal autonomy, in undermining community, and especially in 'invading' the family. The work on specialization and professionalization points towards basic questions about the family, about women, about childhood, about adolescence. Cremin has written about the family as educator, Platt about the 'child savers' and the creation of the concept of juvenile delinquency, Schlossman about parent education, the courts and delinquency, Troen, Fass and Kett about the crystallization, especially in the 1910s and 1920s of the concept of adolescence as a distinct social and psychological category.[33]

The theme of the deliberate undermining of the family is taken to its extreme by Christopher Lasch in his studies of the 'family besieged' and American 'narcissism'. *Haven in a Heartless World* in particular carries the strong central message of 'the shattering impact of policy – the impact of the so-called helping professions – on the family'. Capitalism, he argues, having controlled production, went on to control the workers' 'private life as well, as doctors, psychiatrists, teachers, child guidance experts, officers of the juvenile courts, and

other specialists began to supervise child-rearing, formerly the business of the family'. Probation officers acquired the rights that had
belonged to parents. Parents were declared incompetent, were mys-
tified with 'expert' advice and made to 'cripple the young' at the same
time as offering a 'psychological haven for the cripples, now grown to
maladjusted maturity, whom it had itself produced'.[34] It is an angry,
irritating and worrying analysis and argument which seems to ignore
basic aspects of the nineteenth-century family that had been
'invaded', but the whole direction of discussion about professionalization and specialization points towards it, as does a lot of the work on
schools as alien institutions. All of this represents an important cluster
of concepts which, with the judgements which they confirm or to
which they lead, will inevitably attract a great deal of further discussion.

A final area of analysis – one which brings us much more directly to
questions of the State – is dominated by the concept of 'social control'.
In one guise the concept describes any and every form of education in
all societies. In another, the way it is normally used in the United
States and in Britain, it is equated with social manipulation, with the
intention to control for ulterior purposes, or with powerful forces
which may drive or control the controller, as well as with the
institutions created for the purpose of controlling.

Under the social control umbrella American historians have analysed the history of the education of blacks and immigrants, the
public school and the kindergarten, vocational education and guidance and the whole range of institutions, processes and professions
which constitute or impinge on education. In the 1960s, we have
suggested, American historians rediscovered social class and interpreted reform as what Violas called 'more subtle and effective social
control'. For Spring, in *Roots of Crisis*, schools had become 'the agent
of social order'. To Spivey, the new schoolhouse for the free Southern
blacks was an attempt 'to replace the stability lost with slavery'. For
Lazerson, the kindergarten was 'innovation for traditional goals', a
means by which middle-class progressives could reform the dangerous or un-American aspects of the working-class, poor or immigrant
family: it was a 'means of entering home and neighbourhood'.[35] The
notion of control in all of this literature presented and continues to
present serious problems. First, is it an adequately sensitive explanation of the operation of social class relationships it is mainly supposed
to represent? A review of *Roots of Crisis*, one of the foundation texts of

the analytical trend, complained that it had piled up examples of social control without contributing to a theoretical understanding of it.[36] Feinberg, in *Reason and Rhetoric*, suggested the 'limited nature of the revisionists' appeal to social control'. The fact of social control, he emphasized, was not itself significant: 'What is significant is the direction of that control and the point it is intended to support. . . . While manipulation is a problem exploitation is a more basic one.'[37] From this viewpoint the concept was insufficiently Marxist. In much of this kind of analysis, it is certainly clear, social class and social control were used as blunt instruments, and their relationship with educational processes was often, to say the least, speculative.

A related set of problems has included that of motivation, the confusion of control with the intention to control, the degree of passivity assumed about the 'controlled', and the question of the 'controllers'' degree of conscious motivation as distinct from their roles as unconscious agents in larger historical processes. These problems are reflected perhaps most clearly in attempts to revise previous historical judgements on the educational progressives and reformers and their 'motives' or 'achievements' – especially John Dewey. A good example is Jane Addams at Hull House, Chicago, who used to be presented as the active, liberal, exemplary reformer, working for the advancement of the poor, on the basis of a strong, humane, social conscience. In the 1960s Lasch questioned her motivation, suggesting that it had more to do with personal gratification and problems than awareness of social distress, and he used her as an example in a discussion of progressivism as a new form of manipulation and even repression. In 1974 Phillips placed emphasis on her devotion to the 'traditional values of women', and in 1975 Violas made her the archetype of the establishment of more subtle forms of social control.[38] Reinforcing a point we have made in a previous chapter, Friedman, discussing motivation in American anti-poverty programmes, commented in 1977: 'It is important to peel away surfaces and look at reality underneath; but it is also important not to throw the surfaces away. If we do, we are in danger of ending with the notion that . . . Jane Addams and John D. Rockefeller shared a basic world view and pursued the same goals. . . .'[39] Under the social control style of analysis it can in fact be argued that *all* reform, *all* progress, *all* change, *all* improving motivation, is suspect and illusory, once the structures of exploitation and control are postulated. The controllers become almost inevitably controlled by larger processes. As Katz puts it: 'People of an earlier period may not have been malicious, but they did act on motives rooted, perhaps not even consciously, in their social-class interests.'[40] The analysis contains many such 'mays' and 'perhapses', and at no point is the weakness of much of this historical work revealed more than in the speculative nature of this area of motivation and implementation.

Supporting the social control literature is a substantial and impressive body of 1960s and 1970s historical writing on the growth of the late nineteenth-century corporate state, the processes of liberal capitalism, and particularly the progressive era in American politics. The familiar difficulty is that historians often tend to assume that the discussion of concepts, even if not of the issues, is closed, failing to register the uncertainties that surround them. If it is possible to pile up examples without careful analysis of the theory, it is also possible to pile up theory without confusing it with examples. The historical literature of social control is frequently trapped in the same situation as the one they attribute to past 'liberal' or 'conservative' historians. Violas's *The Training of the Urban Working Class* exemplifies how easy it is, while at some points conducting an important argument, at others to relapse into a repetitive and strident use of over-familiar vocabulary, confusing the intention and practice of control, the equation of wish with actuality, of aim with outcome.[41]

Here lies the difficulty with *Schooling in Capitalist America* by Bowles and Gintis. Since it appeared in 1976 the main and most consistent claim for it has been that it places education in the widest and most relevant socio-political context since, for example, Merle Curti's work in the 1930s. Its central argument is that education has in capitalist society *merely* legitimized inequality by successfully preparing children for their appropriate future roles. Progressive reform, they argue, has enabled capitalist society to do that job more effectively. The discussion begins in what they call 'the thorny and somewhat disreputable facts of economic life'.[42] The book is an impressive exercise in model-making, but seems to have little relevance in any historical discussion, and indeed seems to be one to which historical discussion seems irrelevant. It has unfortunately too often been taken as history. Cohen and Rosenberg have argued that the book substitutes functional analysis for historical explanation, making too facile a connection between the spread of public education in the United States and the economic and social functions 'they *imagine* schooling served'. Mark Stern has accused the book of bad

Marxism, trapped in economic determinism, ignoring the fact that institutions and ideology have a dialectical impact on economic relations, and are not simply caused by them. The role of labour, as presented by Bowles and Gintis, has its foundations, Stern suggests, 'not in history, but in the formal logic of their social model'. The book, indicate Cohen and Rosenberg, is content mostly to illustrate their grand functionalist model 'with a bit of historical material'.[43]

The importance of these judgements for our argument here is that they not only point to profound weaknesses in *Schooling in Capitalist America* but also raise acutely the problem of tension between organizing concepts and historical analysis and interpretation and their relationship to any attempt at an understanding of the present. A concept like bureaucratization or the corporate state can, of course, carry forward the process of understanding and of changing society. Used assertively and statically, it can limit and prevent historical analysis, and in turn its functionalist description can prove to be historically disembodied. There comes a point – and the structuralist fashions of the late 1970s have brought us to it time and again – at which the argument from structure and models and theories may be elegant and comforting, but unless it can respond at some level to rigorous historical analysis and the messages of historical, interpretative debate, it remains in a realm similar to that of abstract art – and whatever else that is it is not history. Nor is it an attempt to engage with the present in order to provide working explanations. In the final analysis *Schooling in Capitalist America* disposes of the need for history. Horlick has suggested that the various kinds of revisionist historian in the 1960s and 1970s have too often neglected the history for the social criticism, failing to examine adequately the processes by which past structures have become present ones.[44] By the end of the 1970s American historians of education were beginning to use the vocabulary of political systems and industrial society more cautiously. Some were carrying the history of education into detailed and sustained attempts at historical analysis of the relationships between education, work, family and other social institutions and structures. The revisionist experience produced important continuities and major hesitations. Discussing social criticism, Lasch talked of its taking the form of 'isolated perceptions that shine for a time and then fade in the glare of the latest revisionism'.[45] That remains an important warning.

It is not easy to translate the story of two decades of American revisionism into British terms, but there are three sets of deductions which may usefully be made.

First, there is the question of the range of what is subsumed in Britain under the concept of education and its history. Even in the 1920s Fred Clarke was discussing the way society educates through a series of sub-systems. In the 1930s he was talking about the 'educational aspect' of housing, public health, social insurance, town planning and industrial regulation. In 1940, as a kind of early-warning Lawrence Cremin, he defined education in terms of a network of formal and informal systems and sub-systems and agencies, including scouts and guides, women's institutes, young farmers' clubs, BBC listening groups, dramatic societies, cinemas, ramblers' clubs, and 'many others in rich abundance'.[46] There has been overwhelming attention in Britain to details of the State, its growth, its agencies, its policies, its legislation, but attention has also been increasingly given to widening the frontiers to include significant analyses of, for example, the history of religion and of the labour movement, of science and of the popular press, of political movements and of the international context. In some of these areas the historical thrusts have been stronger and further than in the United States. In others, particularly in relation to the validity of the organizing concepts and arguments, British historians have gone surprisingly little distance. In approaching the contemporary scene and its institutions and meanings it is obvious that the American efforts at interpretation have crucial messages to offer, but it is equally clear that generalized explanations from bases in the kinds of concepts we have discussed can be of only limited use. The histories are different, and theories of the State, of social control, of bureaucratization, of professionalization, whilst alerting us to common features, stop short of engagements with the present which profit from wide differences in experience and point towards diverse future expectations, ideals and efforts.

Second, and closely related to the first cluster of arguments, is the question of visualizing historically and sociologically the complexity of educational experience. Let us take the 1830s as an example to illustrate the point – and the illustration could be adapted to any other period. If we engage with the educational history of the 1830s we may well have in mind an overall pattern which includes elementary schools, mechanics' institutes, Oxford and Cambridge, London and Durham Universities, the infant school, Robert Owen, Owenite trade union and co-operative educational activities, George Combe, phrenology, the growing urban working class, campaigns for political reforms, the National Union of the Working Classes, Chartism, the radical press, workhouse schools, parliamentary debates and Government grants, the inspectorate, monitorial practices, the Committee of Council, Kay-Shuttleworth, the widening boundaries of towns, factories and factory schools, literacy statistics, the representation of education in literature, the Society for the Promotion of Christian Knowledge, the Society for the Diffusion of Useful Knowledge, libraries, governesses, the curriculum of grammar and public schools, pressure groups, statistical societies, the village, the railway, Irish education, *The Edinburgh Review*, cholera, health, the treatment of children . . . and so on. None of this is unfamiliar, but we may ask whether the extension of range has led to an adequate examination of the analytical frameworks that have been used. It is one thing, in Charles Webster's words 'to sweep the net more widely until the history of education becomes an encyclopaedia of social and intellectual history':[47] historical and contemporary understandings are something different. How adequate, in attacking this agenda of 1830s themes, are our concepts – industrialization, urbanization, specialization, institutionalization, capitalism, social class, socialization, social control, and the rest? To what extent do they explain institutional change, or the contexts of decisions, or the nature and variety of educational experiences and responses, the similarities and diversities of educational developments, the continuities and discontinuities amongst systems, sub-systems and agencies? Are the differences between British and American social and historical preoccupations those of our respective pasts or do they stem from the different political and ideological pressures of our respective presents?

Third, the historical account we have traced raises vital questions about the ways in which a contemporary analysis can be conducted. There is one important sense in which the ground of theory has been evaded in Britain, particularly in relation to the discussion of educational opportunity and social change, and it is imperative for the re-examination of that experience to grapple with the concepts and the theoretical assumptions they have made about the State and social institutions, about economic and political realities, about the nature and distribution of power, for example. The American attempts to explain the educational and social past also indicate how important it is to seek the measure of the concepts within which descriptions and explanations are arrived at. Inadequate though the work of American historians has sometimes been in this respect, it has often been totally absent from the work of British historians. We have previously suggested how, on the political right and left, crude pictures of the present have been buttressed by anti-historical reference to the past. The discussion of *Schooling in Capitalist America* is a reminder of the dangers of postulating social and economic functions and using bits of history to suggest how one *imagines* the functions were and are served by educational agencies. The differences of the American and British endeavours indicate weaknesses and different needs. If a greater concern with the theoretical implications of historical analysis is of major importance in Britain the concern needs to be pursued with two reservations: theoretical questions, not ritualistic gestures, need to be built into the historical search for explanations, and theoretical tantrums which do not attempt to engage with historical commonalities and diversities are of little use in that approach to the social condition which requires understandings and action. The State as a coercive machine, education as an instrument of social control, the subjugation of the individual to bureaucratic and professionalized processes – these are areas of concern which assume meaning only in the search for the kind of historical diversities which this chapter has tried to indicate. Without that search there is no possibility of closer engagement with the present condition, and with the elements which may help us to understand and improve it.

6 Accountability and authority

The issue of accountability presents all the difficulties discussed in the last chapter. Since the major explicit consideration of the concept has taken place in the United States it again raises the problems of comparison. The concept has roots in educational practice and policy on the one hand, and in economic and political pressures on the other. It is therefore amenable to discussion in terms of pure educational theory or of politico-social ideals. It lends itself to possibilities of pragmatic description and of ideological gestures. It can be approached with and without theory, with and without history. If we limit the discussion to teacher accountability, we are faced with the question above all of whether the teacher and the school *are* adequately responsive to social demands – conflicting though they are, and can become *more* so. This gives rise, obviously, to a galaxy of related questions, for example as to the nature and direction of the pressures, the extent of teacher autonomy and accountability, the forms in which accountability may be discussed, and the utility of the whole discussion. Since there are features of the social and economic condition in Britain and the United States which have provoked increased interest in the effectiveness of schools, the concept has crept closer to the centre of socio-educational concerns. It is a short step from a concern about standards and the pivots of public control to that about accountability. It is a further dimension of our previous discussions to see to what extent an historical analysis helps to locate and portray a contemporary issue.

The history in this case is hard to write because the article and the vocabulary are new, even if some of its component parts are recognizable. The education system and the schools have been *responsible* for providing the service required of them by the providers – private or public – but have in less obvious ways been *accountable*. Mary Warnock has pointed out that 'responsibility does not entail accountability', and even though bodies providing a public service may give an 'account' of themselves, they are not normally accountable in any direct way. The Independent Broadcasting Authority, she suggests, can properly be said to be accountable to Parliament and responsible to the public.[1] In this sense private schools have been accountable to trustees, and the State-supported education of the nineteenth and twentieth centuries has been to some extent accountable to school managers and governors, college governing bodies and university councils, and to a lesser extent and in delimited periods, directly to departments or agencies of national or local government. More generally, schools have been placed in a position – especially in the twentieth century – of feeling a responsibility for their activities, a responsibility exercised through various levels of negotiation with governing bodies, local authorities, inspectors and advisers, and parents and the wider community. They have needed to be responsive to administrative, political and social demands, and they have had various measures of autonomy to interpret, implement or resist those demands. There have been changing degrees of pressure to become more specifically or more directly accountable, but on the whole since the mid-nineteenth century the extent of the schools' response and the 'success' of their enterprises have been publicly identified indirectly. The first problem, therefore, in locating 'accountability' historically in Britain in relation to education is to piece together some older categories of discussion and action.

The historian's task is easier in the United States (though historians have barely tackled it)[2] because the processes have been more explicit. There have, for example, been long disputes, especially in the 1920s and 1950s, over 'merit pay' for teachers.[3] The central feature of the American experience of this kind has been that, in one account, 'it infers, from measurable results, judgments about who or what is responsible for those results'.[4] The assumption in many of these – especially twentieth-century – processes has been that responsibility for outcomes can be identified, measured and rewarded or penalized. There have been clear assumptions in such movements about schools, about classrooms, the curriculum, teachers, teaching and learning. The 1970s in particular saw extensive programmes of competency-based education, and a monumental activity of related analysis from many directions.[5] The competency-based education movement reflected concerns about the adequacy of schools and teacher education and in the main emphasized the importance of defined objectives in order to effect improvements. It underlined

the accountability of teachers for meeting behavioural objectives. The graduate of a competency-based program emerges with a given set of behaviours relative to teaching. If these objectives have been chosen as representing minimal standards for effective teaching, then each graduate leaves the program with a demonstrated ability to know and to do those things that are believed necessary for effective teaching.[6]

The movement can also be seen as a response to specific political and economic pressures. 'As schools improve their systems of management,' it was pointed out in 1975, 'they also improve their ability to meet public demands for satisfactory school accountability. . . . If public demands for accountability are not properly answered, proponents of increasing tax monies for other government agencies may succeed in creating a shift of spending priorities.'[7] This is no more than a particularly anxious expression of a commonly recognized relationship between an educational response and public concern about the schools' ability to help solve some specific economic and social dilemmas.

Accountability has been widely discussed and experimented with as such in the United States. Educational performance contracting, for example, not only had its own major experiment, conducted by the Office of Economic Opportunity in 1970–1, but also its own Brookings Institution evaluation. The intention, widely adopted, was to subcontract groups of under-achieving pupils to private agencies, who would be paid only if their teaching methods produced measurable results. The evaluation concluded that progress in achieving effective and measurable improvements in learning would not be achieved without a clearer understanding of 'the process of learning, the working of schools, the characteristics of successful teaching, and other difficult matters'.[8] Such attempts to match school inputs and outcomes more directly have continued to raise central difficulties for the policy-maker, and they are in lines of descent visible to historians of American education. Historians can trace, especially for the twentieth century, attempts to place American education in political, economic and social contexts in which teacher performance and school achievements have been constant focal points of discussion. The vocabulary of 'efficiency' and 'cost effectiveness' has been in regular use in discussions of American education, given the direct connection between American public schooling and local financial appropriations – as well as attempts to apply to American schools and school administration the salient concepts of American finance and business management.

Even movements for the reform of schooling for the benefit of disadvantaged minorities have taken over some of the accountability vocabulary and intentions, and have demanded that the schools be held more accountable for what they achieve, or fail to achieve, on their behalf.[9] In higher education also, if – as the *First Newman Report* put it in 1971 – 'the measurement of cost and performance . . . is somehow regarded as illegitimate', there is at least discussion of the illegitimacy for historians to consider.[10] It was the view of the *Second Newman Report,* two years later, that the greatest challenge of the 1970s would be 'to develop forms of public support and accountability'.[11] For the historian of these American processes there are conference proceedings to analyse, experiments described, self-conscious debates about all levels of education to pursue – from the kindergarten to the university graduate school.

The history of the American accountability movement in education therefore contains three substantial and interrelated elements. *First,* attempts to find ways of measuring, evaluating and improving the management, functioning and performance of education at all levels. The proponents of one or another aspect of accountability have demonstrated a high level of confidence in the ability to identify features to be analysed and influenced in this way, and in general their schémes have sought to apply stringent psychological or management models to education. The accountability movement of the 1970s was based on this tradition, and its tone and style are exemplified by a Rand Corporation report of 1971 prepared for a California school district:

> In its most general sense, accountability is a concept that gives focus and direction to decisionmaking and requires a systematic delineation of responsibilities *within all organizations*. The key to accoun-

tability implementation is an information system that provides rapid, timely feedback to the decisionmaker about the progress being made towards attainment of system objectives. The heart of the information system is the collection, analysis, and dissemination of evaluation data. Evaluation is a monitoring process that measures outputs of the educational system and systematically relates them to inputs so that the educational administrator can make the necessary decisions about program adoption, expansion, or curtailment. . . .[12]

This history of attempts to find a scientific or cost effective basis for approaches to educational performance relates to the *second* aspect of accountability, its political and economic context. Although many features of this history have been presented in terms of educational theory or effectiveness, the self-conscious awareness of public suspicions, criticisms and demands has never been far away. The Rand report went on immediately from talking about 'decisionmaking capability' to the contextual explanation that 'educational decisionmakers are often suspected of making capricious decisions; the ability to make available for public scrutiny the data on which they base their decisions can help to dispel this image'.[13] In American educational institutions the tension between their internal goals and external pressures has often become acute, and the accountability movement has attempted to reconcile these interests by improving mutual understanding and finding operational principles which can allay public anxiety, defuse criticism and be seen to be at least publicly responsive. In higher education Martin Trow has analysed what he calls 'the public and private lives of higher education', suggesting that the central question of the transition to mass higher education had by the mid-1970s become: 'How can the legitimate concerns of the public regarding the cost, efficiency, and expanded functions of higher education be reconciled with the freedom of colleges and universities to maintain their own integrity as institutions committed to teaching and learning?'[14] These kinds of questions have been asked of American higher education since the late nineteenth century, but the dramatic expansion of education in general in the United States from the 1950s almost inevitably led to a revival of accountability pressures. This was particularly the case when a period of expansion ran into the campus and national political conflicts of the late 1960s, together with anxieties about international economic and scientific competition and their reflection in the domestic economy, as well as about international recession. 'The financial problems of the late 1960s,' wrote Earl F. Cheit, 'put increasing pressure on liberal education to be accountable for its product in narrow and measurable terms.'[15]

Doubts about the limiting effects of accountability pressures are the *third* element in the story. The range of these doubts and resistances is wide. At one end are the questions that have been prominent in the 'revisionist' historical literature of the 1960s and 1970s about the relationships between education and American social and economic structures. Some of the most widely read texts of the kind we discussed in the last chapter have argued that schooling in the twentieth century has been, or has increasingly become, accountable not to 'the public', and not to those who are most disadvantaged by the social system, but to 'the corporate state', to 'corporate capitalism'.[16] It has responded to the manpower needs of capitalism by acting, in Joel Spring's analysis, as a 'sorting machine', and in that of Bowles and Gintis as a means of sustaining a self-perpetuating class system.[17] At the other end of the range have been doubts not so much about the *purpose* of accountability pressures, as about their *impact* on schools, focusing attention on basic skills to the exclusion of the humanistic functions of education, forcing classrooms into a common mould, strengthening the competitive ethos, and generally making superficial assumptions about how education works and what it can achieve:

> All of these techniques and movements to establish some method of accountability for educational achievement remain unevaluated. Each has some potential merit in achieving high-quality education, but all focus on some aspect of the organization of the system without adequate evidence that the organizational changes will produce different school environments. . . .[18]

The American versions of educational accountability have related to public perceptions of schools, higher education, social change and economic need – perceptions shaped by dominant features of American society and by the particular tensions within it. From the efficiency movement of the beginning of the century to the interest of the 1970s in competencies and systems run a sequence of historically related attempts to measure, to define and to control in specific ways. Very little of this vocabulary has been indigenous to education in Britain in the twentieth century, and only recently have attempts been

made to domesticate it. This does not mean that schools and universities, teachers and learners, have not been under scrutiny or have not
been under pressure to be responsive to social and economic expectations. It does not mean that sectors of education or specific institutions have not attempted or wished to respond to changed needs or
public interest in being informed or persuaded. It does not mean that
schools, or further or higher education, have not been responsive to
measures of their effectiveness, or proposals for adjustment in their
procedures. It is simply that the historian of education in England and
Wales or in Scotland has first to learn to recognize the older constituent elements of the discussion, the different realities that must
shape the new language of description.

Although there are centuries of explicit relationships between
schools and the charitable bodies responsible for their foundation and
upkeep, it was not until the creation in 1839 of the Committee of the
Privy Council on Education that serious, systematic attempts began to
be made in England and Wales to assess the standards achieved by
schools and to influence them. Created in order to monitor and
supervise the expenditure of Government grants-in-aid to the
National and British Societies for school building, it was operated
through the appointment of Her Majesty's Inspectors – the first
national machinery concerned with obtaining information about the
operation of schools with a view to influencing them. The instructions
provided for the first inspectors were explicit and detailed. The
inspectors of schools aided by grants of public money (which by
definition meant schools for the children of the poor), were to visit
them 'in order to ascertain that the grant has in each case been duly
applied, and to enable you to furnish accurate information as to the
discipline, management, and methods of instruction pursued in such
schools, your appointment is intended to embrace a more comprehensive sphere of duty'. The visits of the inspectors were intended to
be acts of co-operation between the Government and the local committees and superintendents of schools, and the inspectors were to be
a means of diffusing 'information respecting all remarkable improvements . . . whenever affording assistance'.[19] In 1844 the inspectors
were told that they were concerned not only with expenditure on
school buildings, but with ascertaining that adequate funds were
being provided to keep the schools in a 'state of efficiency'. They were
to report on the suitability of the buildings, on their continued
devotion to 'the education of the children of the poor', their respect

for the terms of their trust deeds, and the 'comparative efficiency of these schools'.[20]

The establishment of a national, relatively autonomous inspectorate, with terms of reference which explicitly excluded the desire to 'control' in any direct sense was to have far-reaching consequences. When a Code was drawn up in 1860 bringing together the previous Minutes and Regulations of the Committee of Council, the central functions of the inspectors were described as follows:

> The inspectors do not interfere with the religious instruction, discipline or management of schools, but are employed to verify the fulfilment of the conditions on which grants are made, to collect information, and to report the results to the Committee of Council. No annual grant is paid except on a report from the inspector, after a periodical visit, showing that the conditions of the grant have been fulfilled.[21]

By this stage grant aid had been extended, and included grants to teachers and for the purpose of providing equipment. The inspection was a regular attempt to assess the overall and continuing efficiency of the school (with the exception of the religious instruction, for which the controlling bodies provided their own form of inspection). The inspectors also examined the pupil teachers – under a system of apprenticeship introduced with the Committee of Council's Minutes of 1846. Her Majesty's Inspectors had become a communication system between Government and its main educational agency on the one hand, and the schools for which they provide support on the other. It was the first attempt to make schools publicly accountable, and resulted from the first Government intervention (in 1833) to support mass schooling. The Inspectors of Schools were in this respect different from other Government agents appointed to monitor the working of the Factory Acts or the Poor Law, given the 'more comprehensive sphere of duty' defined for them, and their role in developing a complex process of data collection, information diffusion and the monitoring and influencing of standards.

The development of Government inspection was accompanied by other means of detecting and influencing standards, especially after the middle of the century. The most important of these was the increasingly important role that competitive examinations came to play in education at all levels. Oxford and Cambridge locals and Indian and British Civil Service examinations are crucial examples of how, from the 1850s, the examination came to be seen both as a test of individual achievement and as a guide to institutional standards, a matter of particular concern to the universities: 'raised standards were demanded by parties both within and without the universities and competitive examinations provided a convenient way of achieving them. . . . Competitive examinations led to a general increase in specialist competence.'[22] John Roach describes how, in the second half of the nineteenth century, examinations became an increasingly used part of the educational system, and suspicion grew of the centralized control that they might engender. They were, however, as their proponents understood, basically 'an alternative to a fully state-directed plan of teaching and inspection', and Roach underlines the fact that 'in the twentieth century examinations were to be discussed from the point of view of statistics, of psychology, and later of sociology. In the nineteenth they had been a part of politics. . . . They had furthered an ideal of individual excellence.'[23]

Since the universities were at least in part guardians of the new examination system, they entered the diagram of school accountability. It was through the schools' successes in entrance to the universities and to the Civil Service that the standards they achieved could be increasingly judged. Frederick Rudolph makes the important point about American colleges in the middle decades of the century that 'printed examination questions had a way of being a more revealing test of the course and of the instructor than were the fleeting structures of the oral tradition'.[24] The evolution of examination structures in England proved to be even more revealing as ancient school and university traditions began to be adapted both in the ancient institutions and in their new rivals. New social groups were making new demands on education, and the examination system joined institutional change, the erosion of the traditional curriculum, and other adaptations in educational provision, as indicators of the new relationships. The examination system was an indirect form of quality rating, in an age when the expanding commercial and professional middle class wanted access both to aristocratic traditions and to instrumental forms of schooling.

The moment when a number of these strands came together to form the most articulated version of educational accountability in English history was in 1862, when the Revised Code inaugurated the system of payment by results. The system was to last some three decades, and was a source of intense contemporary controversy. It produced a substantial critical literature, including some of the bitterest discussion of education by Matthew Arnold and Sir James Kay-Shuttleworth. Exactly what it represented, and what was its impact, is still not agreed by historians. That it radically altered the role of the inspectorate for the last three decades of the century, and had a prolonged effect on elementary education, is nevertheless beyond dispute. What the new Code introduced – adapting proposals by the Newcastle Commission and in the first draft of a revision of the 1860 Code – was a system of payment to managers of schools based on an examination of pupils by the inspectors. Payments to teachers were to cease, and the new examination of individual pupils who had completed a satisfactory number of attendances was to be based on their competence in the three Rs as tested on the inspector's annual visit. The level of possible grant per pupil was to be reduced for each pupil's failure in reading, writing or arithmetic. The Department of Science and Art had already based its grants on a 'payment by results' principle, and the new Code was clearly designed to make the elementary schools responsive to the demands of a clearly defined syllabus and procedure. It introduced the concept of income sanctions for failure to reach adequate standards. Sir Lewis Selby-Bigge summarized the Revised Code as having 'adopted the main principle of the Newcastle Commission's Report, that we must look to examination rather than inspection to check, test and secure the efficiency of public education, and that State aid should be determined by the results of individual examinations of children'.[25] Under the Revised Code, wrote Sir G. W. Kekewich, 'the wisdom of the Department prescribed that the worse a school was, the more the means of improving it should be taken away. The larger the amount of money that was needed, the less was given.'[26]

The examination of individual children was not intended to replace the 'general' inspection of schools. Inspectors were told: 'You will judge every school by the standard which you have hitherto used as regards its religious, moral, and intellectual merits. The examination does not supersede this judgement, but presupposes it.'[27] Matthew Arnold in particular now felt, however, that the inspector's possibility of assessing the whole culture of the school was negligible.[28] The examination by the inspectors became more and more perfunctory, and they came to rely on assistants to handle what had become a work explosion.[29] Above all, perhaps, the new situation had changed the status of the inspector and his relationship with the schools. Edmonds describes this as 'the greatest evil of all' introduced by the Revised Code, by elevating the 'status of the inspector, deriving from his increased powers: he could no longer be a friendly critic, for on the nature and results of his examination, the life-blood of the school depended'. He quotes Kekewich: 'Imagine the feelings of the unfortunate teacher when he looked over the inspector's shoulder and saw the failures being recorded wholesale, and knew that his annual salary was being reduced by two and eightpence for each failure.'[30]

The criticisms levelled at the system, including by the National Union of Elementary Teachers, founded in 1870, were concerned with the narrowing effect of the Code on the curriculum, the concentration on rote learning that it provoked, the altered relationship between the teachers and the inspectorate, and the reduction of the status of the teachers *vis-à-vis* their school managers. Critics also pointed to the failure of payment by results to achieve what it most obviously set out to do – provide better 'value for money'. The system was clearly designed to improve the teaching and learning of the basic skills, but as 'specific' and 'class' subjects were admitted for grant and their range extended from the 1870s and 1880s the same criteria of effectiveness were applied across a wide curriculum. Selby-Bigge's verdict on the system summarizes the critical position. 'Value for money', he suggests, is an appealing phrase, but it

> raises the question what constitutes value, and in respect of a social service this question admits of many answers. Mr. Lowe's famous system of 'payment by results' started from the idea of efficiency, but it was really based on a false conception of value, by which it was finally destroyed. It was an attempt to get value for money by making the amount of money dependent on ascertained value, but could only work at all if a very narrow meaning was given to value . . .[31]

The State, pronounced another judge of the system, was seeking value for its money 'before the State itself or anybody representing it had made up its mind as to wherein good value would consist'.[32]

These were majority views among the teachers and educationists. Although the inspectors themselves at first opposed the system, it is probable that a majority came to accept it after two or three years of its operation. The Committee of Council claimed in 1864–5 that of twenty-six reports on elementary schools by inspectors, two-thirds contained favourable judgements on the working of the Code:

'although this estimate was regarded as being a piece of Government exaggeration, it is true that the majority did support the code'.[33] Some recent historians have suggested that the criticisms of the Code, and past acceptance of the criticisms at their face value, have ignored the underlying reality, notably that Lowe's Revised Code was covertly designed basically to strengthen the hold of secular subjects in the elementary schools and to reduce the authority of the Church in education: 'the promulgation and enforcement of the Revised Code constituted a significant victory for the state in its struggle with the Church for the control of education.' The Code indicated 'the state's right to make the content of elementary education meet the wide demands of contemporary society'.[34] This is a difficult argument to conduct, given the relationship of the Code to earlier events (especially the Newcastle Commission proposals of 1861) and the stringent basis on which it was established, but it is certainly true that in its operation it can be related to the secular needs of the changing industrial society of the late nineteenth century. It is equally true that the education service in general expressed a huge sigh of relief when, from 1890, the system began to be relaxed and abandoned. The 1890 Code, wrote Kekewich, 'involved the issue of more humane and more reasonable instructions to the Inspectors', and a more sensible treatment of school finance. While the 1890 Code was 'technically only a change in the conditions on which the State grant was paid . . . in reality it was a revolution in education'.[35]

The end of the Revised Code coincided with the beginnings of a new interest in child study, a period of new interest in curriculum reform and experimentation with teaching methods, and the rapidly growing literature of 'progressive' education after the turn of the century. In the new atmosphere payment by results was widely seen as a prison-house from which teachers, children and the education system as a whole had escaped, even though the effects lingered on. By the beginning of the First World War its abolition still seemed so recent that 'inspection is still a somewhat uncertain quality'.[36] The partners in the educational enterprise were now slowly constructing relationships in a changed society and on different bases. The activities of Her Majesty's Inspectors were to be placed on a different footing, more akin to the terms of reference which they had originally been given, and involving relations with schools which for most of this century have been more tentative and complex than in the period from 1862 to the mid-1890s.

By the end of the century the partnership and the relationships had changed. The School Board era had begun in 1870, and by the first decade of the twentieth century it was being replaced by that of the local authorities. Three important features of the School Boards and their schools need to be singled out for this discussion. *First,* they introduced into the picture the crucial element of local political control over provision, within the context of national legislation. Whatever has changed since, this pattern has remained. The creation of the 'dual system' of State-sponsored and Church-sponsored education became, after the 1902 Education Act, a single system which contained the diversity. By bringing the Church schools into the 'maintained' sector, the 1902 and 1944 Acts produced a system which subjected the mass of schools to the same standards of financial provision, the same criteria of inspection, the same influences for change in the curriculum, child health and welfare, school buildings, and everything that affected the discussion of school standards and achievement or failure.

The *second* feature of importance was the enhanced role provided, within the new political structure, for the elementary school managers. With their responsibility to ensure the proper operation of the schools and to report on them, in some cases they – or the visitors they appointed – acted as a kind of semi-official inspectorate.[37] Their powers were varied and not always clearly defined or understood, but in a new way they brought a substantial lay public into a direct relationship with the schools. The possibility of long-term conflict between the newly unionized teachers and their new lay controllers was perhaps diminished by the *third* feature of these developments – the appointment by the Boards of the first local inspectors. Although the teachers were clearly responsible to the managers and the School Boards, the nearest to a form of accountability in this situation was their relationship with these new inspectors. It was a 'professional' connection, and for the teachers it was the one that most directly affected their position, their reputation, their access to additional school funds, or to promotion. The local inspectors were a response, in Peter Gordon's analysis to

> the need for a more expert evaluation of the work and life of a school than could be provided by managers . . . The erosion of local managers' powers and functions under school boards was an inevitable consequence of the increasing complexity of working . . . and

the consequent greater demands for expertise in a number of fields which the local managers were unable to meet.[38]

The gradual appearance of these local inspectors in the later decades of the nineteenth century meant a change in the accountability equation. The HMIs were an ambiguous element, representing major, uncertain powers and threats – and most directly the judge-and-jury position they occupied until the 1890s. The new Board structures and the management bodies of both Board and voluntary schools meant a change in relationship within which Board school-teachers initially, and then others, felt an enhanced status. The local inspectors – at least partly because they were mainly recruited from the ranks of the elementary school teachers themselves – were more of a bridge to the political and economic masters. The local inspectors provided the most immediate, regular and understandable form of public 'control' over the operation of the elementary schools, and from the beginning of this century over the grammar schools also,[39] as a result of which the university-educated grammar school teachers were brought a step nearer to seeing themselves as part of a 'teaching profession'.

It is important to emphasise the 'professional' component in this new structure of school responsibility or accountability. The elementary school teachers had established the NUET (later the NUT) with 'professional' goals in mind, as well as considerations of pay and tenure. In the last decades of the century their actions, their pronouncements, their publications, reflect an enhanced sense of and concern about status. The beginning of the twentieth century saw a new pattern of discussion of teacher 'professionalism', given the entry of the local authorities into teacher training, the beginnings of the training of secondary school teachers by the universities, and the new pattern of control which pointed towards the possibility of a unified teaching profession, of standardized salaries and even of teacher control over entry to the profession through a Registration Council. By the First World War the much stronger sense of professional identity among teachers had become an important ingredient in their definition of their public accountability – they were judged not only by the HMIs, by the local inspectors, by examination results, by criteria *external* to the school, but also by their peers. Professional norms were increasingly proclaimed, professional 'integrity' was more underlined, the professional organizations had become more important arbiters and spokesmen of the successful functioning of the school system.

One final and distinctive element of the nineteenth-century picture is important, given its strong continuity into the twentieth – the role of the Royal Commission, parliamentary committee or other national investigation or inquiry. From the beginning of the nineteenth century there is a tradition of parliamentary inquiry into social and educational conditions, but it is from the 1850s that the tradition of major national investigations begins. In the 1850s Governments turned this kind of spotlight on Oxford and Cambridge universities and on the elementary schools; in the 1860s on the major public schools and on the grammar and other endowed schools; in the 1870s and 1880s on scientific and technical education. The appointment of the Newcastle Commission in 1858 to inquire into 'the state of popular education in England' is of particular interest, in that it revealed the limits of existing forms of inquiry and began the tradition of using specially appointed assistant commissioners to conduct the necessary detailed inquiries. The Newcastle Commission report of 1861 contains this passage:

> When we entered upon our inquiry, we found that, though various departments of Government were in possession of much information respecting detached portions of the subject, none could furnish a complete account of the state of education of any class of the population, or of any district in the country. . . . [The Inspectors' reports] might at first sight be expected to exhaust the subject. This, however, is not the case. The Inspectors are Inspectors of Schools, not of education. They have no experience of uninspected or private schools, nor have they any means of ascertaining what proportion of the population grow up in ignorance.[40]

What the Newcastle and then other commissions achieved was a form of scrutiny that provided Government and the policy-makers with data as to the quantity, quality and adequacy of sectors or aspects of education. The Revised Code, the legislation of the late 1860s reforming school endowments and management, the Technical Instruction Acts of 1889 and 1891 – these followed from commission inquiries and point to a central feature of these developments, an important supplementary way in which the educational system was made accountable to Parliament. Data and evaluations were brought into the political arena and became a possible basis for legislation.

The teachers, the schools and the system had therefore been made responsive to public scrutiny in another way, and the process by which it was achieved was to be increasingly important in the twentieth century as legislation became more comprehensive, and the administration of the educational system became the business of an increasingly powerful Board of Education, then Ministry of Education and then Department of Education and Science.

In the twentieth century the relationship between education and the wider community has continued to emphasize and to adapt some of these older traditions, and there have been significant continuities and changes. Governments have continued to draw their data and guidance as to the adequacy of the system and its component parts from the inspectorate, as well as from a more diverse use of the mechanism of commission and advisory council or committee. Kogan and Packard stress that in British Government 'it has long been assumed that advisory councils and committees are a necessary part of the policy forming and testing system'. In Britain, unlike other 'equivalent' countries they have been 'a major source of information, of criticism, and of suggestions for change . . . government councils . . . serve the important purpose of articulating beliefs, which might be inert and explicit in the whole society, about how education should be run and how it should be beneficially changed'.[41]

The tendency has been for the findings of such bodies to be used as a basis for adapting the system for purposes of manpower needs and responses to economic change (as in the case, for example, of the Robbins report on higher education or the Dainton Report on the flow of candidates into science in higher education). They have been concerned less with the effectiveness of teachers in classrooms or of schools in their sector than with the national effectiveness of the parts of the system. Nevertheless, the Crowther Report, for example, on the fifteen-to-eighteen age group, the Newsom Report on children of average and below-average ability, and the Plowden Report on primary schools, were at least partly concerned with school processes and curricula, and their effectiveness in relation to specific educational or social problems. Even the 1966 Pilkington Committee on the size of classes and approval of courses in further education went beyond its 'technical' brief to comment that 'all concerned will have to ensure that the scarce resources with which they are entrusted are used to the maximum advantage . . . it is also essential in the national interest that educational standards shall be raised'.[42] In the 1960s and 1970s

Governments became internationally more eager to establish a direct relationship between educational systems and national economic and social needs. Standards became linked more closely to national performance in international competition, to national development, and even to national survival.

In this respect the British experience of examinations and assessment has come to seem even more central, being the most characteristic and effective national means of evaluating school responses to public needs. In a discussion of 'standards and assessment', the Labour Government's 1977 Green Paper, *Education in Schools*, made the following strong statements:

> There must be a coherent and soundly-based means of assessment for individual pupils, for schools and for the educational system as a whole. The professional competence and knowledge of teachers are of prime importance in assessing individual pupils. The Educational Departments (of England and Wales) will encourage the development of diagnostic tests to help them in this task and it is hoped they will be widely used by schools and authorities; greater consistency of practice can only be beneficial.[43]

In the context of our earlier discussion of standards and in relation to accountability these statements indicate one part of the educational landscape that has remained important for more than a century. In terms of the curriculum and of educational standards the 1970s saw distinct attempts being made to arrive at greater direction and guidance from the centre, from the inspectorate, from the Department of Education and Science, and from Government itself. The paradox of the Conservative approach embodied in the Government elected in 1979 was that it needed to use the instruments of central government more powerfully in order to pursue its aim of reducing areas of government control and power.

Other partners in the accountability picture have retained important if changing positions within it. The universities have been consistently involved in the evolution of public examinations. They have sought to influence school curricula and standards in ways which satisfy the entry and other requirements of higher education, but in ways which can be interpreted as responses to public demand rather than parochial university concerns or university interest in power or control. When the American universities abandoned their preparatory departments from the 1870s they turned instead to 'systems of accreditation whereby schools were certified as doing creditable work or where their examinations were accepted as an adequate basis for admission'.[44] The English universities did not 'certify' schools, but went further in that they constructed a public examination system which they either directly controlled or in which they were the dominant partners. From the 1960s, with the advent of the Certificate of Secondary Education, the role of teachers and schools in running the system of public examinations has increased. Given a highly selective and competitive system of higher education, however, the universities have continued to exert a strong influence on decisions about schools and examinations, and to this extent the schools can still be said to have a degree of accountability to the universities. The extent to which schools are successful in public examinations and university entrance is open to public scrutiny and response – and this represents an important form of public accountability.

The public visibility of school management and practices has also remained a significant feature of the system. The effect of national inquiries, national legislation, and national patterns of reorganization (especially of secondary education from the 1950s), has been to make schools and their operation more open to scrutiny from the local agencies responsible for them – the local authorities, the political parties which control them, the officers of the authorities and the local inspectors or advisers. Since the schools have been the subject of extensive controversy since the Second World War, they have seen all their operations closely followed for one purpose or another – their examination results, their teaching styles, their 'progressive' or traditional methods, their curriculum, their response to behaviour problems, their ability to handle precise social problems for which their help is directly sought (authority problems, drugs, consumer awareness and the like). The responses of the schools have been measured in terms of perceptions of their effectiveness, but also through a more direct dialogue between the schools or the teachers and the local and national authorities – through committee and negotiating structures, through conferences, teachers' centres and in-service relationships, through *ad hoc* and standing machineries of many kinds.

New elements, however, have entered this pattern of responsibility and accountability – changes in higher education, the interests of parents and pupils, research and an increased interest in the classroom.

That higher education should itself be discussed in terms of accountability is an indication of how far the range of the discussion widened in the 1960s and 1970s. The creation of the binary system was an attempt to introduce the notion of greater accountability into one part of the higher education system, with the intention of making the 'maintained' sector more immediately responsible to public and national needs and pressures. Student radicalism in the late 1960s, the introduction of new technologies into teaching, the enormous increase in expenditure on the provision of higher education and grant aid for students, dissatisfaction with traditional methods of university teaching and attempts (more successful in the United States than in Britain) to involve students in the assessment of lecturers' effectiveness, the development of evaluation and self-evaluation in higher education – all of these extended the frontiers of the discussion, and also involved new constituencies in making judgements about the higher education they provide, receive or witness. The Council for National Academic Awards strengthened the ability of part of the maintained higher education sector in the 1970s to justify the content, methodology, staffing and other resources involved in their course proposals, and 'validation' became a salient aspect of higher education accountability. Regional planning machinery, national policy-making and interest groups, negotiating machinery, Government audit of the universities, visitations by the CNAA or the University Grants Committee, have become aspects of a greatly diversified need to respond, to justify and to be judged.

When the Taylor Committee reported in 1977 on *A New Partnership for Our Schools* it signalled that an emergent interest in greater parent and pupil participation in school management had become practical politics, or at least an important item on the public agenda. Parents have for the most part in nineteenth- and twentieth-century education been kept at arm's length, involved at closest in parent–teacher associations with no powers. Governing bodies and management committees have at the same time had little or no authority over – or even power to discuss – major areas of school policy, notably the curriculum. Pupils have been admitted to various styles of school 'government', mainly in relation to marginal issues or at a token level. Since the late 1960s there has been a minority, radical call among school pupils to be allowed to play an effective part in decision-making. Since the Second World War there have been parent pressure groups campaigning for greater involvement with and in schools. Since the implementation of the 1944 Education Act there has been a degree of uncertainty as to the extent of the powers of governing bodies. The Taylor Committee put all of these factors together in making its recommendations for a revised management structure of schools, and it did so in terms of the school's accountability. The report indicated in an important passage the possibility of and need for extending the existing boundaries of accountability:

> As a first step in keeping under review the degree to which the school is achieving its goals and making progress towards its aims, the governing body will want to decide what information and advice it will need in respect of those activities of the school which it considers of particular importance as indicators of the school's progress. The primary source of this information and advice will be the headteacher and especially his staff, and the success of the operation will depend upon their contribution. . . . The governing body would also be concerned to obtain information on how the school is seen by the community which it serves. . . .[45]

The conception of a governing body (on which parents, staff and pupils, and the community would be represented) keeping these aspects of the school's life and its external relations under review raises questions about the professional autonomy of teachers, and the hitherto monopoly 'political' role of governing bodies on behalf of political parties and structures. In the context of national and local debate about political and professional issues the proposals met with stiff resistance, but historically they indicate a relatively new element in the overall discussion and – especially in the case of parents – an open frontier for future exploration.

Since the mid-1950s research has considerably extended the framework of discussion. In answer to questions of how or whether an educational institution or process works, research has become of central importance. Do schools improve social mobility? Do teaching styles matter? Has comprehensive reorganization affected examination performance? How is girls' academic performance influenced by attendance at co-educational or single sex schools? In response to questions of this kind researchers have explored the school and the system, diagnosed and even recommended. Research has become a more important ingredient in the accountability discussion by supplementing the means of data collection and evaluation processes developed by the inspectorate and the Government commission. The researcher has in one sense become an expert accountant, developing the means of analysis not available to the participants (though occasionally involving them) or to the casual observer. The difference between the account rendered via research and via the agent of Government relates above all to the relative strengths and weaknesses of the two. The researcher has an uncertain status, his research is geared to long-term and complex understandings, and in this he contrasts with the stronger, ascribed status of the inspector or the commissioner. Nevertheless, the discussion of accountability must take account of research as a recently constructed channel through which important messages about processes and performance now pass.

In many senses, and as a result of many of these developments, the teacher has become more visible in the classroom. There are strong public signals about what teachers *ought* to achieve and what pupils *ought* to learn. There has historically been a strong public feeling that teachers have a straightforward job to do, are provided with the context in which to do it, and should be able to operate in it without difficulty – given their form of expertise, one of the many developed by complex, modern society in order to do specialist jobs *on behalf of* society. The somewhat different roles of the elementary and grammar school teacher were clearly and differently defined in the nineteenth century along social class and cultural lines, in the same way as were those of the grammar and secondary modern school teacher after the Second World War. The period since the 1940s and early 1950s has somewhat clouded this picture. Schools have been as troubled by changing social mores and norms as the world outside them. The community, as we have seen, has looked to the school to take on the extra burdens of solving the new or enhanced social problems. It has radically altered the school structures within which teachers work, and has subjected them to different and often mutually exclusive pressures. The community has then taken an increased interest in how the teacher as professional educator and problem-solver has succeeded or failed in the classroom. Some have asked teachers to solve more, others – including the *Black Papers* – have asked them to solve less (and to stop attempting to be social workers). Classrooms, as well as schools, have become visible.

The interest in the classroom and the teacher's accountability for what he accomplishes within it, has paralleled nation-wide or community-wide interests in social disadvantage – because while nations have evolved anti-poverty or other programmes, or decided on educational priority areas, communities have been concerned about their children with teachers in classrooms. This has always been true, but it has been more strongly felt in recent decades as public policy has pointed to education as an instrument of social policy and improvement, as the demand for more and better education has intensified, as the school leaving age has been raised, and as uncertainties and disappointments have been translated into specific classroom terms. Public anxieties, personal disappointments, and the development of national attempts to monitor school purpose and performance produced the Assessment of Performance Unit in the middle of the 1970s, with its terms of reference 'to promote the development of methods of assessing and monitoring the achievement of children at school and to seek to identify the incidence of under-achievement'.[46] At this level the national machine and the concerns of the classroom come together. The 1977 Green Paper went on from its discussion of the assessment of pupils, schools and the system to indicate that 'tests suitable for the monitoring of pupils' performance on a broader base by local education authorities are likely to come out of the work of the Assessment of Performance Unit. Here again there will be advantage in greater consistency.'[47]

The history of the nineteenth- and twentieth-century elements we have discussed is summarized in that expectation. It contains the teachers and the local authorities, the classroom and the national system, the research and the universities (where some of this research was based). It contains national policy and guidance, with the restrained vocabulary of 'there will be advantage', promoting and seeking to identify. The tensions, however, have become greater for the teacher, who is under more explicit pressures, is being declared more accountable, and being driven in contradictory directions to state the forms and extent of his accountability. The history points in two apparently opposite directions, ones that are familiar in the American as well as the British setting. The second Newman Report on higher education, for example, suggested that there were 'two very different strategies for achieving accountability. Strengthening the tendencies towards central control aimed at rationalizing and ordering the system represents one strategy, strengthening the incentives for self-regulation . . . is quite another.'[48] While the choices are made in different structures and value systems in the United States, this tension between two strategies is becoming evident in Britain also. The agencies of 'central control' have been different and more·

prominent than in the United States, and a more rational, ordered system does not necessarily mean the same or seem as threatening in Britain. That the balance needs to be tilted or at least maintained in such a way as to ensure 'self-regulation' is equally true, however.

There are historically two main dangers in attempting to apply the American interest in accountability to the British situation – apart from the problems inherent in the concept of accountability itself. The first is in failing to see *to whom* the teacher or the school is to be more accountable, and in this connection there are necessary and difficult questions to be asked about the sources of the demand for greater accountability and the forms and channels through which it is to be achieved. That is one way in which the concept and the history raise central questions about power and authority in education and in society. The second danger lies in the narrow base on which the American version of accountability rests, and the forms of control towards which it points.[49] Again, the discussion leads into one about the definition and location of power and authority. Martin Trow underlines the danger in a discussion of pressures on higher education:

> The demands of external agencies for fuller and more detailed justification of the activities and expenditure of colleges and universities, a process under way everywhere, increase the size and importance of central administrations. Since these central bodies are held responsible for the activities of their component units, they respond quite naturally by claiming and exercising greater control over them. In short, stronger pressures for accountability strengthen central authority, both in the institutions and in the system as a whole.[50]

To that extent the American and British discussions share important features. There are obviously, however, differences not only of structure but also in the historical roles of the different parts of those structures. It is not that Britain has no history of accountability in education, it is simply that the history has to be seen as diffused through a variety of interconnected relationships.

The discussion suggests a clear need to determine how the participants – teachers, parents, administrators, politicians and the community at large – view the relationships in these diffuse structures, and how the concept of accountability can or cannot be pressed and responded to. Versions of accountability which set out from narrow hypotheses of ideal and measurable practice, or from political models of right practice, not only seek to impose over-simple patterns on existing complex relationships, but direct attention away from the school-society relationships we have tried to underline. They treat the school not as a part of the social condition, but as an instrument to be moulded or used. Above all, they inhibit teachers from recognizing and acting upon their relationship to the diverse elements in understanding and improving the educational and social condition.

It could be argued that these dangers are present in the American situation and that the discussion in general has little relevance in Britain precisely because a pattern of diffused accountability has been constructed and has been operational in Britain since the mid-nineteenth century. The danger in Britain lies in attempting to superimpose on that pattern a set of accountability criteria which would damage the existing structure and provide nothing valuable in return. What the historical emphases perhaps best indicate in the British situation is the need for and existence of an increasing awareness on the part of teachers of the channels through which they do, can and should communicate with the other partners in the educational structures and processes.

7 Knowledge as power

The most persistent dilemmas in educational debate in this century have been concerned with kinds of knowledge. In terms of school or university curricula, in relation to reorganization and the democratization of provision, in connection with educational ideals of every variety, there has emerged the question of access to knowledge, to the most appropriate knowledge, to one curriculum or another, to knowledge as in itself providing access to further education, to experience, to work. Philosophers have defined the frontiers amongst different knowledges, and sociologists – especially in the 1970s – have considered how access to knowledge and the curricula in which it is embodied are socially determined, politically structured, built in to the mechanisms of power. The school curriculum has been seen, rightly, as a vital battlefield on which competing social and cultural ideals wage war.

How explosive the issue has been can be seen in that passage in T. S. Eliot's *Notes towards the Definition of Culture* when, after examining and rejecting the equal opportunity approach to education, Eliot self-consciously attempts to 'relieve the feelings of the writer and perhaps of a few of his more sympathetic readers' by asserting, almost shouting:

> The culture of Europe has deteriorated visibly within the memory of many who are by no means the oldest among us. And we know, that whether education can foster and improve culture or not, it can surely adulterate and degrade it. For there is no doubt that in our headlong rush to educate everybody, we are lowering our stan-

dards, and more and more abandoning the study of those subjects by which the essentials of our culture – of that part of it which is transmissible by education – are transmitted; destroying our ancient edifices to make ready the ground upon which the barbarian nomads of the future will encamp in their mechanised caravans.[1]

The point here is Eliot's equation of deterioration, adulteration, degradation, lower standards and the end of civilization with the abandonment of culturally essential *subjects*. The world which Eliot in 1948 saw as threatened by the 'headlong rush to educate everybody' was the eighteenth-century one of civilized, liberal values as understood by a leisured, educated class. As Rothblatt points out in his picture of this world in *Tradition and Change in English Liberal Education*, these values were transmissible, and were pervasive and accepted enough not to need the institutional machinery of higher education which was to spread so widely in the nineteenth century:

> Entirely literary in character, focused particularly on the study of classical languages, and requiring therefore only a few cardinal texts, a liberal education did not depend on major research libraries or extensive collections of books. It did not require dons or professors or degrees. Any teacher, provided he had some Latin, a little learning, and the right manner, could undertake the task of liberal instruction.[2]

The nineteenth century, in evolving the now familiar characteristics of the institutional and professional embodiments of higher education, higher culture and liberal values, did not destroy the earlier edifice, but adapted and extended it. Relentlessly, however, in the twentieth century, the adaptation and extension introduced the elements which caused Eliot such alarm.

The 'rush to educate everybody' had from the early decades of this century aroused increasing tensions around the relationship between extended educational provision, the appropriate knowledges to make available, and the forms and structures in which to do so. What was for all, what best reserved for some? Since the 'task of liberal instruction' was now so diverse, and so dependent on diverse structures and interpretations, how was knowledge to be distributed and who was to decide? Those questions obviously relate to the whole range of issues we have located in the discussion of education and the social condition – including opportunity, change, standards, the partners in the system of control, and the structure of power. Although they are questions seen to be central to analyses of education, and present in all the key developments of the nineteenth and first half of the twentieth century, it was not until the massive extension of educational provision in the Western industrialized world after the Second World War that they became explicit and explosive. Eliot's views became submerged in the general preoccupation with expansion, but they presciently forewarned of the major debates to come.

The reorganization of secondary education in Britain was the point at which the curriculum issue developed most acutely, though in the 1950s and 1960s with remarkably little overt discussion. It was widely assumed that the comprehensive school would develop its own characteristic curricular forms to match the underlying purposes of the schools. It was equally widely assumed that this would mean an increasing element of common experience across a broad span of knowledge. Only slowly and uncertainly did discussions begin in the schools and outside around questions of commonality and choice, streaming and mixed ability, and the justice or otherwise of establishing strong biases towards 'academic' and 'vocational' education for different groups of pupils within the schools. G. H. Bantock more than anyone picked up Eliot's message and did battle against the adulteration he saw in the expansion and reorganization of education that was taking place. Bantock saw in the equal opportunity movement and in the curricular implications of the comprehensive school the destruction of values necessary to the continuation of society. By abandoning the underlying virtues of the grammar school curriculum, he argued, we were failing to meet the needs of the 'less able' child, and at the same time depriving the more able of that necessary contact with high standards of transmitted culture. The first step was to recognize the 'radical difference between natures in our society, a radical difference which talks about a "common culture" only serves to obfuscate'. For the average or less-able child, for whom Bantock saw the need of a 'folk' culture to combat the worst elements of the 'popular' culture, he advocated a separate curriculum, the central features of which he outlined in *Education in an Industrial Society* in 1963:

I would support Mr A. W. Rowe's contention, in his *Education of the Average Child*, that 'Many of the traditional subjects, taken over *en bloc* from the grammar school curriculum, are of little use in educating the average child' – a sentiment which I would adopt for less able children. (The common curriculum, indeed, is one of the enormities of the comprehensive school.) We have got to begin by asking what . . . are the essential things in the development of the non-academic child; what fields of interest and importance are relevant to his level of consciousness.

Bantock identified four of these fields – the affective life, the physical life, the domestic life, and the 'environmental challenge of the machine'. From these starting-points he conceived a curriculum which emphasized not intellectual processes but symbol and image – 'handwriting, painting, pottery, weaving, as well as the traditional wood and metal crafts, are what I have in mind' – pointing towards taste in contemporary design, and linking with 'the sort of domestic training that aids home-building'.[3]

This approach to relevant or appropriate curricula for different groups of school pupils obviously ran counter to the dominant interests of educational planning in the 1950s and 1960s, and to the mounting sociological interest in how these apparently educational or cultural categories in fact diguised socially determined definitions. It resurfaced in the *Black Papers*, especially in *Black Paper Two*, where, among others, Richard Lynn defended Britain's 'great cultural tradition of intellectual achievement' against the progressives and the 'destruction of quality education',[4] and where Bantock and Rhodes Boyson attacked discovery methods as a danger to important 'traditional methods of study'.[5] In the meantime, the comprehensive schools were experimenting with different patterns of common early years, common cores, and subject choices. They were coming up against the problems of pupil grouping, teaching styles, competing pressures to offer a continuing 'liberal' education and an increasingly 'relevant' curriculum. They were being offered, especially in the 1960s, a range of new teaching possibilities, based on new technology and confident psychology – including teaching machines, programmed learning and language laboratories. They were being offered new curriculum materials, and were themselves being involved in developing Nuffield and then Schools Council projects across the whole curriculum range, in ways similar to those taking place simultaneously in the United States. New examinations, new forms of in-service education for teachers, new points of change (including teachers' centres), indicated how rapid were the changes in the schools and their curricula, and how strong was the support needed by the teachers in responding to the new demands and uncertainties.

As we have seen earlier, the schools were in the 1950s and 1960s placed under strong conflicting pressures, and were criticized for failing to solve salient social problems. Parents, ill at ease with new curriculum subjects, new mathematics, new teaching methods, were themselves often caught up in the conflicting pressures – wanting their children to have equal access to all that the curriculum had to offer, and at the same time to have unequal or special access to specific subjects or skills useful for expected, precise occupational destinations. The schools were under pressure to teach skills, to prepare for citizenship and life, to engage battle on behalf of equality, justice, race harmony, social justice, moral rectitude, standards of discrimination in the media and popular culture, and a range of other targets urged on the schools by interest groups, popular opinion and the teachers' own sense of rapidly changing social and cultural needs. In the changing conditions of the schools and their environment it was hard to know how to respond to the demands, particularly given the new situations and attitudes of the pupils themselves, their new cultural identities and social expectations. What appeared to be the technical or functional shortcomings of the schools were embedded in confusions which sprang from the political and social changes of which the schools were only one – albeit a highly significant – part.

The discussion of curricula and of knowledge was given a new and different impetus at the beginning of the 1970s, as a result primarily of the 1970 conference of the British Sociological Association on the theme of the sociology of education. A selection of the papers, edited by Richard Brown, appeared in 1973 under the title *Knowledge, Education, and Cultural Change*, but some had already appeared in 1971 in the collection edited by Michael F. D. Young – *Knowledge and Control*. Set against an increasing transatlantic interest in the sociology of knowledge, the two collections represented an attempt to re-examine the assumptions of the sociology of education of the 1950s and 1960s. They attempted to turn attention from questions of structure, access, the economy, and a range of accepted problems which, in Brown's words, left out of account 'almost entirely any consideration of the *content* of education, of what is being taught, of how knowledge is organized, of the cognitive element in the socialization process in the school'.[6] Most of the papers in Young's volume focused on 'the organization of knowledge in the formal educational institutions of industrialized societies'. Young looked towards a sociology of education which would make 'the problems of control and the organization of knowledge and their interrelations its core concern'. One of the central questions in the exercise was 'What counts as knowledge?'[7] 'What we know' was not to be taken as given, but made the object of enquiry.

Involved in this shift of emphasis was an anxiety to turn the apparently neutral and unproblematic nature of school knowledge into an element of social and political analysis at a more fundamental level than that of social class and its attendant features in the previous decades. It was in the school, in the classroom, that lay the key to understanding how class society reproduced itself. From this point on, radical analysis of education was concerned predominantly with this relationship between the curriculum and knowledge on the one hand, and the structure of power on the other. Knowledge was power, or rather different and controlled levels and forms of access to knowledge meant different degrees of access to power. The key to understanding a school, a university, a curriculum project, the place of music or geography or social studies in a school, lay in the question 'What counts as knowledge?', but also by implication 'Who decides what counts?' and who is admitted into which mysteries and in what conditions? The sociology of education was being redefined as the politics-and-sociology of education.

Surprisingly, the interest in knowledge and power was seen in the early 1970s as novel. The point here is not to examine the extent to which the new emphases overturned existing approaches to the sociology of education, or to investigate fine and necessary distinctions that are made in discussions of all the categories involved – notably those of power and control. The point is that the discussion of power and control in the 1970s was in fact part of a long and often neglected tradition of situating knowledge in a context of politics and power. Only in conservative attempts to present 'politico-social ideals' as 'pure educational theory' is the knowledge–power nexus denied. Knowledge as the gateway to participation in the power structures of contemporary society is as important to Daniel Bell and the sociologists of technological society as it is in the radical, deschooling programmes of Reimer or Illich. What is different is the vision of where the power lies or should lie, the nature of the knowledge under discussion, and the means of its delivery.

The 'useless' knowledge sought by the eighteenth-century gentle-man, or the 'useful' knowledge offered to the working class or sought for their own children by the Victorian middle class, or the political knowledge sought by nineteenth-century radical working men, were all conceived in terms of power in one sense or another. Clarke, side-stepping the issue as to whether all knowledge is instrumental, points out that the modern justification of the classical tradition as education for its own sake obscures the fact 'that the classical–human-ist education was deliberately given, especially from the 18th century onwards, as an appropriate training for a *vocation* – that of rulers'.[8] The 'useless' classical curriculum was, and throughout its nine-teenth-century adaptations remained, a badge of respectability, a sign of gentility, a passport to one level or another of government, imperial rule, bureaucratic control, professional status. What 'counted' as knowledge was processed within and by a class which opened and closed the doors of rank and control, guarding them against encroachment and attack. Right knowledge was identified with right social background, right forms of schooling or tuition, right public destinies. Classical learning *was* power in an understood sense. Other learning, in the eighteenth and nineteenth centuries was admitted to respectability, to institutional status and influence, only cautiously, under pressure, and on strict terms. Science gained only the most tentative footholds in eighteenth- and nineteenth-century schools and universities, and many of its advocates had to argue its case on the same grounds as the defenders of the exclusive classical tradition – as a similar form of mental activity, as an abstract intellectual exercise. The establishment of university chairs in new subjects did not mean that the occupants were competent to profess, or that the subjects were taught. Cambridge, Rothblatt points out, reluctantly accepted philosophy and 'a moral tripos had been established in 1851, but as the moral sciences were as yet outside the scholarship network, few students would read it. Consequently the colleges had little need for moral scientists.'[9] The tradition remained strong into the twentieth century, making adaptations, but preserving the link between a particular definition of political power and a particular definition of appropriate knowledge.

Neither of the definitions, however, remained unchallenged. Out of the Enlightenment and rationalism came new conceptions of social organization and of the purposes of knowledge – widening the concern with power to questions not only of power within society, but also of power over nature and over human passions and appetites. Most importantly, however, the period of the French Revolution and the Industrial Revolution saw the transition to political conflict on a new scale and for new ends – the search by those outside 'society' to enter its frontiers. For the British radicals of the 1790s and after knowledge, *any* knowledge, was political knowledge. Popular and working-class radicalism between the 1790s and the middle of the nineteenth century promoted access to knowledge as the central feature of the battle for political and social rights. The messages of the eighteenth-century Enlightenment were most successfully translated into terms understandable in the conditions of the new industrialism in Britain by Robert Owen. Owen's thesis, propounded in the 1810s in *A New View of Society* and then in his *Report to the County of Lanark* in 1820, was that knowledge was now available to demonstrate to all that it was easier to train men to be rational, intelligent and all that went with those qualities than to continue with 'those unpleasant and irrational feelings which for ages have tormented the whole human race'. 'Ignorance, poverty, crime, and misery,' he proclaimed, 'may be prevented.' Owen's new science would open 'a new era to the human race'. Mankind need no longer be 'governed by circumstances', but could be taught to 'govern circumstances'. Owen's plans for rationally organized communities represented a new stage in the achievement of 'full power and control . . . over those circumstances'. It was a far-reaching, a total message, rationalist in its conception, libertarian in its impact, educational in its strategic implications: '. . . the day has arrived when the existing generation may so far control (circumstances), that the rising generations may become in character, without any individual exceptions, whatever men can now desire them to be, that is not contrary to human nature'.[10] It was through the new science of the formation of character, Owen's summary of the rational application of knowledge, that men were to achieve power over the mindless forces that had hitherto controlled their destinies.

For Owen, and for the working-class and radical Owenites of the 1820s and after, knowledge and education were fundamental. The literature of the Owenite movements echoed Owen's preoccupation with education, and underlined the power of knowledge. But it was those working-class radicals who turned towards more direct political action (many of them schooled in the Owenite movement) who made the stronger link between knowledge and power. Picking up the traditions of political radicalism inherited from the turn of the century, alongside the Owenite experience, the working-class radicals of the 1830s put knowledge at the centre of their campaigns. When *The Poor Man's Guardian* appeared in defiance of the stamp duty at the price of one penny in 1831 it carried at the top of its front page a drawing of a printing press which bore the words 'Liberty of the press', the whole surrounded by the motto KNOWLEDGE IS POWER. In defiance of the stamp tax and the threat of imprisonment, the paper called on the public for more than the support of their pennies:

> We must have a moral revolution; we must not allow our tyrants to triumph over us; we must defeat them by the force of reason and opinion; we must hold them to scorn, and, if needs be, fill their prisons with their political victims, until the doors shall open by the mere pressure of their own tyranny . . . you must enable us to publish our papers from the prison . . . you must rebuild our printing presses when they shall have thrown them down . . . circulate our papers – circulate the truths which we write, and you *shall* be free. . . .

The political battle for freedom, for rights, was seen as a battle around knowledge. The stamp taxes were 'taxes on knowledge'. Knowledge and reason were weapons of struggle. The tyrant enemy was invited to 'answer our arguments and show us we are wrong by his superior reason, and we will alter our course', but if he continued to persecute, he was to meet with defiance. The tyrants, 'with all their disgusting boasting of superior knowledge', merely issued unjust and monstrous edicts.[11]

All radical movements in the first half of the nineteenth century made knowledge and its rational application central features of their programmes and action. The class meeting, purchase of books, circulation of tracts, exchange of opinions, familiarity with the poems of Milton, awareness of the history of the fight for freedom, the writing of Chartist hymns, the organization of lectures, infant schools, Sunday schools, and a whole list of similar activities were part of the stream of radical activity throughout the period. In 1836 the London Working Men's Association, forerunner of the Chartists, declared among its objects the promotion of 'the education of the rising generation', the formation of a library 'of reference and useful information; to maintain a place where they can associate for mental improvement'. The Association asked in an Address whether corruption, religious hypocrisy, debauchery, fanaticism, poverty and crime could 'stalk triumphantly through the land – if the millions were educated in a knowledge of their rights?' Injustice, poverty and inequality – the Association declared the following year – were involved in 'giving to one portion of society the blessings of education, and leaving the other in ignorance'. Education needed to be extended 'not as a charity, BUT AS A RIGHT, a right derivable from society itself'.[12] The radical 'curriculum' was inevitably, therefore, conceived at every level. It accepted the Sunday or monitorial school education as a basis on which to build. It included the education of children and adults. It was in turn instrumental, ideological, propagandist and campaigning. The content of the education – even the co-operative knowledge of the Owenite movement – was always, however, less important than the mastery of knowledge itself, the path to enlightenment, the way to right reason, the opportunity to understand and to persuade. It included a large element of self-education, the attainment of which was a form of symbolic power. To a William Lovett or Thomas Cooper, having achieved a high level of personal culture through channels such as these, the pretence of the governing classes to 'superior knowledge' was understandably a 'disgusting boast'.

The underlying sense of knowledge as a political lever of power was lost or diminished from the middle of the century as the Owenite, Chartist and other popular radical struggles receded and confrontations took new forms. Lovett, for example, who had been a key figure in the London Working Men's Association and the Chartist movement, retained the commitment to education, but withdrew from its political definition. 'The most important of our individual duties', he wrote in 1853, 'is the developing and perfecting of our own nature, by intellectual and moral culture.' Individual well-being, he stressed, could not exist without knowledge – 'it being necessary for directing our labours to a beneficial or productive end'. In the home, he added, 'the acquisition of knowledge is equally necessary for strengthening the affections, for the prudent management of the household, and for the teaching and training of the young; so that they may grow up to be wise, good and useful members of the community'.[13] This was only six years away from Samuel Smiles's *Self-Help* with its emphasis on self-control, power over the passions:

It may be of comparatively little consequence how a man is

governed from without, whilst every thing depends upon how he governs himself from within. The greatest slave is not he who is ruled by a despot, great though that evil be, but he who is the thrall of his own moral ignorance, selfishness, and vice.

Smiles stressed the importance of the process of acquiring knowledge rather than the instrumental use of the knowledge itself. School education was 'but a beginning, and is valuable mainly inasmuch as it trains the mind and habituates it to continuous application and study'.[14] Herbert Spencer, writing at the same time the essays which formed his *Education: Intellectual, Moral, and Physical,* stressed a similar point: by making school instruction pleasurable there was 'a probability that it will not cease when school-days end . . . there will be as prevailing a tendency to continue, without superintendence, that self-culture previously carried on under superintendence'.[15] With variations, through Lovett, Smiles, Spencer and a variety of other prominent and influential Victorians, the emphasis had been shifted to self-education, self-control, self-mastery, self-culture, without the political and social objectives with which they had been associated in earlier decades. It is stretching the definition to include them all in the same discussion, but it is necessary to do so. The contexts within which the knowledge was to be gained and applied were being seen differently, for example, in Lovett's discussion of the home, but the sense that knowledge was a form of power remained. The power was simply to be exercised now for different ends.

The same sense of the power or instrumentality of knowledge pervades other and related movements. The phrenologists and advocates of the teaching of physiology and health and social science in the middle of the nineteenth century placed similar emphases. Lovett was connected with all of these through his association with William Ellis and a school which Ellis supported and Lovett ran in Holborn. Ellis, and the schools he created, pressed the place of social science in the curriculum in order to enable the mass of the people to understand the laws of society, to avoid misconduct (such as drunkenness and strikes) and ill health. In a lecture in the same year as the publication of Smiles's *Self-Help* Ellis declared:

As regards knowledge, there are some matters familiar as truisms to the intelligent few, which are unexplained mysteries to multitudes, and which, nevertheless, ought to be known to all . . . The difference between knowledge and ignorance of these matters cannot fail to produce a marked effect upon conduct, and hence upon well-being.

Know your own mental faculties, said the phrenologists, and you will have greater power over your destiny. Know the laws of society, said Ellis and his co-workers in the cause of social science, and you will have 'intellectual and moral weapons' strong enough to defeat 'ignorance and vice, let the iron plating in which they are encased be ever so strong'.[16] The vocabulary of power was pervasive. William Jolly, one of Her Majesty's Inspectors of schools, editor of the works of phrenologist George Combe, in a lecture on physical education in 1875 explained that 'the *Hand* should receive careful training, so as to give our children full power over that wonderful organ. . . . Our girls should further extend their hand-power by all kinds of industrial work, domestic economy and housewifery.'[17] Herbert Spencer, advocating physiological and scientific knowledge for self-preservation, was signalling the same approach to knowledge as *useful* in granting *power* over the irrational or destructive.

The concept of 'useful knowledge' was abroad through most of the nineteenth century, largely – expressed in that form – as a definition of those areas of 'fact' or principle which would be helpful to working men in their occupations. The literature of useful knowledge was a major nineteenth-century industry. In a different sense, however, the concept relates to middle-class attempts to come closer to the centres of social, political and economic power. Middle-class approaches to the secondary school curriculum contained two apparently contradictory trends. The first was the demand for a more utilitarian curriculum, for modern subjects, for book-keeping and modern languages and geography and English. This was the trend which produced the proprietary school in major centres of commerce, in opposition to the classically based grammar school. It was a trend which represented the needs of middle-class parents for an education which would enable their children to cope more effectively with the demands of an expanding and more complicated commerce. It was a search for an instrumental culture which would cement their control over the industrial and commercial machinery of Britain and the world.

On the other hand, however, the middle class sought not only to compete with and wrest political control from the established aristocracy and landed gentry, but also to join them. The new middle class created not only proprietary schools but also new public schools, an extensive network of geographically and economically more accessible schools modelled on the established vehicle of ruling class education. The new provincial universities and university colleges of the second half of the nineteenth century absorbed some of the traditions of the gentlemanly models of Oxford and Cambridge. The search for an instrumental culture to match commercial power was accompanied by the search for ways of acquiring the established badges of status and authority and power. The two trends could not easily be homogenized, but they could co-exist and overlap. Of central importance to our discussion is the fact that either form, pure or adulterated, represented a deliberate identification of knowledge and culture with power. In terms of school curricula the ambiguity was to become of major importance as the absence or weakness of science and other modern subjects in the majority of grammar and public schools became increasingly important and felt on the public pulse. Particularly from the report of the Taunton Commission on the endowed schools in 1868, and during a period of increasing international competition which threatened Britain's pioneering world position, the secondary school curriculum became a focus of competing interpretations of the concept of culture and of appropriate knowledge. Matthew Arnold, Thomas Huxley, Herbert Spencer, Cardinal Newman, and a host of others were drawn into that competition. 'To use a word of Bacon's, now unfortunately obsolete,' said Spencer, '– we must determine the relative values of knowledges.' 'The comparative worths of different kinds of knowledge,' he underlined, 'have been as yet scarcely even discussed.'[18] Those 'relative values' and 'comparative worths' have continued to be hotly debated, in different forms, through the 1960s and 1970s.

By the end of the nineteenth century knowledge had come to be seen as a form or focus of power in a variety of senses. It had by now become more directly necessary as a form of instrumental power, not just useful knowledge or information, for skills, jobs, expertise. Within increasingly State-controlled, State-supported or systematized schooling, technical education and higher education, with longer compulsory schooling and orthodox apprenticeship giving way to new forms of technical training, knowledge-and-skill or knowledge-as-skill became a stronger focus of debate about educational provision. It increasingly affected debates about the curriculum, about the relationship between school and social mobility, school and society.

Expert knowledge itself was acquiring a new status as the power of the professional over all aspects of life became more visible and widespread. Bledstein has vividly described for the United States the emergence and establishment of the new 'culture of professionalism'. He describes the ubiquitous role of the expert, the adviser, the pundit, the source of newly found 'professional authority'. He describes the 'magical' role of expertise, the increasingly dependent role of the mass of people as 'clients', the cultivation of irrationality by the expert discovery of 'abnormality and perversity everywhere', the encouragement of self-doubt, and the construction of a great higher education network by the middle class to produce the professionalized experts.[19] In Britain as in the United States these processes accompanied the emergence of discrete new university-based subjects such as economics and psychology, legitimizing forms of knowledge which served as a basis for expert advice to governments and policy-makers as well as industry, education and the public at large. The power of the expert rested on the authority conferred upon him by his knowledge, knowledge organized and certificated in precise ways. The power of the professional depended on the accreditation of his knowledge. For the nation in general knowledge-as-power had become associated not only with skill and occupation, but also with qualification – with examination, with certificate, with accredited institutions. Rothblatt's description of legitimate eighteenth-century knowledge as unconnected with libraries, collections of books, dons or professors or degrees, no longer applied in the late nineteenth century.[20] Legitimacy was acquired not through desultory contact with knowledge, but through systematic progress over hurdles and prerequisites. Ancient priesthoods and aristocracies had not disappeared; they had been supplemented and were engaged in battle or adaptation.

Just as the early nineteenth-century working class had sought to enter the gates of political power with greater knowledge and reason, so the late nineteenth- and twentieth-century labour movement again identified power with knowledge – this time the knowledge that could be acquired only through secondary education. Tawney's *Secondary Education for All* was not only a major contribution to this process of identification, but also a reflection of the growing labour and socialist concern with education and knowledge in the early decades of this century. 'Knowledge is power' continued to be a catchphrase a century after *The Poor Man's Guardian*. The cross-currents in workers' education reflected conflicting views of the relationship between knowledge and power. Broadly speaking, the National Council of Labour Colleges and the Plebs League represented a Marxist view that the workers' education movement needed to provide an education suited to the socialist aspirations of the working class. The Workers' Educational Association sought a more 'liberal' version of adult education, one which would enable workers to develop the capacity to reason, simply to acquire knowledge, to enhance their personal education. It was an old tension newly expressed. The class-conscious version of the knowledge-as-power theme was expressed at the 1921 Trades Union Congress in this form:

> We shall not be able to grapple with . . . and fight efficiently against the capitalist interest until we have an educated democracy, and particularly so far as concerns our working class movement. We want . . . as far as we can, to organise the common knowledge and education, and give to our people an education that shall not always be directed to serving the capitalist interest. We desire that we shall be able to select the lines of our own studies, have some voice and some choice in the selection of the teachers and the lecturers, and so get together and organise our own colleges and our own curricula. By this means we shall equip ourselves for that larger share in the machinery of government which all of us recognise as coming rapidly to the workers.[21]

Knowledge was by this stage being interpreted as capitalist or anticapitalist, vocational or liberal, and along other axes and antitheses. It related to the structure and content of secondary education and adult education, university education and technical education. Many of the terms contained profound and prolonged ambiguities – Tawney's failure to analyse the grammar school and alternative curricula merely reflecting a wider set of ambiguities about the literary versus utilitarian curriculum in the labour movement in general.

What underlay the period of the implementation of the 1944 Education Act and the anti-poverty strategies of the 1960s, for example, was a diffuse sense of the redistribution of power. Universal secondary schooling, active teaching methods, newly relevant curricula, large comprehensive schools with wider curriculum choices and increased facilities – these and others related to the democratization as well as the structural reorganization of schooling. The intentions were expressed in terms of development of opportunity, but they were also responses to outmoded and therefore politically threatening educational and social structures. The American anti-poverty programmes of the 1960s, including their extensive and elaborate educational components, were at least partly explained in terms of a 'more or less open society, with at least some diffusion of power'.[22] Education as a means of promoting more equal economic and social opportunity became involved with consideration of political perspective in the conditions of the United States and Britain of the 1960s and 1970s. The content of schooling became part of the debate and conflicts around the pluralist society, around the insiders and the outsiders, around power and powerlessness. The preoccupation with structures gave impetus to the 'new' sociology of the beginning of the 1970s to take greater account of the knowledge purveyed within those structures, and the new concern with control and power reopened the debates and battles that had been waged in one form or another throughout the nineteenth and twentieth centuries.

To situate this discussion adequately in its contemporary and historical dimensions there are other directions the account ought to take. It would require some discussion of Marx, Mannheim, Berger and Luckmann, and the sociology of knowledge. It would consider Weber, Durkheim and ways of arriving at theories of society within which to conduct the discussion. It would look to Bourdieu and theories of cultural transmission, and Bernstein and ways of analysing curricula and knowledge structures. It would examine diverse theories of class conflict, Marxist and Parsonian analyses of power, and Foucault's notion of power as diffused, 'from below': 'not something that is acquired, seized, or shared, something that one holds on to or allows to slip away; power is exercised from innumerable points'.[23] The need for these extensions of the discussion lies in the fact that there are variables on either side of whatever equation we establish – knowledge and power, education and politics, school and society. The variables are historical and theoretical. They require considerations of tradition and ideology, regularities and irregularities, functions and dysfunctions, and each requires what we described in the earlier discussion of Clarke as a 'sense of intersection' between past and present. Even in the absence of such a set of detailed discussions, however, it is possible to locate the recent discussions in a historical concern with the social and political stratification of knowledge.

It is possible to see how the concentration of power–knowledge is viewed in our society, and how the sociology of knowledge and of the curriculum highlights some of the contemporary dimensions of the relationship. The discussion of the expert, represented here most strongly by the work of Lasch and Bledstein, is one version of the analysis. The debates about vocational education and integrated subjects and 'relevant' curricula are another. The British and American science curriculum projects, their derivations and forms, are yet another. So also would be a discussion of the role of the university from the point of Rothblatt's analysis in the eighteenth century, through the early nineteenth-century universities of London and Virginia, the American land-grant and state universities of the late nineteenth century and the English university colleges and polytechnics, and the twentieth-century university as the repository of existing knowledge and discoverer of new knowledge necessary for the preservation of civilized values or the material well-being of society. It was Veblen's view in the United States in 1918 that 'the university is the only accepted institution of the modern culture on which the quest of knowledge unquestionably devolves; and the visible drift of circumstances as well as of public sentiment runs also to making this the only unquestioned duty incumbent on the university'.[24] Thirty years later, in England, it was Sir Richard Livingstone's view that 'if you wished to destroy modern civilization, the most effective way to do it would be to abolish universities. They stand at its centre. They create knowledge and train minds.'[25] There are aspects of this centrality that we shall discuss in the next two chapters.

We have considered some historical examples of the interpretation of knowledge, and the forms in which it is encompassed, as routes to power. Some of these suggest how power has been exercised through or identified with certain kinds of knowledge and curricula and education. Others suggest how those who have stood outside the centres of power have seen knowledge as the means of entry (and in addition to the examples of the British working class, we might have taken that of American or British minorities, or that of the social and political position of women and the education of girls). What is clear is that knowledge of itself is neither control nor power, and does not of itself imply how or in which directions it may be applied as power. Knowledge-as-power only has meaning within the historical circumstances in which it is acquired, and in relation to the perceptions, objectives and actions of those who acquire it. The possibilities of exercising control or of being controlled, or wielding or being subjected to power, are not static features of modern industrial societies.

A straightforward equation between knowledge and power is too inflexible or ambiguous to explain what actually happens to individuals, groups or movements in a complex society. The concepts of power and control are relevant only in so far as they are rooted in an awareness of their subjection to changing historical relationships, and of the difficulties of explaining the processes by which people experience influence and control, and react to them. If Spencer was right to suggest that 'the comparative worths of different kinds of knowledge' had scarcely been discussed, it is equally true today that the value attached to different kinds of knowledge as social and political instruments has scarcely been discussed historically. Without such a discussion, the dichotomies between academic knowledge and skill training, types of curriculum, high-status and low-status knowledge, and the rest, remain unnecessarily difficult to approach.

8 Higher educations

To reallocate national priorities in order to sustain growth in higher education was, concluded the Robbins Report on higher education in Britain in 1963, not just a 'probable condition for the maintenance of our material position in the world, but, much more, it is an essential condition for the realisation in the modern age of the ideals of a free and democratic society'.[1] Ten years later, in the United States, the second *Newman Report: National Policy and Higher Education*, began with the statement:

> It is one thing to espouse equal access to college as a goal toward which the nation strives. It is another thing entirely to deal with the implications of that policy as a reality. Today, American society has largely achieved the goal of access, but has yet to make the adjustments in public policy necessary for an era of realistic mass educational opportunities.[2]

Across that period in both countries priorities were in fact being reallocated within a context of economic expansion. Behind the Robbins rhetoric lay a mixture of national motives for the expansion of higher education, including manpower forecasts and technological need, political pressures and new demands. In the much more rapidly expanding higher education network of the United States the question of provision was in fact during this period turning into one of effective action to ensure adequate access *in practice* to the various levels of higher education by underprivileged and minority groups. The expansion, the demand, the changing focus of discussion, coincided in the two countries and internationally with the militancies which on many university and college campuses challenged prevailing university structures and ideologies. By the mid-1970s, however, the scene had fundamentally altered. The debates and the anxieties had begun to take on new forms.

Not, of course, that the old questions had been solved. For example, in Britain there had been by the end of the 1960s a considerable expansion in student numbers at established universities, the creation of new universities, the elevation of the status of a small number of mainly technological institutions to the university ranks, an expansion in technical education, the creation of a bachelor's degree for three- and four-year trained teachers, and the invention of the binary system and the new polytechnics. But, significant as the developments were, basic educational and social realities remained unchanged. With a figure of 8.5 per cent of the relevant age group going on to attend some form of higher education in 1962 (the figure rose steadily in the 1960s and 1970s)[3] the question of 'access' had in Britain been far from solved – especially when international comparisons were made. It was to the United States, again, that attention was primarily turned in this period, given the American explosion of higher education in the decades following the Second World War, and the much-discussed relationships in the United States between higher education and the needs of a rapidly changing social and economic situation. The social condition of black and minority ethnic groups, of urban America, of communities increasingly divided by domestic politics and international policies, was brought into explicit relationship with higher education. How the expanding university, the diversifying structure of two- and four-year colleges, the new on-campus and off-campus processes, were meeting the needs of the American social and economic condition was increasingly a matter of interest to the rest of the world. Berkeley's campus conflicts of 1964 preceded those of the rest of the world. The sit-in, the take-over, the military presence, the death of students, made the weaknesses of the new scales and structures as interesting to the rest of the world as their strengths.

Only slowly, stimulated by the Robbins Report in 1963, did British discussion of the relationship between higher education in general and specific features of the social condition gain momentum. The debates about access to secondary education that had emerged in the late 1950s were being extended to higher education – and the Robbins Committee used a good deal of that earlier evidence in order to focus attention on differential access by social groups to the higher levels of the educational system. Into the late 1960s and 1970s the proportion of unskilled manual workers' children entering higher education remained at around one per cent, while the children from upper income groups had clearly benefited from the expansion of higher education. The proportions of children from immigrant and ethnic racial minority groups entering higher education and the professions in Britain remained low. Access by girls to some areas of higher education and to skilled technical and commercial training through day release and other schemes remained restricted. Economic cuts in the 1970s hit the whole of higher education. The economic and social conditions governing entry to higher education remained as influential at the end of the 1970s as they had done when the Robbins Committee underlined them in 1963:

> The proportion of young people who enter full-time higher educa-
> tion is 45 per cent for those whose fathers are in the 'higher
> professional' group, compared with only 4 per cent for those whose
> fathers are in skilled manual occupations. The underlying reasons
> for this are complex, but differences of income and the parents'
> educational level and attitudes are certainly among them. The link
> is even more marked for girls than for boys.[4]

In Britain as in the United States the question of the diversity of provision, which had been present in the debates of the 1960s, moved into a more central position. In the House of Lords, in December 1963, Lord Robbins reacted against views that had been expressed as to excessive *university* expansion, and against suggestions that

> instead of planning for this we should have devised an extensive
> sub-structure of lesser institutions, transmogrified technical col-
> leges, junior colleges, and so on and so forth. Thus, the present
> atmosphere of universities could be preserved intact and yet a larger
> percentage of the relevant age group could have the kind of higher
> education which is really appropriate to it.

Such views, said Robbins, were not new, and his committee had thought 'long and earnestly' about them, and had inspected 'junior institutions' elsewhere. The Committee had rejected the suggestions decisively on the grounds that 'we knew no tests which *at present levels of entry* would enable it to be said with justice to one young person,

"You may go on to a university", and to another, "You must go to a junior college" ".[5]

In both Britain and the United States there were already wide diversities of provision in 'further' and 'higher' education, and with the introduction of the binary system, the creation of the polytechnics, and in the mid-1970s of colleges and institutes of higher education, the British version of diversity was extended. There is probably near-unanimity of public opinion that the landscape of higher education should contain diverse provision – but the meaning of the phrase, the nature and distribution of that diversity in the conditions of the late 1970s and 1980s, are crucial questions. There are serious pitfalls in the discussion, and again it is essential to see the questions in a clear historical and social perspective. Diversity implies difference rationally conceived, logically planned, properly financed, available as required for varieties of students with different needs – a decent division of function and labour, a sensible specialization of resources. It also implies hierarchy, status, responses to different needs in terms not of knowledge and skill, but of socially governed controls on entry. C. B. Cox and Rhodes Boyson, as editors of *Black Paper 1975*, argued for diversity:

> In higher education there must be no national plan. We need a plurality of institutions offering a wide variety of choice to students of different abilities and aims. Institutions that fail, that cannot attract students, or cannot maintain standards of open debate, should be closed. Transfer from one kind of institution to another, from college of education to university, for example, should be possible for good students.[6]

Whereas the Robbins Report had conceived of a plan within which the colleges of education, for example, were to come closer to the universities, entering into partnership, with differences between them being reduced, the *Black Paper* argued explicitly for hierarchy. It is important to disentangle some of the elements of diversity amongst and within institutions, and again the American and historical perspectives help to make this possible. The necessary starting point is the traditional function of the university.

With the dust of campus battle still in the American air, Horowitz and Friedland dedicated their 1970 analysis of its causes 'To Thorstein Veblen – a half century later'.[7] The dedication seems at first sight eccentric, since Veblen's *The Higher Learning in America* (first published in 1918) is not mentioned in their discussion and the precise problems considered by Veblen do not become apparent in their analysis of the political roots of the 1960s student rebellion. Neverthe-less, the dedication is an acknowledgement from one crisis of higher education to the foremost twentieth-century spokesman of another. Veblen's book, published in 1918, reformulated some underlying nineteenth-century tensions, confronted the industrial and commer-cial pressures on American universities, dissected the roles of scholar-ship, teaching and learning in the universities, and constituted one of the most important works on universities written this century.

There are lengthy lists of books and articles which refer to the 'higher learning' in its national and international variants. At the height of the 1960s crisis Carl Kaysen, for example, in *The Higher Learning, the Universities and the Public*, worried about the former 'teachers' colleges' – now 'state colleges' and offering masters' degrees – and their relationship to 'the true universities'.[8] There are catalogues and bibliographies of works whose titles contain 'higher education'. What Veblen had in mind in his *Higher Learning in America* was the need to separate the higher learning, which was the university's concern, from the teaching of undergraduates, which he believed to be something quite distinct, that should be conducted elsewhere. (That Veblen embedded this argument in an onslaught on business control over the universities makes the whole, more than half a century later, puzzling at first to the British, and probably also to the American, reader.) Robert Hutchins, a central figure in the history of debates about general education, conducted the argument in his 1930s *The Higher Learning in America* around the need to combat vocational-ism, to design an undergraduate curriculum which provided a general base and a commitment to traditional intellectual values. Paul Wood-ring, amidst the turbulence of the late 1960s, levelled his *The Higher Learning in America* against professional specialization in the Ameri-can university and, upturning Veblen, towards greater attention to the teaching of the undergraduate – the 'forgotten man'.[9]

The American literature of the higher learning focused increasingly in the 1960s and 1970s on arguments about the plurality of functions and of institutions, conflicts between teaching and research, between the college (undergraduate in the United States) and the university (in the United States with its graduate, professional and research compo-nents), and between different qualities of institutions – based to various extents on their private and public identities, location, scale, reputation and participation in funded research projects. The British literature is less complex, less fraught with the politics of fund-raising, of Government research support, or even the campus conflicts which produced some of the best and most rapidly forgotten educational literature of the 1960s. When George F. Kneller in 1955 looked at *Higher Learning in Britain* (without obeisance or reference to Veblen) he produced a bland, descriptive document no more memorable than most such literature about British higher education before the Robbins Report and subsequent controversies in the 1960s. Levels and styles of organization in Britain have been debated across the same period in the established context of state and public funding. Accommodations with the Church have been sought (in terms of teacher education) in the framework of a long-established, now almost non-controversial, duality of Church and State in certain aspects of English and Welsh education. Organizational dramas in the university and college sectors have been to do with numbers (for example, expansion and new institutions in the 1960s) and have been mainly in a lower key than in the United States, which developed its higher education in the post-war period on a wider base and a more open philosophy.[10] Or the dramas have had to do with numbers combined with manpower projections and central decision-making (as in the case of the contraction of teacher education in the 1970s) in forms unfamiliar to the United States, which has not had the federal capacity to perform the kind of surgery carried out by British national government and its bureaucracy, particularly after 1973.

In Britain, issues relating to 'graduate schools' and their competition – and triumph over – undergraduate teaching have not rested on the same wide base of higher professional and research training as in the United States since the Second World War, and have tended to assume different forms. The questions in the United States have centred around the effect of major research programmes, the appointment of research professors, the rapid expansion, nature and quality of PhD training, the commitment of university funds to expanding graduate programmes, and the impact of all of this on undergraduate teaching. In Britain the debate – not without echoes of these – has focused more on the conflict between the university teacher's personal research and teaching commitments in general. In both countries the pressures to become involved in administration have been similar. Expansion and new structures have required more complex decision-making; conflict has resulted in more broadly based committee involvement; increased university-based research projects from the 1960s led to more administrative and entrepreneurial concerns.[11] In different ways and for different reasons, as Clark Kerr pointed out vividly in the case of the American 'multiversity' of the 1960s, the university teacher has been pushed, led, tempted, inveigled, away from commitment to the teaching of undergraduates. Reputations and promotions were, in the conditions of the 1960s and early 1970s in particular, earned primarily in research, publication and national professional involvements. Ironically, as Kerr pointed out, 'a superior faculty results in an inferior concern for undergraduate teaching'.[12] The long agony of discussion in the United States in the 1960s and 1970s over federal funding of university research was most acute and guilt-laden in relation precisely to this impact on undergraduate teaching.[13]

In the American context all of these issues have raised important and difficult questions about differences between the university and the college, as well as about differences of quality and prestige within the two categories. Discussions about the nature and purpose of universities, about the validity of radical criticisms of the university from the mid-1960s, about the relationship between institutions of various kinds and the 'higher learning', have continued, in protean shapes, Veblen's attempt to define the right profile for a university in twentieth-century terms. Changing social pressures and changing institutional forms have continued to raise elusive – often explosive – questions about the content of higher education, and about the priorities of the institutions concerned. The pressures on British higher educucation have been mediated differently, and the debate about the shape of the 'higher learning' has been more indirect. The difference between university and college (and for this purpose polytechnic and other new higher education institutions of the 1970s) relates historically in Britain entirely to the power of the one and not of the other to award their own degrees. Within different styles of public funding the distinctions between university and college have included status considerations quite different from those of the United States (where a private college may have considerably higher social status than a public university). There are in Britain colleges where students study for masters' degrees (as in many American state colleges) and, especially in the polytechnics, for doctorates (unlike the American state colleges). There has not been the same unending discussion in Britain about what a university *is*. In British universities *and* colleges there may be or may develop in the future conflicts between the demands, on the one hand, of research, higher teaching and higher learning, and, on the other hand, of lower teaching and lower learning.

The problems, whatever their form, are rooted in a constantly recurring dilemma about the 'esoteric knowledge' which, in Veblen's words, is held in all societies 'in the keeping of a select body of adepts or specialists', in our times by university scholars.[14] The dilemma is not so much regarding the nature of the knowledge of which the university has been the custodian, but what the university should do with it. Veblen's view was that the university was there to guard it, to extend it, and to attract apprentices into the custodial role. Not to *teach* it. That was the job of the college, of someone else. The transmission of knowledge, the lower learning, was a distraction from the central custodial tasks of the university. This dichotomy has been at the heart of twentieth-century debate about the university. Veblen was not lured into what he considered the 'mechanistic' and 'statistically dispassionate' nature of modern learning – which he contemptuously dismissed as a 'highly sterilised, germ-proof system of knowledge, kept in a cool, dry place'. Scholarly enquiry, however, was primary, and university teaching was permissible only if it led to such enquiry, to the further pursuit of knowledge. The university was a 'seminary of the higher learning'.[15]

Veblen's argument is neither eccentric nor romantic when seen against the background of the relentless 'mechanization' of American university learning in the late nineteenth century – its land-grant relationship with commerce, and its growing colonization by the professions. If his vision now looks less than worldly, his world has to be seen as less than settled, and the virtues of the 'capitalist' university less stable than its vices. Without drawing Veblen's deductions, others have looked with degrees of alarm at forces undermining the university's guardianship of esoteric knowledge. The dilemma has been expressed most sharply in the context of the 'politicization' of the university, the radical attack on the scholarly endeavour. But fears have also been expressed about other forms of 'corruption'. Robert Nisbet discusses 'the aura of the sacred that emanated from knowledge', the age-old proposition that 'knowledge of the sacred is sacred' – transformed into the proposition that 'knowledge, that is genuine knowledge, knowledge of a learned discipline, is itself sacred'. Nisbet's analysis took him in the opposite direction from Veblen. It was 'research' that was corrupting the essential dogma of the university, the dogma 'that declares knowledge sacred in and for itself'.[16] Social and physical scientists were rapaciously seizing research monies, becoming a 'new capitalism'. The contours of 'research' itself had changed:

> I firmly believe direct grants from government and foundation to individual members of university faculties, or to small company-like groups of faculty members, for the purposes of creating institutes, centers, bureaus, and other essentially capitalistic enterprises within the academic community to be the single most powerful agent of change that we find in the university's long history. For the first time in Western history, professors and scholars were thrust into the unwonted position of entrepreneurs.[17]

For Nisbet the solution was to get this kind of research out of the campus, and to 'elevate the function of teaching' which had been degraded by this 'profit-, or grant-, or institute-based research'.[18]

Clark Kerr pointed out, in a sentiment that was re-echoed many times across the academic battlegrounds of the late 1960s and 1970s, how aided (especially federally aided) research had led to a lowering of interest in and the 'general deterioration of undergraduate teaching', because of the increased commitment to research and the higher teaching.[19] Ben-David underlines that this has in fact been the case in the United States throughout this century: the existence of outstanding scholars on university campuses may have 'created an atmosphere of intellectual stimulation. But this did not alter the fact that the actual state of the undergraduate curriculum had been determined much more by the needs of the disciplinary teaching of the graduate school than by the purposes of educating the terminal undergraduate.' A vast apparatus of administration and expenditure had produced a myth that universities took the education of undergraduates seriously, but their main interest had always been research and graduate teaching.[20] Here the esoteric knowledge, the sacred, was most visible and most pure. Even an increasing interpretation of knowledge as a productive force did not – especially in Britain – disturb the underlying sense that the university's central concern was with, if not esoteric or sacred knowledge, at least with what Newman called 'universal' knowledge. For Newman the preservation of basic liberal values meant (and the italics were his) *'teaching* universal *knowledge* . . . the diffusion and extension of knowledge rather than the advancement. If its object were scientific and philosophical discovery, I do not see why a University should have students . . . .' Law and medicine and other 'particular studies, or arts, or vocations' were for Newman admissible, and indeed desirable, in the university, but only as branches of a whole, of the university's commitment to a liberal education.[21]

Since Newman, and more explicitly since Veblen, the universities' perceptions of their functions have been increasingly conditioned by the strong and often contradictory pressures on them to respond to social needs. These needs have been expressed in terms of manpower, social service, social responsibility, social justice, national defence, economic and social change, reaction and revolution. In Britain voices proclaiming the primacy of truth, scholarship, unattached research, autonomy, neutrality, objectivity, have been at times shrill and at others muted. British and American universities have had to respond to economic crisis, war, Senator Joseph McCarthy, campus rebellion, rocketing numbers, inflation and affirmative action. Amidst conflict, uncertainty, democratization and reform, the commitment to the guardianship of esoteric knowledge has in some cases sought, and others resisted, new forms. Veblen's emphasis on the 'quest for knowledge', the university as a place of higher learning, has been constantly reinterpreted, in a struggle to retain old and find new identities in a world where stable definitions have become more and more impossible.

At the heart of the university enterprise, however, the questions that Veblen raised more or less explicitly have continued to demand answers. If the university stands guardian over esoteric knowledge, to whom is its guardianship answerable? How does the concept of accountability encroach upon its search for definitions? Does guardianship imply the advancement of knowledge, or the teaching of knowledge, or both? To what extent does the university need to equip successive generations of students for the likely requirements of the world outside? Is the university alone in its guardianship? The demand for knowledge, for education, for training, has spiralled internationally since *The Higher Learning in America*. The concept of higher education has greatly diversified. How do different institutions share out roles, and – as in the case of the *Black Paper* quotation above – what hierarchies do they imply? Is the university still the guardian of the sacred, while others look after the profane? Veblen, defending the university's guardianship against its pollution by the commercial and the professional, saw a total institutional divorce:

The lower schools (including the professional schools) are, in the ideal scheme, designed to fit the incoming generation for civil life; they are therefore occupied with instilling such knowledge and habits as will make their pupils fit citizens of the world in whatever position in the fabric of workday life they may fall. The university on the other hand is specialized to fit men for a life of science and scholarship.[22]

No part of Veblen's thesis was absent from the higher education wars of the 1960s and 1970s.

The expansion of higher education has forced these issues of function further and further centre-stage. At the beginning of this century, for example, research in the United States was, said C. F. Thwing, urgent. The peril of a democracy, however, was that it would 'search for truth not for truth's own sake, but for the sake of what truth will do or bring. It makes investigation into electricity to get light, or heat, or power, not to discover the laws, nature, and relations of electricity.' Truth was primary, and 'the search for truth should therefore be conducted under the most stable and permanent of all human institutions – the university'.[23] Cornell, the land-grant colleges, and the Americanization of the Ph D and research from the 1870s, were one set of responses to pressures for light, heat and power, economic growth and modernization. The English university college, technical college and polytechnic were another set of responses to similar pressures in the last quarter of the nineteenth century. Higher education in the two countries, from different bases and in different political and economic climates, responded slowly in the nineteenth century – more rapidly in its closing decades – to the changing contours of the State, to industrial and agricultural needs, to democracy or the rhetoric of democracy, to new knowledge priorities and the appeals of and for science. In the twentieth century higher education has had to adapt to new stridencies in the voice of the State and of national concerns, mounting pressures from international competition and conflict, new problems of scale and function, and – especially in the United States – not only increased numbers but also a rapidly changing profile of student intakes, as underprivileged sections of the population have gained entrance. In that situation, and in the less dramatically changing version of it in Britain, institutions and systems have had to face basic questions about their curricula, purpose and structures, about their preoccupation with truth, about the relationship between knowledge and heat and light.

Higher education has never, of course, been divorced from those sections of the community on whose behalf it has mainly exercised guardianship. Universities have been for and against kings, have been instruments of civil and ecclesiastical power, as well as creations of class and nonconformity. The establishment of University College, London, in 1828 cannot be separated from the ambitions of a disenfranchized middle class and the Anglican exclusiveness of Oxford and Cambridge. The first two aims propounded in 1818 for the future University of Virginia were:

- to form the statesmen, legislators & judges, on whom public prosperity & individual happiness are so much to depend:
- to expound the principles and structure of government, the laws which regulate the intercourse of nations, those formed municipally for our own government, and a sound spirit of legislation. . . .[24]

Such aims cannot be separated from the political, economic and ideological emphases of post-Revolutionary America: 'American nationalism, which was both a cause and a product of the Revolution, also influenced higher education. The Republic would justify itself in culture as well as in politics.'[25] American and British higher education were both reshaped from the 1870s in the consciousness of international rivalries and domestic needs. An address on American higher education by the president of Cornell University in 1874 began with the words: 'The development of advanced instruction in our country thus far is a matter of which no patriot has much reason to be proud.'[26] Patriotism, the economy, political and social needs, have never been far distant from discussions of the nature and purposes of higher education. Esoteric knowledge has rarely consisted of truth uncontaminated by heat and light, or by considerations of prosperity and legislation.

The forms of social change have, in the twentieth century particularly, dictated emphases in the discussion of the functions of higher education, functions which have become increasingly difficult to discuss in terms of esoteric or universal knowledge, or electricity. Martin Trow has summarized the functions as 'elite' and 'popular'. His argument is that 'at the heart of the traditional university is its commitment to the transmission of high culture' (as defended by Newman and Hutchins). Closely related was 'the shaping of mind and character: the cultivation of aesthetic sensibilities, broader human sympathies, and a capacity for critical and independent judgement.' A second elite function has been 'the creation of new knowledge through "pure" scholarship'. A third, especially important in Europe, has been 'the selection, formation, and certification of a social elite'. The two main popular functions that have emerged for twentieth-century higher education have been 'the provision of mass higher education to nearly everybody who applies for it', and 'the provision of useful knowledge and service to nearly every group and institution that wants it'.[27]

Balancing such functions has been the pivotal problem of American higher education this century, and increasingly so for Britain as it has attempted to expand its higher education base (and in whose case the two 'popular' functions would really need to be more cautiously expressed). Post-war expansion, minimal though it was, produced worries amongst vice-chancellors and principals of British universities about academic standards which, 'once lowered are not retrievable'; the Barlow Committee of 1946 and the University Grants Committee in 1948 were anxious to underline the supreme importance of standards in any discussion of expansion.[28] The Robbins Committee in 1963 summarized the problem of balance between expansion and standards – another version of popular and elite considerations:

> We must demand of a system that it produces as much high excellence as possible. It must therefore be so devised that it safeguards standards. We began our discussion of principles by emphasising the claims of numbers. It is only fitting, therefore, that we should close it by emphasising the claims of achievement and quality. The two ends are not incompatible.[29]

As the report and subsequent events made clear, and as American experience has in different ways confirmed, the reconciliation of the two ends is easier amongst diverse institutions than within a single institution. The tension between the two 'ends' explains the importance of the question of diversity in seeing the relationship between the emergence of higher education (or more properly 'higher educations') as a significant force in discussions of the social condition.

The expansion of higher education, the new social groups for which the expansion was in part intended (but which, in the British case, it largely failed to recruit), the curricular pressures exerted by technological and scientific demands, the development of research, and the attempt to redefine the purposes of adapted institutions, produced tensions of many kinds. Research, as we have underlined, tended to take priority over teaching in the universities. Some American colleges, in a period of growth in graduate education from the 1950s, geared themselves to preparing for graduate schools and became 'university colleges', which, in the new American usage, referred to colleges 'whose primary purpose is to prepare students for graduate work of some kind – primarily in the arts and sciences but also in professional subjects ranging from law and medicine to business and social work'.[30] American commentators began to criticize a higher education structure which did little for the average student: 'the few who intend lifetimes of study, and therefore need academic training least, are almost the sole beneficiaries of formal higher education.'[31] American and British universities shared a dilemma (reflected in the Robbins Report, for example), about how 'specialized' or 'general', how 'liberal' or 'vocational', an undergraduate education should be. In the United States the concern often related to the broad pattern of electives that had developed in many American universities since the 1870s, and the need being formulated in some places after the Second World War to find patterns of study that could genuinely be called a liberal or general education. In Britain, some of the new universities of the 1960s experimented with ways of breaking down the packaged and sequential courses of the traditional universities, and the University Grants Committee acknowledged both that there was need for such experimentation and that the new institutions 'might well be more favourably situated for such experimentation than the established universities'.[32]

The purposes of higher education and of its constituent parts were at least implied in attempts to achieve suitable balances, and the necessary definitions and structures. It was difficult to establish what was a suitable balance between research and training, graduate and undergraduate numbers and programmes, 'professional' and 'vocational' content and 'liberal' content and methods, the demands of the higher learning and of social justice, tradition and experiment, 'universal knowledge' and new ideas, old and new curricula. The dependence of social and economic progress and stability on new knowledge, research – especially scientific research – thrust higher education rapidly from the 1950s into a more and more central position in national planning strategies. The tensions within existing institutions, and between them and new ones being created, became more acute as the pressures mounted and responses became more public, more scrutinized, more subject to wide controversy. Daniel Bell and others pointed in the 1970s to the increasing centrality of knowledge in economic and social development, and it is not necessary to accept all the implications of Bell's analysis of 'post-industrial society' in order to see in the 1970s an increasingly knowledge-based, higher-education-based phase of development.[33] For reasons to do with the progress of scientific knowledge, comments Alain Touraine, the class relations and conflicts of an earlier phase of development have been transferred to the university, which, 'because it is a center of production and diffusion of scientific knowledge, is increasingly becoming the main locus of the social conflicts of our times'.[34]

A basic question for Britain, the United States and other countries, remains how the various levels of conflict in higher education are resolved. The campus rebellions and tensions of the late 1960s and early 1970s illustrated the extent to which these conflicts could be carried within institutions, the features of the various attempts at balance that could be singled out for attack, and vigorous responses or rapid adaptations that might need to be made in order to survive. Within higher education in general, however, attempts to solve the problems of balance, or at least to relieve the pressures entailed, resulted in the widespread creation of new institutions, or the upgrading of existing ones from another, lower sector. Functions were both diversified and redistributed.

New universities were created in Britain in the nineteenth century in order to bypass and break the monopoly of Oxford and Cambridge, and they looked to new geographical and social groups as their constituencies. A response to an economic threat to Britain's pioneer industrial and commercial role in the 1890s was the creation of the London polytechnics. Pressures for expanded higher education provision in the 1960s produced the colleges of advanced technology. The way diversification of function is approached will continue, in Britain and the United States, to be as important as questions of access to higher education in general. Amidst the troubles of the 1960s Martin Trow reaffirmed his admiration of American higher education, which had 'managed both to fulfil its commitments to liberal education and the advancement of knowledge, and also to serve a nation and a people in all the ways it has'. The low participation rate in higher education in Britain makes it possible from a distance to agree with such a verdict on American higher education. What Trow went on to add, however, was that 'the problem now, as it has been for a hundred years, is whether those functions can be performed in the same institutions'[35] (and in the late 1970s Trow was to argue strongly that they could not). The question is whether the university can and should confront the problems of both the 'higher' and the 'lower' learning. The question was to become particularly acute in Britain in the 1970s as the pattern of higher education became increasingly diverse and the nature of the competition between the universities and other elements in the pattern became increasingly debated. By the time the Robbins Committee came to examine and to reject the 'junior college' solution for extending higher education in Britain, the junior or community college was basic to the American higher education experience. It was to continue to transmit important signals to anyone attempting system-building in higher education.

The Robbins Report said,

> It would be a misnomer to speak of a system of higher education in this country, if by system is meant a consciously co-ordinated organisation. The various institutions – the universities, the technical, commercial and art colleges, the colleges for the education and training of teachers – have grown up separately. Moreover, for the greater part of their history, the universities, which were more or less independent of the state, dominated the landscape.[36]

The landscape has become both more and less complex. There are new figures in it – polytechnics, colleges and institutes of higher education. There are, however, new elements of system – greater government control over university affairs, possible further national planning for the 'maintained' sector, patterns of amalgamation and closure in teacher education as part of a national strategy in the 1970s. The Percy Committee on higher technological education proposed in 1944 that the status of the colleges of technology 'must be similar to that of the universities'.[37] British technological institutions have, however, struggled for 'parity of esteem' with the universities, just as the secondary modern schools struggled for such parity with the secondary grammar schools. Both failed. The colleges of advanced technology *became* universities or parts of universities. The polytechnics and some of the new colleges and institutes of higher education have edged towards the status of universities – though the binary line in a sense served to strengthen the position of the universities in the landscape by enabling disturbing levels of applied and technological work to be channelled elsewhere. It has been argued, in fact, that the purpose of the binary system was to achieve precisely that.[38] Ashby expressed the view in 1973 that

> whether higher education is organised in a binary or unitary system is merely a matter of logistics; the boundaries of our binary system are dissolving before our eyes; and a good thing too. Universities have always mixed vocational and non-vocational studies, and polytechnics are already doing the same.[39]

What was happening in the 1970s was in reality less dramatic, however. If the boundaries were becoming a little blurred, they were not dissolving. It was indeed a matter of logistics, but not 'merely' so. The bases on which the parallel sets of institutions rested were different, and were being basically preserved by the binary separation. The existence of areas of overlap did not basically disturb university ideology. Only competition did that, especially when expansion was halted, when students were in short supply, and when prospects for enrolment for the mid-1980s and beyond looked bleak. In status terms, the universities still occupied dominant positions in an altered landscape.

Amidst the diversities of the American 'system' of higher education the two-year college vividly illustrates its tensions and dilemmas. The nineteenth-century 'junior college', in becoming – in the past two decades – the rapidly expanding 'community college', has acquired objectives and structures which do not always easily pull in the same direction. One of the early historians of the junior college discovered 'groups' of purposes ascribed to it by different people, affecting the way the colleges themselves operated, how they reflected back on to the school system, and how they affected the universities. They capped the secondary education system; they prepared some for higher education; they gave terminal vocational education to others. They offered 'two years of work acceptable to colleges and universities', provided opportunities to some for 'rounding out their general education', prepared for occupations, and continued 'home influences during immaturity'. Their teaching methods for this important age group emphasized 'the social control of the individual in small groups', as well as 'better opportunities for training in leadership'. One outstanding virtue, as seen by some later nineteenth-century university presidents, was the colleges' possible role in keeping adolescents away from the university for a longer period, enabling 'real' university work to begin with the third year of a four-year undergraduate education.[40]

The two-year college was seen increasingly, however, as a style and level of education that matched American 'democratizing' needs. Medsker summarized the position in 1960:

> The two-year college was designed to play a special and strategic role in American higher education. This it does in a variety of ways: It is perhaps the most effective democratizing agent in higher education. It decentralizes post-high school opportunities by placing them within reach of a large number of students. It makes higher education available at a lower cost to society. It offers a wide range of educational programs not found in other colleges.

The junior college was also a 'distributing agency', offering terminal formal education, as well as a 'means of identifying students capable of more advanced training'. It extended common schooling and took over its roles in providing for many students 'a means of better civic and vocational education' or simply a 'maturing experience'. In combining all of these it was an equalizer of post-high school opportunities, with great social, economic and geographical advantages – especially as the demand for higher education increased after the Second World War.[41] The community college was widely envisaged as a panacea. It had something for everyone:

> It offers the university a safety valve, the employer a trained worker, the graduate-holder a job. It offers a place for the taxpayer's children, and second, third, infinite chances to people who, for whatever reason, want to go back to school. For the community at large it promises academic and cultural upgrading. Even the police like it because young people, off the streets and under institutional custody, are less likely to get into trouble. Small wonder that the community college has become everybody's darling.[42]

In the 1970s the differences between the two-year college and the university and four-year college in California (which has one of America's widest community college networks) were being described as follows, in terms which had echoes in the claims of other states:

> The community colleges offer the least expensive access to higher

education available in the state to the general public. . . . The community colleges uniquely offer both academic and occupational programs on the same campus (thus, the 'comprehensive college'). . . . The community colleges are required by law to admit any high school graduate and may enrol any student who has reached the age of 18. . . . The community colleges have proven uniquely suited to meeting the educational needs of minority-group students. . . . Community colleges are primarily teaching institutions; that is their reason for existence.[43]

It is the very democratic claims, the range of purposes of the colleges, that constitute the problem.

The 'open door' policy creates the need to sort, counsel, track, students. There are relative prestiges within the colleges between terminal and non-terminal ('transfer') programmes. Medsker pointed out in 1960 how difficult it was for the colleges to combine the two roles: data from 1952 had shown that only about a third of entering students later transferred to four-year colleges, 'yet the same group of institutions reported that ordinarily at least two-thirds of the entering students expect to transfer'. Emphasizing the same point in 1972 he commented that 'the more socially prestigious programme leading to transfer dominates the community college scene for too many students'. The colleges suffered most from 'the faculty's lack of agreement on its purposes'.[44] Another commentator described the 'open door' policy of the colleges in 1973 as 'euphemistic', pointing to a 'gross distortion between written and applied policy':

> When a 'two-year' institution admits anyone and everyone . . . it is often done with a sincere attitude of extending democracy. . . . At this point, however, many institutions discover that they are unprepared or unable to provide adequate programs for 'students' who are unconventional by all traditional criteria. Many community colleges continue to operate as unofficial extensions of the university. . . . The 'cooling-out' function described by Clark is still operating.[45]

The academic 'transfer' courses have the prestige, as have the faculty who operate these 'unofficial extensions of the university'. On this basis some of the colleges have been transformed into four-year colleges. The uneasy alliance of terminal–vocational education and university–preparatory education produces ideological tensions and divisive *internal* structures which parallel those *between* institutions.[46] The Californian claim that the colleges are primarily *teaching* institutions, for example, may have a great deal of substance, but their commitment to teaching and to students in general may not be as strong as some of the claims have suggested. A significant proportion of faculty members have been shown to be at odds with the 'institutional goals' of the colleges, raising what Medsker calls 'at least a question about the fabled institutional commitment of community college staffs'.[47]

If, in addition, the community colleges are 'uniquely suited to meeting the educational needs of minority-group students', they reduce the pressures on four-year colleges and universities to face up to such needs. If the reason for existence of the community colleges is that they are primarily teaching institutions, the priorities of other institutions are redefined accordingly. This point is central in any argument about diversification within a system of higher education: the outcome of diversification is in some way a purification of roles. The presence of the community colleges 'has enabled the four-year institutions not only to become more selective in the students they admit, but to restrict the variety of programmes they offer'. An open admission principle is applied differently in different kinds of institution, and 'many observers suspect that the principle will be adopted as far as systems of higher education go, but that it will never become universally applied to all individual institutions'. The universities, having flirted with the principle, can – especially in a period of economic and other constraints – abandon it to the colleges, and students and costs can be 'rationalized'. Arguments for the expansion of the community college system have often 'been based more on the need to relieve the four-year institutions or to reduce overall costs than on the means by which community colleges can improve undergraduate education or render educational services not previously available'.[48] This is a long way from the more idealistic claims for the community college, expressed in terms of quite different problems to be solved. Describing the variety of often incompatible functions of the colleges, against such a background, Cohen and Bramer conclude that 'we have a penchant for believing that once a problem has been defined and an institution created to deal with it, we no longer need to think about it'. After all, they comment – with international resonances – 'the university has never done an adequate job of educating the student of marginal academic ability'.[49]

The importance lies in the interaction of definitions: the range of community college functions redefines the secondary school and the university, encouraging them to purify themselves in ways similar to other nineteenth- and twentieth-century self-purifications.

The American community college, comments Palinchak, 'is in the delicate position of dealing with various aspects of both secondary and higher education while demanding recognition as a unique institution in American higher education'.[50] The community college is not a replica of the English technical college or college of higher education or polytechnic, and it does not stand in the same relation to other institutions of higher education (the technical college may provide *entry* to the university, but not *transfer*). There are, however, similar 'delicate positions', similar problems of purification, of attention to teaching, of the education of students of 'marginal educational ability', facing institutions on both sides of the Atlantic. The temptation in Britain and the United States is to use institutional diversification to respond to social pressure and to resolve confusions. If it is confusing to have undergraduates and graduates (or liberal and vocational programmes, or undergraduate and pre-degree courses) on the same campus, so – many people respond – remove one or the other! Wolff wants to remove all 'professional' courses from American university campuses, because the problems posed by the combination of under-graduate and graduate programmes is 'a major source of educational confusion'.[51] Kaysen wants to solve problems of specialization and expansion by separating functions: 'the college, not the university, is the appropriate institution for performing the functions of socialization and certification for the representative student.'[52] The process of division of labour has been continuous since the late nineteenth century, accompanied by upward movement of institutions within prevailing hierarchies. For all its virtues, the community college also represents a move towards what Veblen advocated – the university losing 'the drag of the collegiate division and the vocational schools'.[53]

The difficulties of reconciling the different purposes and functions of higher education in general were highlighted by, and contributed to, the crises of the quarter-century following the Second World War. These were not merely institutional crises, they were crises of social purpose and values, basic crises of confidence and identity. They have to be seen in the same context of social change and conflict, the same attempts at adaptation and reorganization, the same difficulties of understanding and responding to the social condition, that we have discussed in terms of, for example, secondary education from the 1950s. As early as 1955 Kneller was finding that in Britain

> within the last generation a series of seismic shocks from the outside world has rocked the very foundations of university thought. Learned men have found themselves perplexed and bewildered by the plague of social and ideational perturbations which has invaded the sanctity of their academic life.[54]

The range of responses to the invasion was not unlike others we have examined. The shocks were to become in the 1960s major confrontations, basic challenges to the university and the social order. Within the universities, as values, curricula and forms were called increasingly into question, the compatibility of the different functions we have discussed in terms of American institutions came to be viewed internationally with less and less certainty.

Scale itself disturbed settled assumptions, thrusting administrative and financial concerns more centrally into university and college consciousness. Jacques Barzun in the late 1960s described the impact of increased scale as follows:

> No adequate idea of the incessantly buzzing and booming academic grove, the harsh orchestration resulting from the disparate purposes carried on there, can be derived from generalities. . . . Nothing short of enumeration will suggest the size of the structure or the complexity of the effort. And even then, the very act of setting items down on paper introduces an order which falsifies the inevitable confusion.[55]

It is impossible and unnecessary here to consider the political and social roots of the campus explosions which began at Berkeley in 1964, swept through many campuses in the United States and throughout the world in the late 1960s, and generally ran out their course by or during the early 1970s. Their importance here is the fact that they spotlighted the confusion of functions and purpose, previously unquestioned assumptions about structures and processes in universities and colleges. The radical student movements proclaimed one thing above all – that the authorities of university and college knew what the institutions stood for, and what they stood for was wrong. The purposes of the institutions, claimed the new radicalism, were corrupt and servile to the warmongering, exploitative State and its agents. Administrators and teachers in higher education knew the fact, and accepted or acquiesced, or else they were dupes, deceived and manipulated. However representative or not the radicals may have been, they carried into debate about higher education questions about the neutrality of scholarship, about the poverty of the curriculum, about the commitment and effectiveness of teachers, about relationships, about teaching as 'a transaction rather than a transmission of fact or truth from older to younger'.[56]

The sustained confrontation focused attention on what Muller called the 'mobilization' and Kerr the 'enlistment' of universities during the Second World War and on through the Cold War.[57] The teaching/research dichotomy assumed a new complexion. The authority of the institution, its administrators, its teachers, its course definitions, its styles of operation, the purposes of its research, were brought into question. At one time or another, to one extent or another, in one way or another, some changes resulted. More open structures were in most of these cases the main result. Curricula were adapted to meet student demands and interests – especially those of black and women students. Assessment procedures were modified. Greater importance was attached to teaching.

These were not to be final seismic shocks. In the less flamboyant times of the mid-1970s higher education came under threat. Student enrolments began to fall. In changed economic conditions graduate unemployment began to deter would-be applicants, and university degrees were described by the International Labour Office as 'fast becoming tickets to nowhere'. Projections of nearly a million surplus university graduates in the United States over the 1974–85 period were being made in 1978, with similar projections for European countries.[58] Throughout all these 'perturbations' higher education came under sterner public scrutiny, under the stronger financial and political pressures of accountability movements. Neither the British nor the American system was 'stable'. Their purposes, functions, forms of control, were constantly having to respond to outside questions and demands. Established institutions nervously began to review their organizational and teaching processes.

Teaching had in previous decades been given low priority in the universities, with only an occasional eccentric senior professor actually preferring to teach undergraduates – very occasionally even first-year students. Much was written in the 1960s and 1970s about the neglect of teaching, about poor teaching methods, about the possibility of improving them. Promotion in the university has been overwhelmingly linked with research and publications – in spite of pressures for teaching and other responsibilities to be given equal consideration. It was foolish, said Flexner in 1908, to select teachers of undergraduates 'according to graduate school standards'.[59] University and college teachers shared with prostitutes, said Jacques Barzun, the distinction of being the only professions 'for which no training is given or required'.[60] The Hale Committee on university teaching methods came to the conclusion in 1964 that little experiment had been carried out on university teaching methods in Britain because 'there is little to tempt a university teacher to give to a study of teaching methods time which inclination and self-interest would lead him to give to research in his own subject'.[61] Not until technology, costs, discontent and riot put teaching methods under scrutiny in the 1960s did the act of teaching itself begin to receive more serious attention, and the balance of university priorities begin to be reassessed against a background of changing constituencies and expectations.

Even where teaching was considered to be important, there were fundamental weaknesses – including routine lectures to large classes, and the dominance of examinations. By the mid-1960s concern about the quality of undergraduate teaching was being sharply voiced. In the same year as the Hale Committee reported in Britain a Committee on Undergraduate Teaching was set up in the United States. It affirmed that 'an impatient expectation of good teaching has spread widely in the present student generation', and that the climate was conducive to the improvement of college and university teaching.[62] With the loss of intimacy of the smaller institution a great deal had been lost, and – in terms of teaching methods and relationships – nothing gained. The Committee quoted an Amherst report which indicated that it was no longer true that even 'where faculty live within easy reach of the campus, close attachments are fostered, students are encouraged to drop in at their teachers' homes for tea or dinner, and faculty members often spend convivial evenings in fraternity houses'.[63] The large urban campus university had developed different priorities and relationships – or lack of them. Another commentator, in the same year, explained the loss of 'conviviality' in terms not just of scale: graduate studies had benefited from the growth of research at the expense of undergraduate contact with faculty members: '. . . the intimacy of contact between faculty and students has disappeared in this era of mass higher education, to be replaced by intimacy centered around research on the graduate levels.'[64]

The 1960s generation, and its expectations, however, were new. In the United States as in Europe students detected traditions laid bare and made vulnerable in the new large-scale enterprise. University and college teaching, it was often felt, perpetuated on the larger scale only what was worst in the traditions. It was an extension of the world described by Flexner before the First World War, when American colleges dictated the shape of eight years of education – half in high school, half in college itself: 'during the first four the college has directed, during the last four completely controlled, the plastic boy.' The college was 'a place for the final training of boys'.[65] Army veterans and large sections of 1960s teenagers did not accept that they were plastic, or in any way similar to the model familiar to Flexner's and subsequent generations.

In the late 1960s and 1970s, nevertheless, there is no indication that the majority of students were dissatisfied with the curricula and the teaching that they were offered. At the height of the American campus disturbances, the Carnegie Commission found that 'some generalized dissatisfaction – even great dissatisfaction – with academic life exists among a minority of students and faculty members, but it is not a substantial cause of political disruption on campus'.[66] This became even more true with the emergence in the mid-1970s of a new generation of students, far more interested than their predecessors 'in getting high marks, a goal to which they are ready to sacrifice all other activities'.[67] But even if they had been only a minority – and in Britain they certainly were – the active radical students had left their mark. Changed economic situations and diminished opportunities for staff promotion and employment were further inducements to a greater concern about teaching. Some American universities made explicit the role of teaching in applications for tenure and promotion – and in some cases student evaluation of teacher performance, a direct legacy of the 1960s, began to be built into the process. Even as promotion prospects began to shrink in Britain in the mid-1970s, greater attention was being paid by the universities to induction, the possibilities of some form of training and to teaching as part of the research–administration–teaching nexus.

The need was for innovation. In terms of undergraduate curricula and teaching there was in the United States what the Hale Committee described as a 'national temperament ever friendly to innovations', and what Ashby later called 'a more favourable environment for good teaching to receive recognition (and for poor teaching to be improved and careless teaching to be reproved) than there is in Britain'.[68] The Hale Committee wanted more experimentation in Britain. One of Kerr's main calls in 1963 in the United States was for 'the improvement of undergraduate instruction in the university', and he pointed to a galaxy of sub-problems that would need to be solved – including how to give recognition to teaching skill, how to create a curriculum that 'serves the needs of the student as well as the research interests of the teacher', and how to 'treat the individual student as a unique human being in the mass student body'.[69] The university was, as we have seen, becoming a – if not the – main 'locus of the social conflicts of our times'. Concern about undergraduate instruction, the needs and treatment of the student, were still at the level of demand and rhetoric when campuses erupted in the second half of the 1960s. The extent of the response by the universities and the higher education system as a whole, then and later, is a matter of interpretation and dispute. To complete the American picture it is worth recording the view of the Newman Report in the early 1970s. The system of higher education had, it underlined, expanded, improved, paid attention to pressing needs – including those of minority groups. On the other hand the system had, in growing, become more homogeneous and less flexible, and had failed to solve major problems that had emerged: 'The system, with its massive inertia, resists fundamental change, rarely eliminates outmoded programs, ignores the differing needs of students, seldom questions its educational goals, and almost never creates new and different types of institution.'[70] Under threat, the universities have made the adaptations necessary for survival. In the encouraging atmosphere of expansion they have made sometimes important modifications. If 'massive inertia' is too strong and all-embracing an indictment of the whole system, it is arguably more appropriate when applied to the universities. The *system* has experimented with community colleges in the United States, and with polytechnics and colleges of higher education in Britain, and part of the purpose of these innovations has been to enable the universities to remain as close as possible to their traditions. If the system *has* managed to create new and different types of institution, it may still be true that they represent neither fundamental changes nor a questioning of educational goals.

The greater autonomy of higher education, as compared with other sectors of education, has led to its remaining – certainly in Britain – more aloof from the continuing disputes about the education–society linkages. It has not been immune, but the function (or mystique) of at least some of its members as guardians of esoteric knowledge – as well as its direct relationship to technological, scientific, medical and other areas of professional leadership – has made argument about higher education more sporadic and less contentious. The questions of diversification, balance and priorities that we have discussed indicate important contextual considerations for understanding developments in British higher education in the past two decades.

9 Higher statuses

Higher education is not what it was in 1961 when the Association of University Teachers could divide a discussion of it into two parts – 'The universities' and 'Other institutions of higher learning', and could open its comments on the latter by pointing out that

> it is taken for granted by most university teachers that, however much the numbers of those taking present university courses are to be expanded, there will be a need for some courses which will differ from present university courses by being wider in scope and lower in standards.[1]

Trow's discussion of elite and popular functions is helpful in the British context. The universities have been edged towards and have occasionally spurted towards, revisions of their popular functions, but other sectors of higher education have developed – and in the case of the polytechnics at least initially and in theory in order to respond more sensitively to those needs. The polytechnics offered a version of diversification different from that of the United States, but in being designed as more publicly accountable institutions and in the priorities intended to be allocated to their programmes they represent a move towards serving popular functions. While the polytechnics in some ways responded to the AUT description of courses 'wider in scope', universities themselves in many ways also widened their scope from the 1960s. From the universities' position in the landscape some degree work in the polytechnics and later the colleges of higher education may have been judged to be 'lower in standard', but the judgement has become increasingly difficult to sustain. As the polytechnics developed their higher degree work and extended their research – and as universities continued to adapt in order to compete and to attract students – their pattern of relationships to the higher and lower learning became less sharply distinguishable.

In the uncertain conditions of the mid-1970s higher education planning and policy-making came under mounting attack, and this was especially true in relation to the colleges of education as they were closed, merged with one another or with universities or polytechnics, and were left to diversify and to be treated by many people as wrecks on the shore – and to be renamed colleges or institutes of higher education. The earlier elevation of technical colleges to the higher status of colleges of advanced technology or polytechnics had – in the context of a binary policy – created anxieties in the universities, but the threat was at least visible and explicitly defined. The emergence of a large number of the new colleges and institutes in the second half of the 1970s was less tangible, and was a threat to both existing sectors, given what was becoming known about the probable decline in higher education numbers from the mid-1980s, and the continual and increasing economic pressures on existing institutions. Involved in the anxieties were long-standing questions of the status of teacher education, questions which had been unresolved after the Robbins Report and which were given greater immediacy by the James Report on teacher education and training in 1972. When forecasts of a declining school population became publicly known after the Committee had reported, and when drastic cuts in teacher education began to be made, confused policy and decisions were met with confused public responses.[2] The appearance (creation would be too strong a word) of the new colleges and institutes of higher education – many, but not all, based on colleges of education – with BA, BHum, professional and other courses alongside their established BEd programmes, was met with some hostility in the universities and elsewhere. Conservative MP Keith Hampson, for example, wrote in July 1977 that the new type of institution had not been created by forward planning on the part of the Labour Government 'as part of a coherent package designed to meet a particular need in an integrated post-school educational system, but simply by default'. He summarized his argument angrily as follows:

My criticism of this Government's policy is therefore fundamental. It is scandalous that an entirely new type of higher education system has emerged in this country as a result of piecemeal decisions, often ill-prepared, and taken in conditions of near total secrecy, and which is simply not geared to meeting the country's most pressing requirements.[3]

Some of the charges of piecemeal decision-making and secrecy could be justified, but the argument as a whole did not see the events of the 1970s in the context of any historical understanding.

The creation of new institutions, new types of institution, new sectors, in higher (or post-school, or tertiary) education has invariably been accompanied by the formulation of precise, explicit aims, the defining of constituencies and curricula. They have been deliberate acts of individuals, of groups, of governments. They have been the outcomes of articulate protest or acknowledged needs, sometimes in a sense of rivalry, sometimes in an effort to extend or complement an existing 'system'.

The movement to create a University of London, for example – which in the event produced University College, London, in the 1820s, was largely and self-consciously a middle-class, nonconformist, urban response to the Anglican monopoly of university education in England. It sought to establish, in the words of its founding council, an institution 'where an enlightened education may be obtained at a reasonable charge, and where persons of every religious persuasion may be freely admitted'.[4] King's College, the Anglican response to such a radical departure, was – explains the college – 'designed to promote a similar range of traditional and modern studies', but with 'the duties of Christianity as inculcated by the Church of England' to be included in the curriculum.[5] The new institutions were created with precise clienteles in mind, with clear curricular intentions in opposition to declared criteria of admission by Oxford and Cambridge.

The later provincial universities and university colleges were, like University College, London, established to bypass tests of religious opinion, and were intended primarily to satisfy local and regional social and economic needs. John Owens in Manchester wished his new institution – when he drafted his will in 1845 – to offer 'such branches of learning and science as are now and may be hereafter usually taught in the English Universities'.[6] In the North and Midlands, however, colleges and universities came generally and more overtly to reflect the industrial and social interests they might hope to serve (though even Owens, creating a university college in Manchester, was responding to a set of local and social needs). These local colleges, wrote the Principal of Firth College, Sheffield, in 1856 were the only places offering a 'scientific training in technical subjects suited to the needs of a Captain of Industry'.[7] Joseph Chamberlain explained the purpose of his new University of Birmingham a decade later as being to 'systematise and develop the special training which is required by men in business and those who either as principals or as managers and foremen will be called upon to conduct the great industrial undertakings in the midst of which our work will be done'.[8] Curriculum and purpose were explicit, and the new institutions shared much common ideology and rhetoric.

The same clear and explicit purposes are apparent with other nineteenth-century institutions which were or became parts of what would now be understood as higher or further education. When the City and Guilds of London Institute, for example, was created at the end of the 1870s, it expressed its purposes precisely in its Charter: 'the advancement, dissemination, propagation, promotion, culture, and application of all such branches of Science and the Fine Arts as benefit or are of use to, or may benefit or be of use to, productive and technical industries especially, and to commerce and industry generally or any branch thereof.'[9] The Central (Finsbury) Technical College, which was one outcome of this development, served explicitly as a model for the new polytechnics created in London after 1883 – and which were sometimes seen as 'poor men's universities'. The South-Western Polytechnic Institute in Chelsea, for instance, began its day work with two main objectives:

(I)   To give that preparatory training which will fit students over fifteen years of age for practical work in the factory or engineer's shop, or prepare them for Colonial life.

(II) The education of pupils, from middle-class and other schools, who are preparing for a higher technical and scientific course of instruction as is provided at the Central Technical College.[10]

A substantial literature of technical education discussed the precise intentions of these and other institutions, given the publicly debated needs both of the country in a situation of severe international economic competition, and of particular industrial and social groups. The Manchester Mechanics' Institution was transformed into a major technical school in the 1880s with the clear intention of making it into 'a regional powerhouse which should serve the industries of the area. . . . On grounds of economic self-interest as well as local loyalty there was need for action.'[11] Institutions were modified as well as created with such clear, explicit intentions.

The foundation documents, early reports and other literature relating to these institutions make it readily apparent that in the conditions of nineteenth-century social and economic development it was possible and necessary to define clear motives – even if it is historically necessary to scrutinize stated purposes with some care. This explicit relationship between institutions, publicly debated needs and voluntary or legislative developments, is obvious in the case of the nineteenth-century university college and polytechnic. It was London University, with its 'external degrees' and 'institutions with recognised teachers' that, more than any other, indicated how the boundaries of higher education could be extended. The technical, art and commercial colleges, concerned generally with preparation for qualifications of professional bodies, the Society of Arts, City and Guilds and the like, had precise terms of reference also, but were lower down the pecking order, and the story of many of them in the twentieth century was to be one of upward struggle or drift. In some cases they were to become regional colleges, colleges of advanced technology in the 1950s (and even technological universities), or a new generation of polytechnics in the 1960s.

The relationship is also obvious in the case of professional and semi-professional education and training, best exemplified by the establishment of the teacher training colleges from the 1840s. Their adaptation to changing circumstances related to batteries of Her Majesty's Inspectors' and diocesan reports, pamphlets, public state-ments and widespread debate. The early colleges were designed not only to train teachers but also to do so with the declared intention of ensuring a continuing denominational presence in the schools. Secu-larist and other attacks on the training colleges claimed, in fact, that the Churches never 'pretended that they felt the slightest interest in anything a man of discernment and sense would call education. They say outright that their concern is for the Church, and for Church principles.'[12] The dispute itself is not important here: the important word is 'outright'. What the Churches did, what the university founders did, what the State did, was in general 'outright'. Their actions in higher education were in general a response – often a growing and solidifying, usually controversial and frequently belated, response – to a social, economic and cultural condition – local, regional or national. In the twentieth century the speed of the response accelerated, but a similar pattern of declared intentions is apparent for most of this century.

New university colleges such as Leicester in the 1920s were locally sponsored and responded to local interests. A proposal for a federal East Midlands University to incorporate Leicester, Nottingham and others, foundered on what Jack Simmons describes as the willingness of Leicester people to 'put up their money largely out of a sense of local patriotism: a patriotism centred exclusively on Leicester'.[13] A policy document a quarter of a century later for the new North Staffordshire University at Keele considered that it should be 'the centre and focus of all higher education in its region'.[14] Local and regional needs continued substantially to influence the nature, curriculum and declared intentions of universities and other institutions of higher education. What became increasingly clear after the creation of Keele, however, was the need for institutions to respond to quite different levels of complexity. By the time the new universities of the 1960s were being created awareness of a world in rapid change had become considerably more acute. Britain and the rest of the Western world had had to respond to the collapse of old empires, Soviet economic and technological challenge, the post-war revivals of Germany and Japan, the increasing speed and scale of scientific research, changing manpower requirements, and the whole range of rapidly changing social and cultural conditions. The creation and adaptation of institutions had previously been innovatory; now they were at least partly seen as sustainers of innovation, constructed almost as symbols of change. The greatest of many excitements in creating a new university, wrote Asa Briggs, lay in 'the opportunity of re-planning the map of learning with which the university will be concerned'. A new university like Sussex could recruit academics precisely because it had set out to exploit 'the freedom to work along new lines and the power to plan new combinations of subjects and new curricula'.[15] The University Grants Committee was in 1964 endorsing 'the need for more experiment in the structure of degree courses, in the content of curricula, in methods of teaching and in university organisation'.[16]

The pressures to which institutions had to respond, therefore, had been joined by a new one – constant pressure to experiment, and a realization that however unwelcome experimentation might be survival might just depend on it. This was not the only new pressure. The constant demand for expansion was another – expressed in terms both of economic development and of the right to higher education for all qualified to enter it. This was the central message of the Robbins Report – one that was coupled, as we have seen, with a concern about the maintenance of academic standards. As Naomi McIntosh put it in describing the position: 'it is no use extending access and giving to more people the right to enter, if that right simply becomes a right to fail.'[17] The Robbins Report not only signalled the arrival of planning on a new scale, but also the targets to be aimed at in meeting the challenge of the new complexities: instruction in skills, the promotion of the general powers of the mind, the advancement of learning, and the transmission of a common culture. It was from that starting point that it went on to discuss in detail the principles on which the future pattern of higher education, and each of its component parts, should be built. The higher education world after Robbins changed swiftly and in some ways unexpectedly. As one response to the strategies outlined by Robbins the colleges of advanced technology were promoted. The binary policy and the creation of the new polytechnics was an unpredicted attempt to use part of the system as a corrective device. The increasingly dominant factor had become national economic and manpower planning, the gearing of higher education more closely to national policies, the integration of higher education into a national, State-administered and increasingly sensitive strategy for facing national and international change.

This is not to say, of course that once they had been established a batch of universities, or a clutch of colleges of advanced technology, or a flock of polytechnics, all set off in the same direction. It is intriguing to consider why, in fact, they immediately started to pull in different directions, often as a result of internal tensions amongst groups eager to establish novel courses or compete with university ones – at all events, to attract students, achieve status, and survive. The colleges and polytechnics did not award their own degrees – that, as everyone understood, was the main difference between the universities and the rest. It gave the universities and the Council for National Academic Awards, which acted for this purpose as a university, the power of promotion or constraint, and their patronage of the 'validation' process further strengthened and legitimized the dominant role of the universities in the new landscape. The colleges and polytechnics therefore had the universities, a national council, professional bodies of various kinds, and others, controlling or strongly influencing their examinations, syllabuses, and much else. Local authorities managed them more directly than the universities were managed by any outside body – an uneasy arrangement that resulted in the Oakes Report of 1978, and the subsequent debates about the management of public sector higher education. In spite of national and local controls, however, the CATs and then the polytechnics of the 1960s began to pull away from their declared frameworks of technology and applied studies. Polytechnics developed liberal arts courses at the same time as universities were attempting to expand – and to recruit students for – their technology and applied science courses.

What some of these historical considerations suggest is a way of approaching the 'terms of reference' of the colleges and institutes of higher education of the 1970s, and the pattern of statuses into which they were projected. Before commenting further on their 'piecemeal' character and their responsiveness to the country's 'most pressing requirements', there are two points that need to be underlined.

First – we have looked at some examples of historically located *intentions*. The further one looks into the twentieth century, the more the original intentions and structures have been modified in answer to increasing pressures. Universities have ceased to be 'local'. Their curricula and recruitment have not remained tied closely to local and regional interests. They have adapted in response to Government pressures (including financial ones), manpower forecasts and demographic vagaries. They have adjusted their pattern of research, accepted international roles, modified their curricula in order to attract students to shortage or unpopular areas, altered their structures and governance, and become more sensitive to national issues. The examples we have used describe institutions as seen through the eyes of their founders, not as they were in the last quarter of the twentieth century. *Second* – all institutions of higher and further education have become less and less able to state their purposes in the single-minded terms available in the nineteenth century. 'Learning' and 'curriculum' cannot be divorced from 'democratic needs'; manpower is part of a discussion that also includes human rights; expansion and contraction create academic problems, but are part of economic and social strategies; demographic decline means competition for students, and adaptations in order to survive. Distinctions amongst institutions have – as we have underlined – become more obscure, in spite of constant attempts at redefinition. Institutions would not now be able with confidence to predict that they do not intend to alter their entrance requirements, examination procedures, departmental structures, curricular or other policies, over the next five, or even the next two, years.

Only against that background of uncertainty and change can the Colleges and Institutes of Higher Education be discussed. Those which had been colleges of education had never had a glamorous status in the map of higher education, but they had been distinct and understood. As they were merged, absorbed or left to diversify, some retained a majority of their places in teacher education, in others the balance went the other way. Alongside some of the colleges of technology and art that had remained poised uncertainly between lower level further education and the charted waters of higher education, they looked for new identities. The colleges and institutes emerged, therefore, from teacher education or from bases in engineering or management, commerce or art and design. Some had been earlier aspirants for polytechnic status. Some brought into a single institution many hitherto separate and disparate units. Some were combinations of similar and geographically related colleges – including denominational colleges of education. In other cases a new identity emerged from a single diversifying institution. The new colleges and institutes form the only example in our discussion of a sector coming into existence at a moment of demographic and economic contraction. They are examples of survival and adaptation, not of creation. They were the first instance in British higher education of a new sector being born *without* clear terms of reference. This very fact made the new institutions as appropriate to the 1970s and beyond as earlier generations of higher education had been in their contexts. The decisions about the new sector may have been taken in piecemeal fashion, under duress or by default, but they may have been the right decisions for all that. Intentions, declared or secret, may encompass more than they know.

It was either impossible or difficult or inappropriate in the conditions of the 1970s to define 'coherent packages' or even 'pressing requirements'. At the end of the 1970s was the need for more research, more technician training, longer undergraduate programmes, the admission of more students, the recruitment of more minority group students, the expansion of electronics or computing at the expense of the social sciences, or the expansion of the social sciences? The expansion or contraction of the universities, or the polytechnics, or higher education across the board, or in individual cases? And in relation to principles of finance, demography or need? And what *were* suitable packages in which to include the former colleges of education (given that no consensus about the location and control of teacher education had been reached since the Second World War)? And how *does* higher education relate to national economic performance? Since there was in the late 1970s no agreed answer to any of these questions, the colleges and institutes of higher education may have been the right response to the uncertainties of change at many levels.

It is not that the polytechnics and universities have not needed to be, or have not been, unresponsive. In seeking their different places in the higher education landscape the new institutions of the late 1970s had by definition to be adaptable – to measure and re-measure local, regional and national needs, to re-think their community relation-ships, their position as small- or medium-sized, often residential, colleges with strong traditions of student counselling and welfare, in some cases with a high proportion of part-time students, and often attracting a significant proportion of mature students. They found themselves torn between different models of development – either as the small institution doing what the university does but smaller and different; or the American-style community college – a wide-open staging post into higher education for mature and second-chance students, combined with the vocational and 'terminal' courses associ-ated in the United States with the community colleges and in Britain in the past with the technical and 'further education' colleges. Some tried to combine the two. Some moved into social work and other professional training, new types of combined liberal arts degrees, masters' degrees, and research.

The development of polytechnics and colleges and institutes of higher education is a central, necessary case study in any discussion of present relationships between higher education and social and economic change. A full discussion of the responsiveness of higher education would also, however, need to encompass the Open Univer-sity. Such a discussion would involve not only a further analysis of the 'pool of ability' for which provision has been inadequate, but also similar questions of institutional direction and change. The social composition of the Open University's student body is in practice less weighted towards the lower social and income groups than was originally envisaged. The processes of 'distance learning' have raised considerable problems. But what the Open University has done more strikingly in terms of our present discussion is reveal that the 'pool of ability' is not only not exhausted – as the Robbins Committee had clearly demonstrated – but that the concept itself was outdated. More provision of this kind not only responds to existing demand, but encourages new demand. The universities, as well as the new sectors of higher education, are having to come to terms with the new concepts of learning and the new categories of student that the Open University has helped to make more central to discussions of education. Through the agency of the Open University, and under other pressures, the discussion of established categories of 'mature', 'part-time', 'adult' and other kinds of student and education has been vastly altered. Parallel developments in the universities and the Open University, polytechnics and colleges have brought higher education to the brink of new possibilities and new expansions of the whole conception of further, higher and continuing education. The American experience of the 1960s and 1970s has important messages for the discussion of future patterns, alternatives and difficulties. Policies of restricting public expenditure in these fields could have damaging and dramatic effects not only on the *level* of provision but also on the possibilities of serious consideration being given to the *nature* of provision for all the changing categories of student need and demand. Parallelism and pluralism in British higher education have gone a long way since the early 1960s. Higher education has a long history of upward drift by aspiring institutions, and the dangers of excessive ambition, parallelism and competition are real. Whatever the benefits of a 'rational' division of labour in higher education, it can equally be argued that research, graduate teaching and undergraduate teaching – with an increasing emphasis on expanding the recruitment of relatively under-represented sections of the population – ought to be indivisible. The dangers of separating off 'teaching' and 'research' institutions (and of isolating different kinds of problems in different kinds of institution) are greater than the dangers of parallelism and competition. Strong, separate identities encourage institutions to identify other people's problems in order no longer to think about them. The main argument against the binary system has always been that it strengthens the elite functions of the universities, and separates off the popular functions in at least partially truncated or lower status institutions. On both sides of the binary line the needs of teaching and of students, the relationship between the higher and the lower learning, the nature of new institutions, have been placed in the wrong perspectives. Existing structures have been solidified. In concentrating attention on the needs of particular groups of students in specific institutions, they have encouraged others to feel exempt from facing up to the functions concerned. Viewing one kind of institution as an 'undergraduate teaching' institution, or a teacher training institution, has encouraged others to have a weak commitment to undergraduate teaching or the education of teachers.

If it is crucial in Britain to extend the number and range of students entering higher education, it is equally important – as emerged in our last chapter – that in a diversified structure the lower learning retains *everywhere* a central presence, and is everywhere amenable to similar pressures. The argument since Veblen illustrates the difficulties of dividing amongst or of combining within institutions the different varieties of the higher and the lower learning. After decades of the kinds of changes and pressures discussed in this and the previous chapter the greater danger now lies in cementing precise institutional definitions, which inevitably encourage greater attention to elite functions – especially on the part of the universities.

Diversity, as we have emphasized, also implies hierarchy. It would be unrealistic to attempt to conjure it away, but it would be a retreat from whatever gains might have been made in the 1960s and 1970s to interpret those changes in ways which strengthen, and indeed, extend the higher education hierarchy. The creation of the polytechnics and the later colleges and institutes of higher education was attended with confusions within which the universities had to reconsider their own self-definitions. The polytechnics grew out of the further education sector. The Labour Government's 1966 White Paper, *A Plan for Polytechnics and Other Colleges*, explained that the new institutions were necessary in order to ensure that

> the rapidly mounting demand for higher education within the system of further education is met in such a way as to make the best possible use of these resources without prejudicing opportunities for the tens of thousands of less advanced students who wish to take courses at intermediate or lower levels.[18]

What this new combination was to mean was discussed two years later by former Secretary of State for Education and Science, Patrick Gordon Walker. In some ways, he told an audience, the polytechnics will be like universities. The intention is, for example, that they should concentrate on higher education. Where other levels of work are being done they will be given up as soon as satisfactory alternative arrangements can be made. . . . Universities are selective institutions catering mainly for students wanting to pursue degree courses. In contrast the polytechnics will be comprehensive institutions providing courses at every level of higher education.

The polytechnics, he added, would be encouraged to develop research of kinds which arose naturally out of their teaching activities.[19]

There is in these statements every conceivable degree of ambiguity and uncertainty – about what is meant by higher education, about the nature of these all-through, comprehensive institutions, about what would happen to the other work if they 'concentrated' on higher education, about whether the lower level work would remain or not remain. And the similarities and differences between the polytechnics and the universities were here, in other statements, and in practice, impossible easily and confidently to define. The very act of seeking to define the polytechnics as something intangibly different, however, helped the universities to confirm their established and superior status. The universities, after all, were the traditional home of the higher learning, the seminaries of a liberal education, the route to the higher professions. In the United States from the end of the nineteenth century the range of professions served by the universities had been considerably extended, as the social sciences established themselves as discrete disciplines in the universities, and as new occupations graduated to 'professional' status. There, as in parts of Europe, the range of 'professions' encompassed more than in Britain. Engineering, for example, had not gained the same status in Britain as in Germany or France, and however much ambiguity there was internationally about the professional status of social work and similar activities, their ability to reach a status matched by university acceptance was the more difficult, the slower, and the more hotly resisted in the British university environment. In the United States – with all the repercussions and resistance we suggested in the last chapter – the universities and their graduate schools extended their professional training commitments – as Rudolph puts it:

Crafts on their way to becoming professions, skills once learned on the job or in the field – mechanical engineering, journalism, architecture, business – used the university schools and departments as environments in which was determined who the professionals would be and how they would be trained.[20]

In this sense, as Bledstein argues, the universities and colleges of the late nineteenth and early twentieth centuries, were indeed *used* by the middle class to extend their ranges of status and power. The newly reformed American college curriculum and the newly created state university represented an expansion of functions but also the consolidation of class status.

Whereas much of this is true of the new university colleges and universities of late nineteenth-century and early twentieth-century Britain, the scale was smaller and the range narrower. However much, as we have suggested, the creation of new institutions was intended to meet geographical and social needs, at the heart of the university enterprise was the strong tradition of Oxford and Cambridge, prolonged resistance to utilitarian pressures, the classical interpretation of the higher learning – an interpretation which the new institutions had adapted, but had not abandoned. In Britain the concept of the 'university' remained wedded more closely to the 'elite' functions than in the United States. In relation to our discussion the crucial point is the strong connection retained in the twentieth century by the universities with the education of the senior professions. The historian of the Association of University Teachers describes the university teacher as the 'key profession' in the twentieth century, because

> In a world increasingly dominated by the professional expert, on whose competence, reliability and integrity not merely the functioning of our complex industrial society but the very survival of our civilization, if not of the human race itself, has come to depend, university teachers have become the educators and selectors of the other professions.

The university teacher was the 'principal agent in the process of selection for the key posts in industry, commerce, government and the other power-structures of modern society'. Even more:

> it is the sole profession in an increasingly specialized world which still embraces the whole gamut of knowledge and professional skills . . . it is the sole profession which has the time . . . the means and

the skill not merely to make new discoveries . . . but to do society's fundamental thinking for it . . .[21]

It would, of course, be possible to attempt to extend these definitions to apply to the *university and college* but the reality is different. The universities select for precisely those 'other professions' which are involved in the key posts described. The power structures are not just the political and industrial ones indicated, but also those professions which occupy key status and instrumental roles in our society – including the law and medicine. The polytechnics and colleges of higher education will not be acquiring medical schools or pointing in obvious ways to top careers in the Civil Service. In the landscape of higher education such fortresses are more or less unassailable.

It would be equally unrealistic to imagine that the new generations of higher education institutions will – like the university colleges of earlier decades – become universities, or acquire charters enabling them to grant their own degrees. They may come into closer partnership with the validating universities or the CNAA, but it is likely that this formal distinction across the binary line will remain. If higher education in general, however, is to be responsive to 'pressing social requirements' the distinctions need to be further broken down, the definitions weakened wherever possible. The fact that a university trains doctors does not exempt it from the whole range of social concerns about the recruitment of minority and underprivileged students, about the adequacy of undergraduate teaching, or about innovative responses to social change. That a polytechnic or college of higher education is concerned with social work or para-medical training, with the undergraduate education of teachers, or with part-time adult students, does not exempt it from the need to pursue research and to have the higher learning represented in whatever ways might be possible. Diversification as launched in Britain in the 1960s and 1970s in higher education has altered the landscape, but has not seriously undermined old hierarchies and statuses.

The problem of bringing a discussion of higher education into the same visible relationship with the social condition as other parts of the system have is that it still, as a system and as separate institutions, bears historical overtones of being a minority or elite social concern. The American situation is in this connection of major importance. It is not a model – it is a set of structures and strategies which is based on a different range of assumptions, and in the evolution of higher education it is inescapable to pay serious consideration to that experience, those institutions, those possibilities, and those dangers and weaknesses. It is likely that the diversification of higher education, even in an age of economic slow-down or contraction, will need to be seen in relation to a series of changing features of the social condition. We shall need to put under scrutiny the rhythm of higher education and work (or unemployment), the validity of our concepts of full-time and part-time higher education, the timing and length of periods of study, the relationships between higher education and social and economic re-adaptation, the fading distinctions between liberal and vocational education, the ways of ensuring that higher education becomes more sensitive to the social condition, as well as to changes in the structure of knowledge and to the needs of economic policy and planning. If the institutional changes discussed in the last two chapters seem more remote from crucial, current social dilemmas than issues to do with, for example, the control and accessibility of schools, and related questions of opportunities and achievement, it is all the more important that the higher education landscape should be widely explored. There was never a more important time in which to press for more, to experiment with the different, and to bring what we offer to all ages of our post-school population closer to the centre of our debates about where we are as a society.

10 Teachers and adolescents

If the ability of higher education to respond to social pressures and invitations is strongly conditioned by questions of status, the ambiguous position of teacher education within the system has been most strongly conditioned by such considerations. The position of teacher education has reflected the uncertain position of the teacher. On one terrain the teacher can be seen to wield authority, but on a wider one he or she has neither authority nor power. The teachers have been centrally involved in operating the structural changes of recent decades, with at best a marginal role in making the decisions. In the salary stakes the teachers have followed behind the field of stronger, or more influential and status-wielding, professions. With the professionalization of teacher training in the nineteenth and early twentieth centuries, the power over training and selection and entry moved firmly into the hands of the universities, the training colleges and the employers. In the accountability diagram we have sketched in a previous chapter the teachers have been advised, cajoled, bullied, and in recent decades consulted mainly in relation to those areas of education decision-making which are not central to any power structure. And in an effort to preserve their apparent power in 'professional' areas – mainly the curriculum – they have resisted pressures to admit parents and the community into their 'expert' field. In resisting the Taylor Committee's proposals for a wider partnership in the government of schools, the teachers protected their frontiers blindly. In a period when central government and its educational agents were strengthening their position in the decision-making structure, the teachers failed to respond to proposals which could have brought parents, for example, into an important alliance – not, as many of the teachers saw it, into a position of interference in the teachers' legitimate, professional field. Over this, as over most issues of concern relating to the educational and social condition, the teachers have responded with profound status anxieties. It is not difficult to understand why.

Elementary school teachers in the nineteenth century were in the main, like their pupils, from working-class families. Teachers of the children of the poorer classes, wrote a prize essayist in 1839, 'are not removed from the level of those classes'. Their life was a 'harassing struggle' and they were 'merely tolerated in society'. The schoolmaster, wrote another essayist at the same time, was paid at a rate 'scarcely above that of the parish pauper's allowance'. Society, and even legislation, defined for the teacher 'the humblest station in society as that beyond which he shall *not* rise'. This was not true of the Oxford or Cambridge graduate in the better-endowed grammar or public school, but, in general, education in the early nineteenth century shared none of the prestige of the other professions. As one of the essayists put it in 1839: 'education, as a profession . . . obtains but little respect from society, and confers no social advantages on its members.'[1] In 1973 a sociologist could still accept an analysis of 'the semi-professional or marginally professional status of schoolteaching, in relation to the established professions'.[2] Since the early nineteenth century the teaching semi-profession has changed its status, composition, training requirements, organization, and almost everything else connected with it, but it has retained permanently bizarre social characteristics. It has moved towards militancy and away from it; it has identified itself more and less with the organized labour movement; it has concerned itself to changing extents with matters of 'professional' concern other than salaries and conditions of service – including teaching methods, school organization and curriculum content. Their strategies have more often than not been directed towards overcoming the 'but little respect from society' and the lack of 'social advantages'. The difficulties and uncertainties of the semi-profession, however, have not deterred recruitment.

One obvious and consistent source of pressure to enter teaching has been necessity. The young Oxbridge graduate without immediate prospects of advancement in the Church in the nineteenth century might be driven to the endowed grammar school. The working-class boy and girl seeking some form of stable, non-manual employment, might be driven, from the middle of the last century, to pupil-teaching. For him or her, however, an uncertain and bewildering social status was waiting. One of Her Majesty's Inspectors visiting Chester Training School in the 1840s, for example, found it striving not to separate the future teacher from 'the classes out of which he is taken', but to confirm his working-class identity, to strengthen his sympathies 'with his own people'.[3] The elementary school teacher was working-class, and although other training colleges took a different view from Chester's and sought to 'improve' the working-class entrant by an induction into middle-class culture, his or her status hovered uncertainly between the class from which most elementary teachers came and the professional middle class to which they aspired. They were in many respects divorced from the former, and were largely rejected by the latter. They had no hope of entering the world of the endowed grammar or public school. Their pay and conditions ranged from poor to abysmal. And yet to their families and to the parents of their pupils they visibly enjoyed a form of participation in the non-working-class world: even if they were servants of the church or the school board, at the same time they *represented* those whom they served. They wielded authority and imposed sanctions, at the same time as being at the mercy of other authorities and other sanctions. They had relatively stable positions and salaries. They had crossed the divide which separated the class from which they came and the first levels of the classes where power and authority lay. However little of these the teachers enjoyed, and however close to the working-class community they remained, the teacher's schoolhouse, style of work, social relationships, symbols of authority, and search for adequate professional and social status, inevitably produced ambiguities and tensions. The elementary teacher achieved what Asher Tropp calls 'social isolation',[4] abandoning one status without acquiring another, driven partly by lack of any alternative into the social no-man's-land that D. H. Lawrence in this century experienced so acutely.

For a small minority the motive and the achievement were to pass through teaching to a 'real' profession and a secure status. At the top of the hierarchy the schoolhouse might just lead to the manse. At the bottom, two years in the residential teacher training college in the second half of the nineteenth century might, after a period of teaching, lead beyond it to a career elsewhere – including in the nonconformist Churches. For the vast majority of entrants to teaching, however, the prospects beyond teaching were probably never entertained, and the trap they entered held tight. As the number of elementary school teachers increased, the scale of recruitment of working-class and lower-middle-class girls increased, though in the case of both boys and girls in the late nineteenth century new career opportunities in commerce and industry competed for the attention of those able to put together the requisite education, stamina and ambition.

The education 'profession' also changed. New day training colleges were established at the end of the century. The National Union of Teachers campaigned from the 1870s on salaries, tenure, conditions – and the quality of education. The Board schools, improvements in training, and the establishment of pupil teacher centres, helped to raise standards and status. Teacher training as a step towards social mobility, especially for the children of skilled working-class and tradesmen's families, became a larger ingredient in motivation to enter teaching. In the twentieth century – particularly with the establishment of the Burnham negotiating machinery after the First World War – social mobility, security of tenure and improved status became crucial objectives of the teachers now seeking a stronger professional identity. In the case of the elementary teachers this was coupled with the aim of the unification of training and of the class-divided profession – since the grammar school was still predominantly a middle-class preserve, and the elementary school remained separate, and predominantly working-class.

By the 1920s the elementary schools were still staffed largely by working-class recruits, but with an admixture of lower-middle-class children coming through the elementary schools (and entering into competition for the new 'scholarships' to the grammar schools). A committee on the training of elementary school teachers assumed in 1925, 'just as our witnesses have assumed, that all but a few of those who ultimately qualify as teachers in Elementary Schools begin their education in Elementary Schools'. Of increasing importance to would-be teachers was now the establishment of central elements in professional identity – security of tenure, and nationally agreed salaries and pension arrangements. Even attacks on these conditions in the Government economic policies of the 1920s served to cement professional solidarity. The 1925 Committee stressed that where salaries were low, as in teaching, recruits might 'attach at least as much importance to security as to adequacy . . . in Elementary School teaching, where a teacher's financial hopes can never be more than modest, the value of security rises'. For recruits in search of social mobility and a meal ticket, security compensated for poor working conditions and, in the committee's words, the fact that elementary school teaching particularly 'does not take a high place in popular regard'.[5] It was still a semi-profession, but it was a secure meal ticket – an important factor in this century especially in the recruitment of male teachers.

Even since the Second World War some of these features of teaching have remained relatively constant. First, the struggle for professional recognition has continued, with now one now another aspect of teaching becoming prominent – salaries, school conditions, superannuation. . . . One of the central obstacles to this recognition has been the low status of teacher training. The low regard in which teacher education was held in the 1960s was reflected in a systematic questioning by the National Union of Teachers of the appropriateness of the education and training of teachers in Britain.[6] This was also an 'outstanding fact' of the evidence to and report of the James Committee on teacher education in 1972. Second, teaching has continued to rely to an important degree on the recruitment of children of skilled manual and lower-middle-class families. The social composition of the colleges of education in the 1950s and 1960s was different from that of the universities. The Robbins Committee pointed out that in 1961–2, 54 per cent of students in teacher training came from middle-class homes, compared with 71 per cent in universities. Lower percentages of college students had fathers in professional or managerial occupation than did university students, and a higher proportion of college students (11 per cent) had fathers who were semi-skilled or unskilled workers than did university students (7 per cent).[7] The teaching profession overall had since the 1930s become more attractive to middle-class recruits, as postgraduate training for secondary education gained ground, and as the three-year certificate and then the B Ed were introduced. Floud and Scott found in the mid-1950s that the picture of the teaching profession across the different kinds of schools was being affected by the increased percentage of teachers from lower-middle-class backgrounds entering the grammar schools. The diminution of class differences between teachers in different sectors of public education was accelerated by the introduction of the B Ed, by comprehensive reorganization, and by the enhanced status of the primary school in post-war Britain.

While we know a little about the social and educational background of entrants to teaching in the nineteenth and twentieth centuries, their motives have been and are for the most part a matter of speculation. They have in recent years been faced with conditions, salaries, prospects and a status more attractive than in previous decades, but they still constitute a 'marginal profession' riddled with ambiguities. June Purvis explains, for example, that teaching does not satisfy the 'career' conditions normally associated with a profession. It does not have the same pattern of progression: '. . . the career structure within the school is flat rather than hierarchical. The majority of practitioners are on the same level with a minority holding posts of responsibility.' This leads to 'horizontal rather than vertical career patterns' – teachers move more than other professions not for advancement but for greater job satisfaction, and not necessarily for improved grade or status.[8] In the conditions of retrenchment of the late 1970s this analysis of teaching as a career with low expectations of promotion became even more true.

Until the mid-1970s deterrents to teaching were increasingly balanced by such inducements as training opportunities, the ease of entry into teaching, job security and ease of transfer between jobs – the last particularly attractive in the case of married women teachers. Mobility and a meal ticket had strong appeal. From the mid-1970s this was no longer true to anything like the same extent. Entry qualifications for teacher education began to be raised, and recruitment for teacher training places in the colleges was dramatically cut. At some levels of teaching and in some subject areas qualified teachers began to face unemployment, as the education service itself began to be reduced. Promotion prospects became harder. The easy re-entry of women teachers after having families came to a halt. Part-time teaching posts became almost impossible to obtain. Geographical mobility was curtailed. Compulsory transfer or redundancy or early retirement began to enter the teacher's consciousness. Uncertainties of a new magnitude surrounded school-teaching – and even within the reduced quotas for teacher education it proved difficult to attract sixth-formers into the B Ed. Student teachers in the late 1970s on occasion occupied their colleges or made other gestures of protest against unemployment and cuts, and further forewarned the next generation of students that the meal ticket had been withdrawn.

The 'value of security' took a hard knock as a result of economic uncertainties, demographic vagaries, political confusions, and the national decisions taken in response to them. Two factors were beginning to assume importance, however, in balancing out the undermining of the 'meal ticket' incentive to enter teaching. The first was the tendency in the 1960s and 1970s to recruit more 'socially idealistic' students than in the past. Teaching has been so much talked about in recent years as a kind of social work, or as a form of social commitment, that the colleges and departments have recruited at least a proportion of students with an ambition to use the schools as their sphere of social involvement. Since the reality of schools does not always make it easy for the teacher (and certainly for the student teacher) to act within the framework of a strong social conscience, and since many teachers in any case resist this interpretation of their role, students with this kind of ideal have often become disenchanted during training or during their early careers. Changes, nevertheless, have taken place which bring considerations of this kind more to the surface: within the opportunity debates and strategies that we have discussed there have been increased emphases on home–school links, the community school, the wider responsibilities of the teacher. In spite of any general decline of confidence in the school–society relationship it is possible that more of such committed students may find their way into training and the schools. For the student with high professional motivation or explicit social ideals the continuing uncertainties of the teaching professions may not prove to be important as a deterrent.

The second counterbalancing factor has been the tightening of entrance requirements and a search for higher standards in training, which could enhance professional status and encourage recruits with a different pattern of motivation from that of some past students (and which could also affect the social composition of the teacher–education component of the colleges of higher education and polytechnics). Past experience should prevent too optimistic a view of how effectively teacher education can respond to sharp social and educational challenges. Roger Webster has told the story of Sir Gordon Russell lecturing on contemporary furniture design. At the end of the talk 'one of the audience commented that it was easy enough to design modern furniture. What he wanted to know was, How could the design of antiques be improved?' In the 1970s, Webster suggested, 'in reforming the curriculum and organisation of educational institutions we are trying to do just that: to improve the design of antiques', adding a coat of varnish, tacking on a 'decorative knob'.[9] A history of teacher training in recent decades would need to indicate in detail the changes, the crises, to which teacher education might be expected to have responded, and to evaluate the nature, speed and adequacy of the responses. We have underlined in previous chapters the changes most influential for educational processes – including urban and family change, the impact of changes in ethnic and racial balances, swiftly changing ethical and political attitudes, and the altered cultural experiences and social expectations of different groups in the population. Teacher education across the period of these major changes was slow to react – even to the directly educational features of these events.

There would be a variety of ways in which these questions of teachers and teacher education could be further developed, and case studies of particular issues would be the most helpful. It would be possible to follow through questions of the responsiveness, or otherwise, of teacher education to major ethical and political changes, to changes in social and economical structures. The inability of teacher education to design 'contemporary furniture', or to understand what it was doing to antiques, would be perhaps most clearly evident by trying to relate historically the education of teachers and the concept of an approach to adolescence in recent decades. An examination of the extent to which teachers were prepared for the world actually inhabited by the adolescents some of them were to teach would be the sharpest way of pursuing Webster's point, and it may be interesting to suggest how the analysis might be conducted.

It was said of Keate, headmaster of Eton in the early nineteenth century, that he possessed one qualification for a headmaster which Arnold of Rugby did not have, notably 'the knowledge of God Almighty's intention that there should exist for a certain time, between childhood and manhood, the natural production known as boy'.[10] We have come in the twentieth century to accept the equivalent knowledge of a fixed category and status known as adolescence. The nature of that knowledge is critical to an assessment of the training of teachers for secondary education in particular. We have suggested in an earlier chapter that the concept of adolescence was effectively established as a generalized social category in the early decades of this century. G. S. Hall, publishing *Adolescence*, the first major work on the subject in 1904, turned the concept for the first time into an important educational tool. The 1910s and 1920s made adolescence a problem. Selwyn Troen has pointed how in the United States – and the same was true in Britain – easy access to unskilled jobs by young 'teenagers' (to use a later term) was barred by technological advance. Cash registers, pneumatic tubes and telephones, for example, greatly reduced the need for messengers: the department stores, which had been among the largest employers of unskilled young adolescents, radically cut this labour force after 1900. Office work declined. The job market contracted, and compulsory schooling was extended.[11]

The 'problem' profile of adolescence became sharper during the First World War. Concern about juvenile behaviour in Britain before the war was intensified during the war by an increase in juvenile delinquency, especially among young teenagers, by the relative financial independence of those over fourteen on war-related employment, and anxieties about post-war employment and public morality.[12] Children who left school before the age of fourteen, pointed out a Royal Commission on venereal diseases in 1916, could not be adequately educated in sound moral principles.[13] Wartime educational demands included the strong one for post-war continuation classes up to eighteen. The Lewis Committee of 1917 asked whether the conception of a juvenile as 'primarily a little wage-earner' could be replaced by 'the conception of the workman and citizen in training'.[14] It is this tension between adolescence as a period of late childhood, as prematurely entering the labour market, and as a period of pre-adulthood, that accounts for the establishment of the concept from the 1920s particularly as one related to fundamental problems and anxieties. The psychologist did not create the category, but was rapidly engaged in diagnosing the problems associated with it.

The lengthening of the period of compulsory schooling was in part a response to this situation, and what it achieved was a constantly increasing period of dependence, or what Wall describes as the increasing 'semi-dependence' of the second decade of life, as a result of the 'democratization' of adolescence through the spread of educational opportunities for this age group.[15] The group came more and more, especially after the Second World War, to be seen as autonomous and rootless. The age of onset of puberty had steadily lowered, the authority of parents and established institutions in imposing sexual restrictions was felt to be diminishing, and the financial autonomy of the 'affluent teenager' became part of the sense of threat on the part of an older generation whose moral, social and political values seemed challenged. The raising of the school leaving age, together with increased opportunities for full-time and part-time post-secondary education, steadily lengthened the period of 'semi-dependence'. One American view of the position in the mid-1970s suggested that there was now a 'new stage of American man – almost endless adolescence'. If students were adolescents, and if adolescent culture contained a significant student-based ingredient, then it had to be remembered that the average age of students was rising, and the numbers participating in undergraduate and graduate studies were increasing. Adolescence was therefore no longer 'the relatively fleeting "transitional stage" of textbook and popular lore but a substantial segment of life which may last 15 or 20 years'. The discussion of 'youth culture' had reflected

the prolongation of adolescence, since it is not surprising that a period of life which may last from age 12 to age 35 might develop its own cultural style. . . . There is thus an enormous stratum of persons caught in the tension between their experience of peak physical strength and sexual energy on the one hand, and their public definitions as culturally 'immature' on the other.[16]

It is against this background that British, American and other societies discovered – especially in the 1960s – the dissatisfaction of youth. The schools became involved with the whole range of intensifying problems associated with behaviour, discipline, rejection of authority, permissiveness, the cults of rock idols and the fashions of dress, group behaviour and the constant search for new cultural identities. The schools were faced with the importation of a rapidly changing social scene into the classroom. Coping, surviving, understanding changing attitudes and phenomena, were the basic vocabularies of teachers in the majority of the schools caught up in swiftly changing social and cultural situations. The preparation of students for teaching in these situations, however, was caught up in different currents – establishing the academic and professional respectability of the teacher training exercise itself, drawing the philosophical, sociological, psychological and other maps which students might use to master the educational terrain. Teachers complained that students were not prepared for the practicalities and difficulties of the job; students complained that the world of training and the world of the schools did not match; many teacher trainers merely refurbished their antique curriculum. The mismatch could be presented in different ways – the most common being that of the conflict between theory and practice. The important conflict, however, is that between the realities of social change and the levels of educational reponse. If the *Black Paper* response was to cling to the known and the established, that of the majority of schools was to cope as well as possible, and that of the majority of teacher education was to delay any response, or to hope that none was necessary.

The point about the history of adolescence is that it is based on a constant conflict and accommodation amongst the social and economic situation of the young, the anxieties and definitions of older generations, and the educational and other institutional arrangements made to handle changing perceptions of the problem. Adolescence has not been a fixed category in this century. Perceptions of its problem content have changed markedly. Institutional arrangements in response have included juvenile courts, youth clubs, longer compulsory schooling, proposals for part-time, post-school education, and a range of others. The preparation of teachers has included aspects of developmental psychology, sociology, and occasionally 'field' work to meet the problems. But the curriculum of teacher education for the most part in the 1960s and 1970s prevented sustained involvement with and analysis of these crucial areas of social change, because the priorities of teacher education were dictated by quite different commitments to solving other problems – the outstanding one being the status of teachers in the schools, and the status of teacher-trainers in their parent institutions. These priorities did not mean that no adaptation took place, or that no confrontation with such fundamental areas of experience as that of adolescence took place. They meant that teacher education was at best slow to come to terms with salient social changes, and even with major educational changes. It was long after the comprehensive school had taken root in the 1950s and 1960s that university education departments were willing to admit that not all of their graduate certificate students were going to teach in grammar schools.

The discussion of adolescence and teacher education is a further reminder that the whole range of educational issues – curriculum, skills, preparation for adulthood, the training of teachers, society's expectations of schools . . . is bound up with the location of power in the making of educational decisions, and the position and status of teachers in relation to decisions and the social changes they attempt to encompass. The student entering teacher education and intending to join the teaching profession is entering a world of ambiguities and conflicts, competing statuses and profound and unresolved questions about his or her position in a power structure or a partnership, his or her responsibilities and accountability. Teacher education is not merely an instrumental process by which to enter a profession. Teaching is neither a fixed category nor a secure meal ticket.

11 Change

It is difficult at the beginning of the 1980s to talk optimistically about change. The end of economic expansion and of the widespread search for suitable accompanying strategies for educational and social change produced in the 1970s an increasing climate of disappointment and uncertainty. The climate was one, by the end of the 1970s, in which cuts, retreats, conservative counter-attacks, could gain momentum. Some radicals even set out to defend what they had previously attacked as palliatives or illusory advances. American assessments of the anti-poverty action of the 1960s weighed gains and losses to produce a balance which offered little guidance as to future policy. In Britain the thrust of positive discrimination strategies had by the end of the 1970s been dissipated amidst resource cuts and ideological controversy. Some Marxist or radical theories denied the possibility of real change within capitalist structures – or gave the impression that such was the case. Karabel and Halsey point out that neo-Marxists in the 1970s were suggesting an almost 'perfect fit' between schooling and other social institutions:

> There is a tidiness about the family–school-work triumverate that in the neo-Marxist view serves to transmit inequality from generation to generation, but the process seems to work so smoothly and is based upon such an imposing system of domination that one must wonder how it is that educational change ever takes place.[1]

One argument, of course, is that it doesn't – or at least that it takes place at a level which impinges only negligibly on the social condition. The basis of the functionalist Marxist argument conducted by Bowles and Gintis is that educational change within capitalist structures has been either impossible or trivial or – when it has occurred – has merely reinforced ruling-class power. Reimer, Illich, the deschoolers and the reluctant schoolers, identified school *as such* with Establishment, exploitation, domination, dehumanization. The painful discussion of whether schools affected anything anyway produced only occasional spasms of light or optimism – weakly as in the 1974 American survey, *How Effective Is Schooling?*, and more strongly in 1979 in Britain by Rutter and colleagues in *Fifteen Thousand Hours*.[2] The times were not propitious for serious reconsideration of questions of education and social change.

By the end of the 1970s, it could also be argued, the market for panaceas had also collapsed, and the way forward was precisely through a reconsideration of the weaknesses in the grand and lesser designs of the previous decades. The careful assessment of American and European policies, social and educational theories, and practical endeavours, of the 1960s and 1970s could perhaps begin to take place most usefully when they did not and could not point to short-term cosmetic decisions. The end of the 1970s was perhaps the sort of situation in which to ask, again, basic and familiar questions of the kind we saw formulated by Clarke in the 1940s, and present throughout the varied educational and social efforts of the following decades. The dialogue between present concerns and past experience, the much-explored frontier (if that is what it is) between sociology and history, takes on particular significance in such an effort to formulate and locate adequate questions. The historical dimension provides neither answers nor confidence. The dangers of seeing the past experience in a frame constructed in the present are major and serious. Bernard Bailyn demonstrated clearly in the American situation of 1960 how fundamentally American educational history had been misread in the context of twentieth-century concerns. American revisionist historians have demonstrated how fundamentally the re-reading of the past can remain locked in other, changed, contemporary concerns. Historians have still not sufficiently engaged in the dilemmas raised by the sociology of knowledge, by Mannheim's discussion of 'relationism', by the varied directions taken by Schutz, Lukács and others. There is still in educational and social history a strong element of 'celebration', of a search for lineage and genealogy, for a *justification* of the present or of a critique of the present. The dangers are real, but a situation of uncertainty is a good one in which to make an historical safari which attempts to evade such dangers. A dialogue, not between present and past confidences, but precisely between present and past uncertainties is what is most needed in examining educational and social policy at the beginning of the 1980s. Confidence that nothing has changed or can change is in this situation equally as dangerous as certainty that it has not and cannot.

Central to the re-examination of our social condition and its educational concerns, therefore, is a restatement of questions and a review of what it is that the questions are about. It is no longer adequate simply to repeat questions about education and society, education and social class, opportunity, standards, accountability. These concepts and relationships need to be re-examined at the intersection of theoretical controversy and recent experience. What in Clarke's world is the same and what is not? What measures have been used and could be used to judge the social impact of educational decisions, and the educational impact of social changes? How do categories such as disadvantage, privilege, poverty, power, stand up for examination after the immense service they were called upon to give in the 1960s and 1970s? How effectively *do* schools sort and prepare students for social and economic roles? How efficiently do they, or should they, equip students for the legal profession, plumbing or unemployment? These are more complex questions than they are often made to appear, and none of them is new. These and all the other questions involved in our excursions into the relationship between education and the social condition are dictated by the continuing confusions and conflicts of our own experience and of the historical record. That experience and that record indicate choices, successes, failures – and controversy around them and their meanings. Over-arching explanations of the kind we discussed in terms of American educational history often prove short-lived and unhelpful, unless the organizing concepts are seen to be interrelated and subject to historical change. The single-minded pursuit of explanations in the failure of British social democracy may ultimately prove as crude as American attempts to place the burden of explanation on the corporate state or on professionalization or on bureaucracy.

This is not to deny that socio-political explanations need to be sought. It is not to deny the continuing relevance to the discussion of, for example, social class and the State, and it is not to remove such a discussion from its central position. It is merely a warning that the re-examination needed is endangered by unilinear history, by ritualistic political judgements, by single-minded, closed-minded, gestures made through established jargons and vocabularies. The dangers of moving from strong theory to historical explanations and policy formulation are most obvious in a period when other factors have produced a decline in confidence in political and social policy and planning. The main danger in this connection lies in what is claimed as 'knowledge' of underlying structures and inevitable historical processes. This 'knowledge', with its *assumed* historical processes, its untested explanations and correlations, its denial of choice and experience and difference and the possibility of decision and change, prevents questions and disarms the actor. Contemporary structuralist theory, functionalist theory (including the Marxist kind), the critical theories of many of the movements of the left, make it difficult to know what is *not* a palliative, what does not merely add another small piece to the controlling logic of capitalist society and its deep structures. The exclusion of reform, experience and motive from the discussion of social and political 'realities' enfeebles or frustrates action. The constant reference back to exploitation or social control is helpful in the analysis only if these and other such organizing explanations are conceived as historical variables. It is as meaningless to generalize about schools as in themselves instruments of repression as it is to generalize about knowledge as in itself a source of power.

The period since the Second World War has produced, internationally, an enormous range of styles of educational and social analysis. The need now is to rescue from that multiplicity of efforts to understand and to change at least a strong awareness of how deeply education was established as a social process in those decades. To that awareness needs to be linked a sense of the forces seeking to destroy it – and those forces include the search for theoretical purity, the reassertion of a conservative ideology of pure education, and an uncritical acceptance of evidence of failure. With all of these needs to be associated a strong historical reappraisal of experience – one which can debate and interrelate with theory and ideology and evidences. If it is a radical reappraisal that is needed, it has to be remembered that radicalism is not exclusive to Trafalgar Square or people who wear badges. It may involve identification with a movement, and support for a programme or policy. It may involve a choice of contemporary national and international symbols and realities and causes with which to be associated, but the exclusiveness of those identifications often courts the danger of cutting off involvement with understandings at other levels. There are choices to be made in the infant classroom, in the technical college, in the academic board and senate, in the staffroom, in the construction of the time-table, in the day-to-day experiences involving pupils and teachers and parents and administrators and all the elements that constitute the current condition of the society. It is a time to resist forces, from whatever direction, which weaken a sense of the social processes at work in those situations, and the choices that need to be made there, for the whole system and its parts and processes. It is a time, in reviewing recent experiences, to start the fresh questioning from the most important and most confident educational achievement of recent decades – the understanding that education cannot be discussed apart from its relationship with, its position in, the social condition. 'We have been thinking of education throughout,' said Clarke in *Education and Social Change*, 'as a process conducted and conditioned by social forces, all of which have a history, and aiming at the further development of the potentialities of worthy living in a community.'[3] Whatever reservations and adaptations we may wish to underline four decades later, the field delineated by Clarke and under such fundamental threat at the beginning of the 1980s, is one that must not be abandoned.

References

CHAPTER I   THE SOCIAL CONDITION: A FRAMEWORK FOR
DISCUSSION

1 Quoted in Frank W. Mitchell, *Sir Fred Clarke: master-teacher 1880–1952* (London, 1967), p. 45n.
2 ibid., pp. 165–6.
3 ibid., p. 106.
4 Sir Fred Clarke, *Education and Social Change: an English interpretation* (London, 1940), p. 44.
5 ibid., p. 31.
6 ibid., pp. 49–50.
7 ibid., pp. 45–6.
8 ibid., p. 43.
9 ibid., pp. 6–9.
10 ibid., p. 66.
11 W. F. Connell, *The Educational Thought and Influence of Matthew Arnold*, Introduction by Sir Fred Clarke (London, 1950), p. xiii.
12 ibid., p. ix.
13 ibid., p. xiii.
14 Mitchell, op. cit., pp. 166–7.

CHAPTER 2   EDUCATION AND SOCIAL POLICY

1 R. H. Tawney, *The Attack and Other Papers* (London, 1953), pp. 32–4.
2 R. H. Tawney, *Education: the task before us* (London, 1943), p. 13.
3 Sections 17 and 19, Education Act, 1918, in K. E. T. Wilkinson, *A Guide to the Education Act 1918* (London, 1920), pp. 83–7.
4 Bolton King, *Schools of To-Day: present problems in English education* (London, 1929), p. 5.

5 Department of Education and Science, *The School Health Service 1908–1974* (London, 1975), p. 35.
6 Susan Isaacs, *The Children We Teach* (London, 1932), p. 172.
7 Ministry of Education, *Report of the Committee on Maladjusted Children* (London, 1955) p. 12.
8 ibid., p. 9. See, for example, H. Crichton Miller, 'The Psychological Understanding of the Adolescent', in T. F. Coade (ed.), *Harrow Lectures on Education* (Cambridge, 1931), and his foreword to The Home and School Council of Great Britain, *Advances in Understanding the Child* (London, 1935).
9 Board of Education, *The Education of the Adolescent* (London, 1926), pp. xix, 41.
10 Grace Paton, *The Child and the Nation* (London, 1915), p. 84.
11 R. H. Tawney, *Secondary Education for All: a policy for Labour* (London, 1922), p. 16.
12 Ministry of Reconstruction, Adult Education Committee, *Final Report* (London, 1919), pp. 5, 168.
13 Board of Education, Adult Education Committee, *Adult Education and the Local Education Authority* (London, 1933), p. 18.
14 Board of Education, *An Experiment in Rural Reorganisation* (London, 1933), p. 25. See also, for example, Board of Education, Adult Education Committee, *Pioneer Work and Other Developments in Adult Education* (London, 1927), ch. VII, 'Special Problems of the Countryside'; Board of Education, *The New Prospect in Education* (London, 1928), sections 53–9, 'The Rural Area'; Board of Education, *Adult Education and the Local Education Authority*, para. 262, 'The Rural Problem'.
15 M. Alderton Pink, *Procrustes: or the future of English education* (London, n.d.), pp. 10–16; J. H. Garrett, *Mass Education in England* (London, 1928), pp. 27–32.
16 Workers' Educational Association, *The Public Schools* (London, 1943), p. 18.
17 Nuffield College, *The Open Door in Secondary Education* (London, 1943), p. 17.
18 Sir Richard Livingstone, *The Future in Education* (Cambridge, 1944), p. 1.
19 Board of Education, *Report of the Committee Appointed by the President of the Board of Education to Consider the Supply and Training of Teachers and Youth Leaders* (London, 1944), p. 31.
20 Sir William Beveridge, *Social Insurance and Allied Services* (London, 1942), pp. 6, 170.
21 Staples' 'Reconstruction' Digests, III, *The Spens Report and After* (London, 1943), p. 27.
22 Women's Group on Public Welfare, *Our Towns: a close-up* (London, 1943), pp. xvii–xviii.
23 Susan Isaacs (ed.), *The Cambridge Evacuation Survey: a wartime study in social welfare and education* (London, 1941), p. 180.
24 Women's Group, op. cit. p. 105.

25 *Report of the Commissioner of Education for the Year Ended June 30, 1912*, (Washington, D.C., 1913), vol. I, p. 491.
26 Sir Richard Livingstone, *Education for a World Adrift* (Cambridge, 1944), p. 9.
27 Education Act, 1944, section 7.
28 Shena D. Simon, *The Education Act 1944: provisions and possibilities* (London, 1945), p. 3.
29 Lord Butler, *The Art of the Possible* (London, 1971: edition of 1973), p. 127.
30 Beveridge, op. cit., p. 6.
31 National Insurance Act, 1946, section 1 (1).
32 National Health Service Act, 1946, section 1 (1).
33 Ruth Glass (ed.), *The Social Background of a Plan: a study of Middlesbrough* (London, 1948), p. 83.
34 London County Council, *London School Plan* (London, 1947), p. 7.
35 National Union of Women Teachers, *The Education Act 1944: promise and fulfilment* (London, 1948), p. 4.
36 Ministry of Education, *The New Secondary Education* (London, 1947), p. 29.
37 H. C. Dent, *Secondary Modern Schools: an interim report* (London, 1958), p. 201. See also Harold Loukes, *Secondary Modern* (London, 1956).
38 John Newsom, *The Child at School* (Harmondsworth, 1950), pp. 83–4.
39 *The Times Educational Supplement*, 23 October 1964, p. 707.
40 Department of Education and Science, *Circular 10/65*, p. 1.
41 J. E. Floud (ed.), A. H. Halsey and F. M. Martin, *Social Class and Educational Opportunity* (London, 1956); J. W. B. Douglas, *The Home and the School* (London, 1964). For extracts from and a discussion of these and other contributions to this literature, see Harold Silver (ed.), *Equal Opportunity in Education* (London, 1973).
42 Ministry of Education, *Half Our Future* (London, 1963), p. 6; Ministry of Education, *Higher Education*, vol. I, p. 53.
43 Department of Education and Science, *Children and Their Primary Schools* (London, 1967), pp. 50, 55.
44 Department of Education and Science and the Scottish Education Department, *Higher Education into the 1990s: a discussion document* (London, 1978), p. 9.
45 Angus Maude, 'The Egalitarian Threat', *Fight for Education (Black Paper One)* (London, 1969), p. 7.
46 Gordon Bowker, *Education of Coloured Immigrants* (London, 1968), p. 1.
47 Department of Education and Science, *Education in Schools: a consultative document* (London, 1977), p. 2.
48 ibid., p. 11.
49 Fabian Society, *Planning for Education in 1980* (London, 1970), p. 1.
50 ibid.
51 John Alderson addressing the British Association, reported in the Stoke on Trent *Evening Sentinel*, 6 September 1978.

CHAPTER 3   EQUALITY OF EDUCATIONAL OPPORTUNITY:
THE MAP OF UNCERTAINTY

1 DES, *Children and Their Primary Schools*, ch. 5 and p. 57.
2 Basil Bernstein, 'Education Cannot Compensate for Society', *New Society*, 26 February 1970.
3 Christopher Jencks *et al.*, *Inequality: a reassessment of the effect of family and schooling in America* (New York, 1972: edition of 1973), p. 261.
4 Department of Education and Science, *Educational Priority*, vol. 3 (ed. Jack Barnes), *Curriculum Innovation in London's EPAs* (London, 1975), pp. 244, 248.
5 A. H. Halsey, 'Whatever Happened to Positive Discrimination?', *Times Educational Supplement*, 21 January 1977, p. 23.
6 Harry Rée, 'School Report: 1. The Death of Dad', BBC Radio 4, September 4, 1975 ('There's been a great decrease in automatic, unthinking acceptance of authority. I've heard it called the Death of Dad. . . . In fact, if, in Genesis, the world began with the fall of man, it took a new turn in the 20th century with the Fall of Father.') See, similarly, the chapter on 'The Changing Parent: the substitution of influence for power' in Frank Musgrove, *The Family, Education and Society* (London, 1966).
7 Barry J. Hake, 'Some Problems of Educational and Social Equality Strategies', *Paedagogica Europaea*, vol. 9 (1974) (*Compensatory Education*), p. 10. See also Michael Flude, 'Sociological Accounts of Differential Educational Attainment', in Michael Flude and John Ahier (eds), *Educability, Schools and Ideology* (London, 1974), p. 15; Charles I. Norris, Introduction, in Nelson F. Ashline *et al.* (eds), *Education, Inequality, and National Policy* (Lexington, Mass., 1976), p. xvii.
8 A. H. Halsey, 'Would Chance Be a Fine Thing?', *The Guardian*, 11 February 1975, p. 20. See also Stuart Maclure, 'High Jencks at OECD', *Times Educational Supplement*, 17 January 1975; Paul Moorman, 'The Great Obstacle to Equal Opportunity Is Inherited Wealth', *Times Higher Education Supplement*, 24 January 1975, p. 9.
9 Quoted by Norris in Ashline, op. cit., p. xvii.
10 See the discussion in Silver, op. cit., p. xxvii.
11 Colin Greer, *The Great School Legend: a revisionist interpretation of American Public Education* (New York, 1972), pp. 3, 152.
12 Carl Bereiter, 'IQ Differences and Social Policy', in Ashline, op. cit., p. 146.
13 Arthur R. Jensen, *Genetics and Education* (London, 1972), p. 65. See also Preface to Jensen's *Educational Differences* (London, 1973), and 'Inequality of Schooling', in Jensen, *Educability and Group Differences* (London, 1973).
14 Melvin Tumin, quoted by Edmund W. Gordon, 'Toward Defining Equality of Educational Opportunity', in Frederick Mosteller and Daniel P. Moynihan (eds), *On Equality of Educational Opportunity* (New York, 1972), p. 427.

15 Geoffrey Bantock, 'An Alternative Curriculum', in C. B. Cox and Rhodes Boyson (eds), *Black Paper 1977* (London, 1977), p. 79.
16 Mary Warnock, *Schools of Thought* (London, 1977), especially pp. 31–47.
17 See, for example, James A. Coleman, 'The Concept of Equality of Educational Opportunity', in Donald M. Levine and Mary Jo Bane (eds), *The 'Inequality' Controversy: schooling and distributive justice* (New York, 1975).
18 Daniel Bell, *The Coming of Post-Industrial Society* (New York, 1973: edition of 1976), p. 428.
19 Walter Feinberg, *Reason and Rhetoric: the intellectual foundations of 20th century liberal educational policy* (New York, 1975), p. 265.
20 Torsten Husén, 'The Equality-Meritocracy Dilemma in Education', in Ashline, op. cit., particularly pp. 45–57.
21 A. H. Halsey, 'Towards a More Noble Alternative', *The Guardian*, 27 May 1975, p. 20.
22 Remi Clignet, *Liberty and Equality in the Educational Process: a comparative sociology of education* (New York, 1974), p. 6.
23 Maurice Chazan et al., *Just Before School* (Oxford, 1971), pp. 5–6.
24 William Labov, 'The Logic of Non-Standard English', in Nell Keddie (ed.), *Tinker, Tailor . . . the myth of cultural deprivation* (Harmondsworth, 1973), p. 55.
25 Warnock, op. cit., p. 58.
26 See Marvin Lazerson, *Origins of the Urban School: public education in Massachusetts, 1870–1915* (Cambridge, Mass., 1971), pp. x–xi and chs. 3–6.
27 See Wilbur B. Brookover et al., 'Quality of Educational Attainment, Standardized Testing, Assessment, and Accountability', in C. Wayne Gordon (ed.), *Uses of the Sociology of Education. The seventy-third yearbook of the National Society for the Study of Education* (Chicago, 1974), pp. 162, 168, 180–1.
28 Dan Finn et al., 'Social Democracy, Education and the Crisis', in *Working Papers in Cultural Studies 10: On Ideology* (Birmingham, 1977), p. 196.
29 Paul E. Willis, *Learning to Labour: how working class kids get working class jobs* (London, 1977), p. 178.
30 An excellent discussion of Rawls's importance for this educational debate is Tyll van Geel, 'John Rawls and Educational Policy', in Samuel K. Gove and Frederick M. Wirt (eds), *Political Science and School Politics* (Lexington, Mass., 1976).
31 Wilma S. Longstreet elaborates on this 'trivialization' charge in *Beyond Jencks: the myth of equal schooling* (Washington, D.C., 1973), especially pp. 3–7. A similar argument is conducted by Christopher Lasch, 'Inequality and Education', in Levine and Bane, op. cit. Harold Entwistle raises the trivialization issue in *Class, Culture and Education* (London, 1978), p. 24.
32 See Jensen, *Genetics and Education*, p. 66; *Educational Differences*, p. 381.

33 Robert L. Bailey and Anne L. Hafner, *Minority Admissions* (Lexington, Mass., 1978), p. 40.
34 Samuel Bowles and Herbert Gintis, *Schooling in Capitalist America: educational reform and the contradictions of economic life* (London, 1976), especially pp. 9, 103, 130.
35 Longstreet, op. cit., p. 1.
36 There is a discussion of this aspect of American experience in Robert L. Church and Michael W. Sedlak, *Education in the United States: an interpretive history* (New York, 1976), p. 437.
37 Longstreet, op. cit., p. 7.
38 Michael Rutter and Nicola Madge, *Cycles of Disadvantage: a review of research* (London, 1976), ch. 4.
39 Michael Rutter et al., *Fifteen Thousand Hours: secondary schools and the effects on children* (London, 1979), pp. 177–80.
40 Lasch, op. cit., p. 49.
41 Jencks, op. cit., p. 263.
42 Van Geel, op. cit., p. 124.
43 Peter R. Moock, 'Education and the Transfer of Inequality from Generation to Generation', *Teachers College Record*, vol. 79, no. 4 (1978), p. 748.
44 Barnes, op. cit., p. 274.
45 Robert Thornbury, *The Changing Urban School* (London, 1978), p. 201.

CHAPTER 4   SCHOOLS, SOCIAL CHANGE AND STANDARDS

1 See Richard Johnson, 'Edward Thompson, Eugene Genovese, and Socialist-Humanist History', *History Workshop*, no. 6 (1978); E. P. Thompson, 'The Poverty of Theory: or an orrery of errors', in *The Poverty of Theory* (London, 1978).
2 David F. Noble, *America by Design: science, technology, and the rise of corporate capitalism* (New York, 1977).
3 Malcolm Skilbeck, 'The Flight from Education', *Education News* (Australia), vol. 15, no. 10 (1976), p. 31.
4 C. B. Cox and Rhodes Boyson, 'Letter to MPs and Parents', *Black Paper 1975* (London, 1975), p. 5.
5 'Black Paper Basics', in ibid., p. 1.
6 G. H. Bantock, 'Progressivism and the Content of Education', in ibid., p. 18.
7 ibid., p. 20.
8 The notion of equality is attacked in several of the articles in *Black Paper 1975* (particularly by Eysenck), and support for the concept of equality of opportunity is implied in the 'Black Paper Basics' quoted above, unlike, for example, Angus Maude's attack on the concept in 'The Egalitarian Threat', in the first *Black Paper, Fight for Education*, p. 7.
9 'Black Paper Basics', in *Black Paper 1975*, p. 1.
10 Derwent Coleridge, *The Teachers of the People* (London, 1862), pp. 43–4, 71–3.

11 *Report of the Commissioners Appointed to Inquire into the State of Popular Education in England*, vol. I (London, 1861), pp. 155–7, 234–5.

12 Lyon Playfair, 'Address on Education', *Transactions of the National Association for the Promotion of Social Science, 1870* (London, 1871), pp. 42–3.

13 John Morley, *The Struggle for National Education* (London, 1873), pp. 18, 26–7.

14 Coleridge, op. cit., pp. 15, 43–4.

15 *The State of Popular Education in England*, p. 157.

16 C. B. Cox, 'Examinations: Seven Questions', *Black Paper 1975* (London, 1975), p. 34.

17 Reba N. Soffer, *Ethics and Society in England: the revolution in the social sciences 1870–1914* (Berkeley, Calif., 1978), p. 138.

18 Letter in *The Times Educational Supplement*, 15 January 1965, p. 108.

19 H. G. Rickover, *American Education – A National Failure: the problem of our schools and what we can learn from England* (New York, 1963).

20 George Weber, 'Reading Instruction in America', *Black Paper 1975* (London, 1975), p. 14.

21 C. B. Cox and A. E. Dyson, 'Letter to Members of Parliament', *Black Paper Two* (London, 1969), p. 3.

22 Department of Education and Science, *Children and Their Primary Schools* (London, 1967), p. 201.

23 Department of Education and Science, *A Language for Life: report of the Committee of Inquiry . . . under the Chairmanship of Sir Alan Bullock* (London, 1975), p. 10. ·

24 Ray Hopkins, 'Whose Standards?', *The Times Educational Supplement*, 31 December 1976, p. 9.

25 Maude, op. cit., p. 8.

26 Cox and Dyson, 'Letter to Members of Parliament'. *Black Paper Two*, p. 14.

27 Richard Lynn, 'Comprehensives and Equality', *Black Paper Two*, p. 27.

28 S. H. Froome, 'The Mystique of Modern Maths', *Black Paper Two*, p. 108.

29 E. J. R. Eaglesham, *The Foundations of Twentieth-Century Education in England* (London, 1967), ch. 4, 'Education for Followership'.

30 James Callaghan, 18 October 1976, reprinted in *The Times Educational Supplement*, 22 October 1976, pp. 1, 72.

31 Neville Bennett and Noel Entwistle, 'Informal or Formal: a reply', *The Times Educational Supplement*, 21 May 1976, p. 2.

32 *Children and their Primary Schools*, p. 210.

33 Shirley Williams, at the North of England conference, reprinted in *The Times Educational Supplement*, 14 January 1977, p. 8.

CHAPTER 5   PUBLIC CONTROL, CHOICE AND THE STATE

1 National Commission on the Reform of Secondary Education, *The Reform of Secondary Education* (New York, 1973), p. 16.

2 David Tyack, 'A Choice of Education?', *New Society*, 7 April 1977.

3 Study Commission on Undergraduate Education and the Education of Teachers, *Teacher Education in the United States: the responsibility gap* (Lincoln, Neb., 1976), pp. xi-xii, 6, 12.

4 Jennings L. Wagoner jun., 'Historical Revisionism, Educational Theory, and an American *Paideia*', *History of Education Quarterly*, vol. 18, no. 2 (1978), p. 201.

5 Joan Simon, 'The History of Education in *Past and Present*', *Oxford Review of Education*, vol. 3, no. 1 (1977), p. 72.

6 Bernard Bailyn, *Education and the Forming of American Society* (Chapel Hill, N.C., 1970).

7 Lawrence A. Cremin, *The Wonderful World of Ellwood Patterson Cubberley*, (New York, 1965), p. 48.

8 Lawrence A. Cremin, *Public Education* (New York, 1976), p. 30.

9 Simon, op. cit., pp. 72-4.

10 For Massachusetts see Michael B. Katz, *The Irony of Early School Reform* (Cambridge, Mass., 1968); Marvin Lazerson, *Origins of the Urban School: public education in Massachusetts, 1870–1915* (Cambridge, Mass., 1971); Stanley K. Schultz, *The Culture Factory* (New York, 1973). For New York City see Carl F. Kaestle, *The Evolution of an Urban School System* (Cambridge, Mass., 1973); Diane Ravitch, *The Great School Wars* (New York, 1974). For St Louis see Selwyn Troen, *The Public and the Schools* (Columbia, Mo., 1975). For Chicago, see David Hogan, 'Education and the Making of the Chicago Working Class, 1880–1930', *History of Education Quarterly*, vol. 18, no. 3 (1978), prefiguring a forthcoming book on Chicago.

11 In addition to the works cited in note 10, see also David B. Tyack, *The One Best System: a history of American urban education* (Cambridge, Mass., 1974).

12 This is one of the themes of Tyack's *The One Best System* and Michael B. Katz, *Class, Bureaucracy, and Schools* (New York, 1971).

13 Schultz, *The Culture Factory*, p. 305.

14 David B. Tyack, 'The Perils of Pluralism: the background of the Pierce case', *The American Historical Review*, vol. 74, no. 1 (1968); Lloyd P. Jorgenson, 'The Oregon School Law of 1922: passage and sequel', *Catholic Historical Review*, vol. 54, no. 3 (1968).

15 John W. Meyer, *et al.*, 'Education as Nation-Building in America: enrolment and bureaucratization in the American states, 1870–1930', research report, Boys Town Centre for the Study of Youth Development, Stanford University, n.d.

16 David B. Tyack, 'The Spread of Public Schooling in Victorian America', *History of Education*, vol. 7, no. 3 (1978).

17 Michael B. Katz, *Class, Bureaucracy, and Schools* (edition of 1975), p. 149.

18 David B. Tyack and Michael Berkowitz, 'The Man Nobody Liked: toward a social history of the truant officer, 1840–1940', *American Quarterly*, vol. 29, no. 1 (1977); David B. Tyack, 'Pilgrim's Progress: toward a

social history of the school superintendency, 1860–1960', *History of Education Quarterly*, vol. 16, no. 3 (1976).

19 Donald R. Warren, *To Enforce Education: a history of the founding years of the United States Office of Education* (Detroit, Mich., 1974).

20 Clarence J. Karier, 'Testing for Order and Control in the Corporate Liberal State', in Clarence J. Karier, Paul C. Violas and Joel Spring, *Roots of Crisis* (Chicago, Ill., 1973); Paul D. Chapman, 'Schools as Sorters: testing and tracking in California, 1910–1925', paper presented to the American Educational Research Association, San Francisco, April 1979.

21 David B. Tyack, 'Ways of Seeing: an essay on the history of compulsory schooling', *Harvard Educational Review*, vol. 46, no. 3 (1976).

22 David J. Rothman, *The Discovery of the Asylum* (Boston, Mass., 1971).

23 Steven L. Schlossman, *Love and the American Delinquent* (Chicago, Ill., 1977); Steven L. Schlossman, 'End of Innocence: science and the transformation of progressive juvenile justice, 1899–1917', *History of Education*, vol. 7, no. 3 (1978); Allan Stanley Horlick, *Country Boys and Merchant Princes: the social control of young men in New York* (Lewisburg Pa., 1975); Barbara Brenzel, 'Lancaster Industrial School for Girls', *Feminist Studies*, March 1975; Barbara Brenzel, 'The Girls at Lancaster', Harvard University Ph D thesis, 1978.

24 Michael B. Katz, 'Origins of the Institutional State', *Marxist Perspectives*, vol. 1, no. 4 (1978).

25 Christopher Lasch, 'Origins of the Asylum', in *The World of Nations: reflections on American history, politics and culture* (New York, 1962).

26 Frederick Rudolph, *Curriculum: a history of the American undergraduate course of study since 1636* (San Francisco, Calif., 1977).

27 Mary O. Furner, *Advocacy and Objectivity: a crisis in the professionalization of American social science 1865–1905* (Lexington, K., 1975); Thomas L. Haskell, *The Emergence of Professional Social Science* (Urbana, Ill., 1977).

28 See, for example, David Riesman, *Constraint and Variety in American Education* (Lincoln, Neb., 1956); Christopher Jencks and David Riesman, *The Academic Revolution* (New York, 1968); Gerald Grant and David Riesman, *The Perpetual Dream: reform and experiment in the American college* (Chieago, Ill., 1978); Martin Trow, 'The Public and Private Lives of Higher Education', *Daedalus*, vol. 2 (1975); Martin Trow, 'Aspects of Diversity in American Higher Education', in Herbert Gans (ed.), *Essays in Honour of David Riesman* (Philadelphia, Pa., 1979).

29 Haskell, op. cit., pp. 13–17.

30 Furner, op. cit., especially ch. 2.

31 Carol S. Gruber, *Mars and Minerva: World War I and the uses of the higher learning in America* (Baton Rouge, L., 1975).

32 Burton J. Bledstein, *The Culture of Professionalism: the middle class and the development of higher education in America* (New York, 1976), especially chs. 2 and 3 (for 'vertical vision' see p. 111).

33 See for example, Lawrence A. Cremin, 'Family–community Linkages in American Education: some comments on the recent historiography',

Teachers College Record, vol. 79, no. 4 (1978); Anthony M. Platt, *The Child Savers: the invention of delinquency* (Chicago, Ill., 1969); Steven L. Schlossman, 'Before Home Start: notes towards a history of parent education in America, 1897–1929', *Harvard Educational Review*, vol. 46, no. 3 (1976); Selwyn K. Troen, 'The Discovery of the Adolescent by American Educational Reformers, 1900–1920: an economic perspective', in Lawrence Stone (ed.), *Schooling and Society* (Baltimore, Md., 1976); Paula Fass, *The Damned and the Beautiful: American youth in the 1920s* (New York, 1977); Joseph Kett, *Rites of Passage: adolescence in America 1790 to the present* (New York, 1977).

34 Christopher Lasch, *Haven in a Heartless World: the family besieged* (New York, 1977: edition of 1979), pp. xx–xxi, 16, 39. See also Christopher Lasch, *The Culture of Narcissism* (New York, 1978), and for a critical discussion of Lasch's thesis and other recent work on the family, Joseph Featherstone, 'Family Matters', *Harvard Educational Review*, vol. 49, no. 1 (1979).

35 Paul C. Violas, *The Training of the Urban Working Class* (Chicago, Ill., 1978), p. 216; Joel Spring, 'Education as a Form of Social Control', in Karier, op. cit., p. 30; Donald Spivey, *Schooling for the New Slavery: black industrial education, 1868–1915* (Westport, Conn., 1978), p. 17; Marvin Lazerson, 'Social Reform and Early-Childhood Education: some historical perspectives', *Urban Education*, vol. 5, no. 1 (1970), p. 93; Marvin Lazerson, 'Urban Reform and the Schools: kindergartens in Massachusetts, 1870–1915', *History of Education Quarterly*, vol. 11, no. 2 (1971), p. 126.

36 Barry Franklin, 'Education for Social Control', *History of Education Quarterly*, vol. 14, no. 1 (1974), p. 132.

37 Walter Feinberg, *Reason and Rhetoric: the intellectual foundations of 20th century Liberal educational policy* (New York, 1975), pp. 255, 258.

38 Christopher Lasch, *The New Radicalism in America (1889–1963): the intellectual as a social type* (New York, 1965) – see especially essays on Addams and on 'Politics as social control'; J. O. C. Phillips, 'The Education of Jane Addams', *History of Education Quarterly*, vol. 14, no. 1 (1974), p. 60; Paul C. Violas, 'Jane Addams and the New Liberalism', in Karier, op. cit.

39 Lawrence M. Friedman, 'The Social and Political Context of the War on Poverty: an overview', in Robert H. Haveman (ed.), *A Decade of Federal Antipoverty Programs* (New York, 1977), p. 43.

40 Katz, op. cit., p. 173.

41 Violas, *The Training of the Urban Working Class*, passim, for the use of a vocabulary of 'control', 'manipulation' and 'function' as little examined as the vocabulary of the historians attacked by the revisionist historians.

42 Samuel Bowles and Herbert Gintis, *Schooling in Capitalist America: educational reform and the contradictions of economic life* (London, 1976), p. 25.

43 David K. Cohen and Bella H. Rosenberg, 'Functions and Fantasies:

understanding schools in capitalist America', *History of Education Quarterly*, vol. 17, no 2 (1977), pp. 120, 123; Mark Stern in ibid., pp. 155–7.
44 Allan Stanley Horlick, 'The Rewriting of American Educational History', *New York University Education Quarterly*, vol. 5, no. 4 (1974), p. 28.
45 Lasch, *Haven in a Heartless World*, p. xix.
46 Sir Fred Clarke, *Education and Social Change: an English interpretation* (London, 1940), pp. 40–1.
47 Charles Webster, 'Changing Perspectives in the History of Education', *Oxford Review of Education*, vol. 2, no. 3 (1976), p. 203.

CHAPTER 6   ACCOUNTABILITY AND AUTHORITY

1 Mary Warnock, 'Accountability or Responsibility – or Both?', *Independent Broadcasting*, November 1974, pp. 2–3.
2 There is a brief but interesting chapter on 'The Historical and Contemporary Foundations of Accountability' in Don T. Martin, George E. Overholt and Wayne J. Urban, *Accountability in American Education: a critique* (Princeton, N.J., 1976).
3 See, for example, Stayner F. Brighton and Cecil J. Hannan, *Merit Pay Programs for Teachers: a handbook* (San Francisco, Calif., 1962).
4 Martin, *et al.*, op. cit., p. 31.
5 A crucial text for this movement and analysis is W. Robert Houston and Robert B. Howsam (eds), *Competency-Based Education* (Chicago, Ill., 1972). The relationship between the competency-based movement and public demands for accountability is treated at many points in Robert T. Utz and Leo D. Leonard (eds), *The Foundations of Competency Based Education* (Dubuque, Ia., 1975). For a survey of the state of developments in and controversy about an important aspect of this movement – 'minimum competency testing' – see *Phi Delta Kappan*, vol. 59, no. 9 (1978).
6 Richard W. Burns, 'The Central Notion: explicit objectives', in Houston and Howsam, op. cit., p. 24.
7 Alfred P. Wilson and Tony L. Stansbury, 'Contemporary Trends and Competency Based Education', in Utz and Leonard, op. cit. p. 137.
8 Edward M. Gramlich and Patricia P. Koshel, *Educational Performance Contracting: the evaluation of an experiment* (Washington, D.C., 1975), p. 76. For a bibliography of this movement see G. R. Hall *et al.*, *A Guide to Educational Performance Contracting* (Santa Monica, Calif., 1972).
9 See Wilbur B. Brookover, 'Quality of Educational Attainment, Standardized Testing, Assessment, and Accountability', in C. Wayne Gordon (ed.), *Uses of the Sociology of Education. The seventy-third yearbook of the National Society for the Study of Education* (Chicago, Ill., 1974), pp. 161, 183–5.
10 *The Second Newman Report: national policy and higher education* (Cambridge, Mass., 1973), p. xii.
11 ibid., p. xxiii.

12 Marjorie Rapp, *Data Requirements for Accountability: prepared for the Los Angeles Unified School District* (Santa Monica, Calif., 1971), p. 2.
13 ibid.
14 Martin Trow, 'The Public and Private Lives of Higher Education', *Daedalus*, vol. 2 (1975), p. 115.
15 Earl F. Cheit, *The Useful Arts and the Liberal Tradition* (New York, 1975), p. 12.
16 See for example, Clarence J. Karier, Paul C. Violas and Joel Spring *Roots of Crisis* (Chicago, Ill., 1973); Joel H. Spring, *Education and the Rise of the Corporate State* (Boston, Mass., 1972).
17 See Samuel Bowles and Herbert Gintis, *Schooling in Capitalist America: educational reform and the contradiction of economic life* (London, 1976).
18 Brookover, op. cit., p. 189.
19 'Instructions to Inspectors of Schools', *Minutes of the Committee of Council on Education . . . 1840–41* (London, 1841), pp. 1–2.
20 *Minutes . . . 1844*, vol. 1 (London, 1845), p. 122.
21 *Copy of Minutes and Regulations of the Privy Council on Education, Reduced into the Form of a Code . . . 1860*, p. 6.
22 Robert J. Montgomery, *Examinations: an account of their evolution as administrative devices in England* (London, 1965), p. 242.
23 John Roach, *Public Examinations in England 1859–1900* (Cambridge, 1971), pp. 279–81, 285.
24 Frederick Rudolph, *Curriculum: a history of the American undergraduate course of study since 1636* (San Francisco, Calif., 1977), p. 146.
25 Sir Lewis Amherst Selby-Bigge, *The Board of Education* (London, 1927: edition of 1934), p. 129.
26 Sir G. W. Kekewich, *The Education Department and After* (London, 1920), p. 57.
27 Quoted in Henry Craik, *The State in Its Relation to Education* (London, 1884: edition of 1896), p. 74.
28 See Matthew Arnold's general reports for 1863, 1867 and 1869 in Sir Francis Sandford (ed.), *Reports on Elementary Schools 1852–1882 by Matthew Arnold* (London, 1889).
29 See Gillian Sutherland, *Policy-Making in Elementary Education 1870–1895* (London, 1973), pp. 71–2, for the views of Sir Joshua Fitch.
30 E. L. Edmonds, *The School Inspector* (London, 1962), p. 81.
31 Selby-Bigge, op. cit., pp. 48–9.
32 Thiselton Mark, *Modern Views on Education* (London, 1914), p. 56.
33 B. J. Johnson, 'The Development of English Education, 1856–1882, with Special Reference to the Work of Robert Lowe, Viscount Sherbrooke', Durham University M Ed. thesis, 1956, p. 175. Gillian Sutherland, op. cit., p. 192, claims that criticism of the Code was expressed by a vociferous minority.
34 John Hurt, *Evolution in Education* (London, 1971), p. 202.
35 Kekewich, op. cit., p. 56.
36 Mark, op. cit., p. 56.

37 Edmonds, op. cit., pp. 93–4.
38 Peter Gordon, *The Victorian School Manager* (London, 1974), pp. 150–2.
39 See P. H. J. H. Gosden and P. R. Sharp, *The Development of an Educational Service: the West Riding 1889–1974* (Oxford, 1978), pp. 7–9, 78, for a discussion of early local inspection of elementary and grammar schools.
40 *Report of the Commissioners Appointed to Inquire into the State of Popular Education in England*, vol. I, pp. 7–8.
41 Maurice Kogan and Tim Packard, *Advisory Councils and Committees in Education* (London, 1974), pp. 1–7.
42 Committee on Technical College Resources, *Report on the Size of Classes and Approval of Further Education Courses* (London, 1966), p. 5.
43 *Education in Schools*, pp. 41–2.
44 Rudolph, op. cit., p. 161.
45 Department of Education and Science, *A New Partnership for Our Schools* (London, 1977), 55–6.
46 The terms of reference are contained in various publications of the Department of Education and Science dealing with the Assessment of Performance Unit. For an early discussion of the APU and its context see Joanna Mack, 'Assessing Schools', *New Society*, 25 November 1976, pp. 401–3.
47 Department of Education and Science, op. cit., p. 42.
48 *The Second Newman Report*, p. 83.
49 For a discussion on these dangers see John Elliott, 'Preparing Teachers for Classroom Accountability', *Education for Teaching*, no. 100 (1976).
50 Martin Trow, 'Aspects of Diversity in American Higher Education', in Herbert Gans (ed.), *Essays in Honour of David Riesman* (Philadelphia, Pa., 1979).

CHAPTER 7   KNOWLEDGE AS POWER

1 T. S. Eliot, *Notes Towards the Definition of Culture* (London, 1948), p. 108.
2 Sheldon Rothblatt, *Tradition and Change in English Liberal Education: an essay in history and culture* (London, 1976), p. 75.
3 G. H. Bantock, *Education in an Industrial Society* (London, 1963), pp. 203–17.
4 Richard Lynn, 'Comprehensives and Equality', *Black Paper Two*, p. 31.
5 G. H. Bantock, 'Discovery Methods', in ibid., pp. 110–18: Rhodes Boyson, 'The Essential Conditions for the Success of a Comprehensive School', in ibid., p. 62.
6 Introduction to Richard Brown (ed.), *Knowledge, Education, and Cultural Change: papers in the sociology of education* (London, 1973), p. 3.
7 Introduction to Michael F. D. Young, *Knowledge and Control: new directions for the sociology of education* (London, 1971), pp. 2–3, 8–9.
8 Sir Fred Clarke, *Education and Social Change: an English interpretation* (London, 1940), p. 22.

9 Sheldon Rothblatt, *The Revolution of the Dons: Cambridge and society in Victorian England* (London, 1968), p. 135.
10 Robert Owen, 'Report to the County of Lanark', in *A Supplementary Appendix to the First Volume of the Life of Robert Owen* (London, 1858), vol. I, pp. 288–94.
11 *Poor Man's Guardian*, 24 June, 1831, pp. 1–2 (unnumbered).
12 *Life and Struggles of William Lovett in his Pursuit of Bread, Knowledge, and Freedom* (London, 1876: edition of 1920) vol. I, pp. 94–5, 99, 139, 142.
13 William Lovett, *Social and Political Morality* (London, 1853), pp. 27–8.
14 Samuel Smiles, *Self-Help* (London, 1859: edition of 1908), pp. 3, 369.
15 Herbert Spencer, *Education: Intellectual, Moral, and Physical* (London, 1861: edition of 1919), p. 124.
16 William Ellis, *An Address to Teachers on the Importance of Imparting the Principles of Social Science to Children* (London, 1859), pp. 7, 16.
17 William Jolly, *Physical Education for Common Schools* (Edinburgh, 1875), p. 18.
18 Spencer, op. cit., pp. 6, 8.
19 Burton J. Bledstein, *The Culture of Professionalism: the middle class and the development of higher education in America* (New York, 1976), ch. 3.
20 Rothblatt, *Tradition and Change in English Liberal Education*.
21 C. G. Ammon of the Union of Post Office Workers, T U C *Annual Report* 1921, p. 362, quoted in Douglas Bourn, 'The Development of Labour Party Ideas on Education with Special Reference to the Period 1918–1944', Keele University Ph D thesis, 1978, p. 67.
22 Lawrence M. Friedman, 'The Social and Political Context of the War on Poverty: an overview' in Robert H. Haveman (ed.), *A Decade of Federal Antipoverty Programs* (New York, 1977), p. 28.
23 Michel Foucault, *The History of Sexuality*, vol. I, *An Introduction* (first English edition, London, 1979), p. 94.
24 Thorstein Veblen, *The Higher Learning in America* (New York, 1918: edition of 1957), p. 11.
25 Sir Richard Livingstone, *Some Thoughts on University Education* (London, 1948), pp. 7–8.

CHAPTER 8 HIGHER EDUCATIONS

1 Ministry of Education, *Higher Education* (London, 1963), vol. I, pp. 266–7.
2 The *Second Newman Report: national policy and higher education* (Cambridge, Mass., 1973) p. 1.
3 Ministry of Education, op. cit., vol. I, p. 16. For a later discussion of the 'age participation rate' see Department of Education and Science and the Scottish Education Department, *Higher Education into the 1990s: a discussion document* (London, 1978).
4 Ministry of Education, *Higher Education*, vol. I, p. 51.

5 Lord Robbins, *The University in the Modern World* (London, 1966), pp. 42–3.

6 C. B. Cox and Rhodes Boyson, 'Letter to M Ps and Parents', *Black Paper 1975* (London, 1975), p. 5.

7 Irving Horowitz and William H. Friedland, *The Knowledge Factory: student power and academic politics in America* (Chicago, Ill., 1970: edition of 1972).

8 Carl Kaysen, *The Higher Learning, the Universities and the Public* (Princeton, N.J., 1969), p. 15.

9 Robert Maynard Hutchins, *The Higher Learning in America* (New Haven, Conn., 1936); Paul Woodring, *The Higher Learning in America: a reassessment* (New York, 1968), p. 185.

10 See, for example, Martin Trow, *The Expansion and Transfiguration of Higher Education* (New York, 1972); Joseph Ben-David, *American Higher Education: directions old and new*, reprinted as *Trends in American Higher Education* (Chicago, Ill., 1974), ch. 1.

11 See a discussion of research and these new concerns in Clark Kerr, *The Uses of the University* (New York, 1964: edition of 1966), pp. 42–9, 64–80.

12 ibid., p. 65.

13 A perceptive discussion of this issue is Philip C. Ritterbush, 'Adaptive Response within the Institutional System of Higher Education and Research', *Daedalus*, vol. 99, no. 3 (1970).

14 Thorstein Veblen, *The Higher Learning in America: a memorandum on the conduct of universities by business men* (New York, 1918: edition of 1957), p. 1.

15 ibid., pp. 2–5, 11–15.

16 Robert Nisbet, *The Degradation of the Academic Dogma: the university in America, 1945–1970* (New York, 1971).

17 ibid., pp. 72–3.

18 ibid., pp. 223–4.

19 Kerr, op. cit., pp. 64–5.

20 Ben-David, op. cit., p. 50.

21 John Henry Newman, *On the Scope and Nature of University Education* (London, 1915: edition of 1943), pp. xxxiii, 159–60.

22 Veblen, op. cit., p. 15.

23 Charles F. Thwing, *A History of Higher Education in America* (New York, 1906), p. 471.

24 *Report of the Commissioners for the University of Virginia* (Rockfish Gap, Va, 1818, University of Virginia, Manuscripts Department).

25 Oscar and Mary F. Handlin, *The American College and American Culture* (New York, 1970), p. 20.

26 Andrew D. White, 'The Relation of National and State Governments to Advanced Education', *Journal of Social Science*, no. 7 (1874), p. 299.

27 Martin Trow, 'Elite and Popular Functions in American Higher Education', in W. R. Niblett (ed.), *Higher Education: demand and response* (London, 1969), pp. 182–4.

28 University Grants Committee, *University Development from 1936 to 1947* (London, 1948), p. 32, also quoting a note of the Committee of Vice-Chancellors and the Barlow Committee.

29 Ministry of Education *Higher Education*, vol. I, p. 10.

30 Christopher Jencks and David Riesman, *The Academic Revolution* (New York, 1968), p. 24.

31 Ritterbush, op. cit., p. 655.

32 University Grants Committee, *University Development 1957–1962* (London, 1964), p. 93.

33 Daniel Bell, *The Coming of Post-Industrial Society* (New York, 1973), especially ch. 3.

34 Alain Touraine, *The Academic System in American Society* (New York, 1974), p. 279.

35 Trow, 'Elite and Popular Functions in American Higher Education', p. 20.

36 Ministry of Education, *Higher Education*, vol. I, p. 4.

37 Quoted in Kneller, *Higher Learning in Britain* (Berkeley, Calif., 1955), p. 77.

38 See Peter Scott, 'The Prophet Who Had His Way' (interview with Sir Toby Weaver), *The Times Higher Education Supplement,* 10 February 1978, p. 9.

39 Eric Ashby, *The Structure of Higher Education: a world view* (New York, 1973), p. 10.

40 Leonard V. Koos, *The Junior-College Movement* (New York, 1925: edition of 1970), pp. 19–23, 235–8.

41 Leland L. Medsker, *The Junior College: progress and prospects* (New York, 1960), pp. 4–5, 17–22.

42 Arthur M. Cohen and Florence B. Bramer, 'The Community College in Search of Identity', in *Inside Academe: culture in crisis* (New York, 1972), pp. 164–5.

43 Sidney W. Brossman and Myron Roberts, *The California Community Colleges* (Palo Alto, Calif., 1973), pp. 8–9.

44 Medsker, *The Junior College*, p. 24; Leland L. Medsker, 'The American Community College: its contribution to higher education', in W. Roy Niblett and R. Freeman Butts (eds), *The World Year Book of Education 1972/3: universities facing the future* (London, 1972), p. 321.

45 Robert Palinchak, *The Evolution of the Community College* (Metuchen, N.J., 1973), p. 3.

46 For a discussion of the social-class basis of student enrolments and routes taken in the colleges, see Jerome Karabel, 'Community Colleges and Social Stratification: submerged class conflict in American higher education', in Jerome Karabel and A. H. Halsey (eds), *Power and Ideology in Education* (New York, 1977).

47 Medsker, 'The American Community College', p. 322.

48 ibid., pp. 317–20.

49 Cohen and Bramer, op. cit., pp. 165, 172.

50 Palinchak, op. cit., p. 5.
51 Robert Paul Wolff, *The Ideal of the University* (Boston, Mass., 1969), pp. xi, 12.
52 Kaysen, op. cit., p. 78.
53 Veblen, op. cit., p. 209.
54 Kneller, op. cit., p. 100.
55 Jacques Barzun, *The American University: how it runs, where it is going* (New York, 1968), pp. 12–13.
56 W. Roy Niblett, *Universities between Two Worlds* (London, 1974), p. 58. On the political roots of American student militancy see Horowitz and Friedland, op. cit. On the social background and composition of student movements see Seymour Martin Lipset, *Rebellion in the University* (London, 1971).
57 Steven Muller, 'A New American University?', *Daedalus*, vol. 107, no. 1 (1978), p. 1: '. . . the American university was mobilized for war by the federal government in 1941, and demobilization did not occur until twenty-five years later.' Kerr, op. cit., p. 48: 'the major universities were enlisted in national defence . . . as never before'.
58 Reported in *The Chronicle of Higher Education*, 22 May 1978, pp. 8–9.
59 Abraham Flexner, *The American College: a criticism* (New York, 1908), p. 185.
60 Barzun, op. cit., p. 36.
61 University Grants Committee, *Report of the Committee on University Teaching Methods* (London, 1964), p. 118.
62 C. Easton Rothwell *et al.*, *The Importance of Teaching: a memorandum to the new college teacher* (no publisher, n.d.), p. 9.
63 ibid., p. 17.
64 Peter H. Rossi, 'Researchers, Scholars and Policy Makers', *Daedalus*, vol. 93, no. 4 (1964), p. 1160.
65 Flexner, op. cit., pp. 5, 47.
66 Carnegie Commission on Higher Education, *Reform on Campus: changing students, changing academic programs* (New York, 1972), p. 2. See also Lipset, op. cit., ch. 2.
67 Martin Seymour Lipset, 'The American University – 1964–1974: from activism to austerity', in Paul Searby (ed.), *Universities in the Western World* (New York, 1975), p. 143.
68 Eric Ashby, *Any Person, Any Study: an essay on higher education in the United States* (New York, 1971), p. 66.
69 Kerr, op. cit., pp. 118–19.
70 *Report on Higher Education (First Newman Report)*, quoted in *Second Newman Report*, p. ix.

CHAPTER 9   HIGHER STATUSES

1 Association of University Teachers, *Submissions to the Committee on Higher Education* (London, 1961), p. 8.

2 See especially David Hencke, *Colleges in Crisis* (Harmondsworth, 1978), ch. 2.

3 Keith Hampson, 'Murder, he says', *The Guardian*, 19 July 1977.

4 'Statement by the Council of the University of London', 1827, in Michael Sanderson (ed.), *The Universities in the Nineteenth Century* (London, 1975), p. 60.

5 'A Sketch of the Development of King's College', in King's College London, *Calendar 1973–1974*, p. 21.

6 *Extracts from the Will (dated 31st May 1845) of John Owens . . .* (Manchester, n.d.).

7 W. M. Hicks, *Local Colleges and Higher Education for the People* (Sheffield, 1886), pp. 8–9.

8 Letter by Joseph Chamberlain, 1899, in Sanderson op. cit., p. 216.

9 A. M. Holbein, *The Work of the City and Guilds of London Institute* (London, 1949), p. 2.

10 Harold Silver and S. John Teague (eds), *Chelsea College – a history* (London, 1977), p. 22.

11 M. J. Cruickshank, 'From Mechanics' Institution to Technical School', in D. S. L. Cardwell (ed.), *Artisan to Graduate* (Manchester, 1974), p. 145.

12 National Education League, *The Training Schools under Government Inspection, 1870–71, in England, Wales, and Scotland . . .* (Birmingham, 1872), p. 18.

13 Jack Simmons, *New University* (Leicester, 1959), p. 73.

14 R. A. Lowe, 'Determinants of a University's Curriculum', *British Journal of Educational Studies*, vol. XVII (1969), p. 43.

15 Asa Briggs 'Drawing a New Map of Learning', in David Daiches (ed.), *The Idea of a New University: an experiment in Sussex* (London, 1964), p. 60.

16 University Grants Committee, *University Development 1957–1962* (London, 1964), p. 104.

17 Naomi E. S. McIntosh, 'Access to Higher Education in England and Wales', in Robert S. Pike *et al.*, *Innovation in Access to Higher Education* (New York, 1978), p. 182.

18 Quoted in Peter Scott, 'At Last the New Polytechnics', *The Times Educational Supplement*, 31 May 1968, p. 1836.

19 Quoted in ibid.

20 Rudolph, *Curriculum*, p. 180.

21 Harold Perkin, *Key Profession: the history of the Association of University Teachers* (London, 1969), pp. 1, 227–8.

CHAPTER 10   TEACHERS AND ADOLESCENTS

1 John Lalor, 'The Social Position of Educators', in *The Educator* (London, 1839), pp. 79, 81; James Simpson, 'On the Expediency and the Means of elevating the Profession of Educator in Public Estimation', in ibid., p. 425.

2 June Purvis, 'Schoolteaching as a Professional Career', *British Journal of Sociology*, vol. 24 (1973), p. 43.

3 Henry Moseley, 'Report on the Chester Diocesan Training School for Masters', Committee of Council *Minutes 1845*, p. 369.

4 Asher Tropp, *The School Teachers: the growth of the teaching profession in England and Wales from 1800 to the present day* (London, 1957), p. 34.

5 Board of Education, *Report of the Departmental Committee on the Training of Teachers for Public Elementary Schools* (London, 1925), pp. 39–41.

6 National Union of Teachers, *Teacher Education: the way ahead* (London, 1970), p. 8. See also National Union of Teachers, *The Reform of Teacher Education* (London, 1971), Introduction and p. 10.

7 *Higher Education*, vol. II (B), p. 71.

8 Purvis, op. cit., pp. 46–7.

9 Roger Webster, 'The Future of Teacher Training', in Michael Raggett and Malcolm Clarkson (eds), *Changing Patterns of Teacher Education* (London, 1976), p. 146.

10 David Newsome, *Godliness and Good Learning: four studies on a Victorian ideal* (London, 1961), p. 49.

11 Selwyn K. Troen, 'The Discovery of the Adolescent by American Educational Reformers, 1900–1920: an economic perspective', in Lawrence Stone (ed.), *Schooling and Society: studies in the history of education* (Baltimore, Md, 1976).

12 Lilian Fleet, 'Some Margins of Compulsory Education: some limitations on the concept of universal compulsion with special regard to raising the school leaving age and educational minority status', Bristol University Ph D, 1976, pp. 134–51 ('Social Control and Discipline in Adolescence'), p. 143.

13 ibid., p. 142n.

14 Quoted in ibid., p. 143.

15 W. D. Wall, *Adolescents in School and Society* (Slough, 1968), pp. 3–4.

16 Bennett M. Berger, 'The New State of American Man – Almost Endless Adolescence', in Burton R. Clark (ed.), *The Problems of American Education* (New York, 1975), pp. 110–12.

CHAPTER II CHANGE

1 Jerome Karabel and A. H. Halsey, 'Educational Research: a review and an interpretation', in Jerome Karabel and A. H. Halsey, *Power and Ideology in Education* (New York, 1978), pp. 40–1.

2 Harvey A. Averch *et al.*, *How Effective is Schooling? a critical review of research* (Englewood Cliffs, N.J., 1974); Michael Rutter *et al.*, *Fifteen Thousand Hours: secondary schools and their effects on children* (London, 1979).

3 Clarke, *Education and Social Change*, pp. 66–7.

Index